Richard. Judi

Jill D Wilkins

Catriona

DS

Gerry

Social Understanding and
Social Lives

ESSAYS IN DEVELOPMENTAL PSYCHOLOGY

North American Editors:
Henry Wellman
University of Michigan at Ann Arbor
Janet Werker
University of British Columbia

UK Editors:
Usha Goswami
University of Cambridge
Claire Hughes
University of Cambridge

Essays in Developmental Psychology is designed to meet the need for rapid publication of brief volumes in developmental psychology. The series defines developmental psychology in its broadest terms and covers such topics as social development, cognitive development, developmental neuropsychology and neuroscience, language development, learning difficulties, developmental psychopathology and applied issues. Each volume in the series will make a conceptual contribution to the topic by reviewing and synthesizing the existing research literature, by advancing theory in the area, or by some combination of these missions. The principal aim is that authors will provide an overview of their own highly successful research program in an area. It is also expected that volumes will, to some extent, include an assessment of current knowledge and identification of possible future trends in research. Each book will be a self-contained unit supplying the advanced reader with a well-structured review of the work described and evaluated.

FORTHCOMING TITLES

Trehub: *Infants and Music*

Vosniadou: *Children's Cosmologies*

ALSO AVAILABLE IN SERIES

Goldin-Meadow: *The Resilience of Language*

Inagaki and Hatano: *Young Children's Naïve Thinking about the Biological World*

Perez-Pereira and Conti-Ramsden: *Language Development and Social Interactions in Blind Children*

Byrne: *The Foundation of Literacy*

Tager-Flusberg: *Autism and William's Syndrome*

Meins: *Security of Attachment and Cognitive Development*

Siegal: *Knowing Children (2nd Ed.)*

Mitchell: *Acquiring a Conception of Mind*

Meadows: *Parenting Behavior and Children's Cognitive Development*

Langford: *The Development of Moral Reasoning*

Hobson: *Autism and the Development of Mind*

White: *The Understanding of Causation and the Production of Action*

Smith: *Necessary Knowledge and Constructivism*

Cox: *Children's Drawings of the Human Figure*

Howe: *Language Learning*

Sonuga-Barke and Webley: *Children's Saving*

Sprenger-Charolles, Colé and Serniclaes: *Reading Acquisition and Developmental Dyslexia*

Barrett: *Children's Knowledge, Beliefs and Feelings about Nations and National Groups*

For updated information about published and forthcoming titles in the *Essays in Developmental Psychology* series, please visit: **www.psypress.com/essays**

Social Understanding and Social Lives

From toddlerhood through to the transition to school

Claire Hughes

Psychology Press
Taylor & Francis Group

LONDON AND NEW YORK

First published 2011
by Psychology Press
27 Church Road, Hove, East Sussex BN3 2FA

Simultaneously published in the USA and Canada
by Psychology Press
711 Third Avenue, New York, NY 10017

Psychology Press is an imprint of the Taylor & Francis Group, an Informa business

Typeset in Times New Roman by RefineCatch Limited, Bungay, Suffolk
Printed and bound in Great Britain by TJ International, Padstow, Cornwall
Cover design by Lisa Dynan

This publication has been produced with paper manufactured to strict
environmental standards and with pulp derived from sustainable forests.

British Library Cataloguing in Publication Data
A catalogue record for this book is available
from the British Library

Library of Congress Cataloging-in-Publication Data
Hughes, Claire.
  Social understanding and social lives: from toddlerhood through to the
transition to school / Claire Hughes.
    p. cm.
  Includes bibliographical references and index.
  ISBN 978–1–84169–735–2 (hb)
  1. Social perception in children.   2. Socialization.
3. Child development.   4. Child psychology.   I. Title.
  BF723.S6H84 2011
  155.42′38—dc22

                                                            2010031824

ISBN: 978–1–84169–735–2 (hbk)

For Andrew, who makes everything seem possible, and for our three wonderful children, Alistair, Elora and Malaika, who teach me something new every day.

Contents

PART IV
Conclusion   167

Acknowledgements

The Toddlers Up study, presented in this book, was funded by an initial grant from the Health Foundation and two further grants from the Economic and Social Research Council. It has been very much a team study, and so I'd like to start by acknowledging all those who have worked in the Toddlers Up study over the past six years. Chief among these is Dr Rosie Ensor (now a British Academy postdoctoral research fellow), who has been pivotal to the study's success, from recruitment all the way through to analyses and dissemination. In particular, Rosie ran the study during the months that I was on maternity leave, and most recently has led the way in making the leap from traditional statistical approaches to latent variable model fitting. The Toddlers Up study also owes much to the work of Dr Alex Marks, Dr Anji Wilson, Ms Martha Hart and Ms Lorna Jacobs. Many of the observational methods adopted in the Toddlers Up study were inspired by earlier collaborative work with Professor Judy Dunn, at the Institute of Psychiatry, in London. I would also like to thank Judy Dunn, Janet Astington and Lynne Murray for their supportive and insightful comments on the first draft of this book. Without the support of the participating families and schools, none of this would have been possible, and so my warm thanks go to them also. Other studies described in this book include: (i) collaborative work with Dr Serena Lecce, who now runs a parallel research programme at the University of Pavia in Italy; and (ii) recent work from one of my PhD students, Rory Devine, and a clutch of talented undergraduate students, including John Mills, Sarah Scott and Rebekkah Tennyson. Finally, warm thanks for her constant support go to Professor Susan Golombok, Director of the Centre for Family Research, at Cambridge University.

Introduction

Brief history of three decades of research

What children understand about their own and others' minds and how children reach this understanding are questions that have attracted remarkable levels of research interest for more than thirty years. In its first decade, research in this field was characterized by heated polemical debate between different theoretical camps, including proponents of innate and modular cognitive systems, or of constructivist models of cognitive development, or simulation accounts (in which children learn about the mind through imaginative leaps rather than through theory testing). Over time, many of these distinct strands have been woven together to produce hybrid accounts in which the salience of specific processes varies with children's developmental maturity. For example, the findings from autism research provide strong evidence that very early milestones in children's awareness of other minds are likely to have an innate basis (U. Frith & Frith, 2001). Conversely, studies of children who have hearing impairments (and whose parents are not fluent users of sign language) demonstrate the importance of access to rich linguistic environments for later milestones in social understanding (Peterson & Siegal, 1995).

This shift from polemical debate to integrative frameworks has been accompanied by a change in the kinds of questions that have preoccupied researchers. For example, while early research emphasized the dramatic nature of developmental changes in the preschool years and was heavily focused on documenting the nature and timing of these changes, later studies expanded the scope of this research in two ways. First, the "watershed" model of dramatic change in the preschool years was replaced by a more gradual model of development, which highlighted the need for researchers to investigate developments that occurred both before preschool (i.e., in infancy and toddlerhood) and later in development. Second, studies that included larger and more diverse samples and/or task batteries highlighted the magnitude of individual differences in children's understanding of mind, prompting questions about the origins of these individual differences. Most recently, this new generation of research has begun to address questions of stability and predictive utility. For example, do preschoolers who lag behind their peers in acquiring an understanding of mind still show similar lags at school age, and do these individual differences predict significant contrasts in children's social development?

Given the intensity of research in this area, it is rather surprising that it has taken nearly a quarter of a century for investigators to address these issues. Babies who begin to crawl or walk later than other babies typically catch up with their peers within a matter of months (Clark, Whitall, & Phillips, 1988). In contrast, babies who babble or talk later than other babies do appear to be at risk for language disorders, including dyslexia (e.g., Koster et al., 2005). In other words, some early individual differences appear more significant than others, such that the predictive utility of early individual differences in children's understanding of mind needs to be tested directly. Moreover, theoretical accounts of the evolutionary advantages of having a concept of mind highlight both Machiavellian intelligence (e.g., Dunbar, 2003) and collaborative skills (Tomasello, Carpenter, Call, Behne, & Moll, 2005). This indicates that children's understanding of mind may best be viewed as a socially neutral tool, suggesting that early individual differences should be examined in relation to both positive and negative social outcomes. In short, research on children's understanding of mind has, over the past thirty years, expanded considerably in scope and now includes studies of developmental changes across a relatively broad age-range as well as studies of the origins and consequences of individual differences. This book aims to touch on all of these questions.

Why the title "Social Understanding and Social Lives"?

Choosing a title for this book led to a dilemma: should I use the term "theory of mind", now very widely adopted within academic research on young children's cognitive development (e.g., searching for "theory of mind" and "children" produces more than 1500 hits), or adopt the broader term "social understanding"? In the end, this broader term "social understanding" won the day, for two reasons. First, it encompasses more than just the ability to pass tasks that tap into children's understanding of false belief (and are widely used as a litmus test for crediting children with a "theory of mind"). This heavy focus on a single task within the "theory of mind" literature led to intensive research on the preschool period but, as outlined below, the Toddlers Up study spans from toddlerhood through to early school age. Reflecting this extended developmental scope, the study includes not only classic false-belief tasks, but a variety of different measures ranging from children's conversational references to thoughts, feelings and desires, to their performance on tasks that tap into the ability to engage in pretend play or simple deception, or to understand different feelings and their causes, or to grasp that people can have mixed emotions, second-order false beliefs (i.e., false beliefs about beliefs) and emotions that are based on false beliefs.

Second, adopting the term "social understanding" provides a means of drawing the reader's attention to the possibility that how children perform on the above array of tasks may be related to the quality of their social relationships, both within and outside the home. Previous studies of potential family influences on children's social understanding have led to the identification of a variety of potentially important family features, of which perhaps the most significant are: (i) the frequency/quality of mother–child talk about inner states (e.g., Dunn, Brown, &

Beardsall, 1991a); and (ii) cooperative interactions between siblings (e.g., Hughes, Fujisawa, Ensor, Lecce, & Marfleet, 2006). One aim of the Toddlers Up study was to assess the significance of individual differences in the *trajectories* for each of these domains. This developmentally dynamic perspective requires longitudinal observations for a sizeable sample, and so is beyond the reach of many studies.

Note also that although children's "mindreading" skills are widely assumed to be salient for their social interactions, the evidence to support this view is remarkably thin, especially given the intensity of research in this field over the past 30 years. Three features of the Toddlers Up study made it well placed to contribute to this knowledge base. First, unlike previous work, which focused heavily on the preschool years, the Toddlers Up study spans a broader developmental period, from toddlerhood through to the transition to school. Second, the study stands apart from others in the field by virtue of the breadth and detail of the data collected. These include: (i) detailed coding from video observations of the children interacting with multiple social partners (mothers, siblings, friends, unfamiliar peers); and (ii) interview- or questionnaire-based ratings from multiple informants (mothers, teachers and the children themselves). Third, each time-point in the Toddlers Up study also included standard language ability assessments and a set of executive-function tasks (tapping into children's planning, working memory and inhibitory control), enabling the specificity and relative importance of predictive relations between early social understanding and later social outcomes to be addressed.

How this book is organized

The structure of this book took a little time to resolve: originally, my aim was to make it a game of two halves, with the first half devoted to predictors of individual differences in children's social understanding and the second half devoted to outcomes associated with these individual differences. In fact, it quickly became clear that the first of these two issues has received much more research attention than the latter, such that the book plan lacked balance. My solution has been to divide the book into three main parts. The first part adopts a straightforwardly cognitive perspective on developments and individual differences in children's social understanding. Thus, Chapter 1 is devoted to documenting milestones in children's growing understanding of mind. This chapter draws heavily on a chapter co-authored with Janet Astington, which is to appear shortly in the *Oxford Handbook of Developmental Psychology* (Astington & Hughes, in press). In the chapter, apparently paradoxical findings from infants and preschoolers are reconciled by proposing a developmental shift from intuitive to reflective understanding. Chapters 2 and 3 then address two hot topics in this research field, namely the nature of associations between individual differences in children's social understanding and in their "executive functions" (i.e., their ability to show flexible, goal-directed control of their actions) and their language skills (considered at several different levels, from semantics to syntax and pragmatics). The studies reviewed in Chapter 2 involve both typically developing children and atypical groups and address the nature of this association between executive control and theory of mind: is it general or specific, direct or indirect, universal or culturally bound? In Chapter 3, cross-cultural work, studies of bilingualism, training studies and research with distinct clinical groups – children with hearing impairments, specific language impairment (SLI) and autism spectrum disorder (ASD) – are reviewed in order to highlight multiplicity of relations between language and social understanding. This first part of the book is aimed primarily at students and researchers who are interested in these three distinct but closely related aspects of children's cognitive development.

The second part of the book examines predictors of children's social understanding from a sociocultural perspective, and may be of interest to parents as well as students and researchers working in the field of children's family relationships. Chapter 4 describes how individual differences in children's linguistic environments may contribute to variation in their social understanding. This chapter begins with an overview of distinct theoretical perspectives, before drawing on examples of conversations, taken from two families participating in the Toddlers Up study (which is described in more detail opposite) to present a developmentally dynamic model of how children's exposure to certain types of talk (specifically connected conversations about thoughts and feelings) may contribute to their growing social understanding. This model has emerged from PhD and post-doctoral research conducted by Dr Rosie Ensor, who has been pivotal to the success of the Toddlers Up study at all stages, from the recruitment of participants to the video-based coding and data analysis. Chapters 5 and 6 then review the literature on associations between social understanding and children's experiences in their relationships with parents and siblings respectively. The first half of Chapter 5 charts historical changes in research on parenting (which has generally focused on how children are socialized by their parents), while the second half reviews three distinct strands of research that have directly addressed links between parenting and children's social understanding: attachment research, studies of parent–child conversations and cross-cultural studies. Chapter 6 also draws on examples of family conversations taken from the Toddlers Up study to illustrate the myriad ways in which siblings may directly or indirectly, and deliberately or inadvertently, contribute to young children's growing social understanding. This chapter also summarizes developmental findings that have emerged from work conducted by Dr Alex Marks, another key player in the Toddlers Up team, as part of her doctoral thesis.

The third part of the book then turns to the question of whether individual differences in young children's social understanding help to explain variability in their behaviour and adjustment to school and is, I hope, of interest to parents and educators, as well as to students and researchers interested in children's relationships with peers and friends and adjustment to school more generally. Chapter 7 reviews research on links between social understanding and individual differences in children's antisocial behaviour and is organized by five themes. These include: viewing children's understanding of others as a socially neutral tool; adopting a developmental perspective; considering deviance as well as delay; recognizing that links between social understanding and bullying are heterogeneous; and bringing deontics (i.e., the understanding of social norms or values) into the picture. Chapter 8 examines links between social understanding and children's positive interactions with friends. Three themes are used to organize this chapter. The first of these is the developmental synchrony of cognitive and social milestones; the second is the question of whether social understanding is a more salient predictor of behaviour for typically developing or at-risk groups of children; and the third is a focus on discourse as a consistently strong correlate of individual differences in children's social understanding. Chapter 9 brings us to children's transition to school, examining links between children's social understanding and their success in starting school from three different viewpoints: that of their peers, their teachers and the children themselves. As a result, topics addressed in this chapter include links between social understanding and children's: (i) peer status (i.e., the extent to which children are noticed and liked by their classmates); (ii) social competence (as rated by teachers); and (iii) self-concepts, sensitivity to criticism and self-reported relationships with teachers and peers. Chapter 10 provides a brief summary of the findings from Chapters 1 to 9 before outlining three emerging themes. These concern: (i) developmental change and continuity; (ii) observations of children as a valuable research tool; and (iii) moderating and mediating factors involved in relations between social understanding and its antecedents and sequelae. This chapter ends with two new directions: the potential educational implications of (and influences on) children's social understanding; and the value of combining research on children's mentalizing skills and on their awareness of how behaviour is also constrained by social norms.

A short account of the Toddlers Up study

The project of writing this book was motivated by a desire to bring together findings gathered over several years from a longitudinal study in Cambridge, UK, dubbed the "Toddlers Up" study, and funded originally by the Health Foundation and later by two grants from the Economic and Social Research Council. This study was originally conceived as a "prequel" to a London-based study of 40 hard-to-manage preschoolers (also funded by the Economic and Social Research Council, and conducted in collaboration with Professor Judy Dunn from the Institute of Psychiatry). Our findings from this London study demonstrated that at the age of 4, when they were first recruited, these hard-to-manage preschoolers displayed a myriad of problems, ranging from cognitive deficits (e.g., problems in inhibiting maladaptive prepotent responses, and in understanding emotions and engaging in moral reasoning; Hughes & Dunn, 2000; Hughes, Dunn, & White, 1998), peer problems (e.g., frequent displays of anger and aggression towards friends; Hughes, Cutting, & Dunn, 2001; Hughes, White, Sharpen, & Dunn, 2000b) and family problems (e.g., lack of positive and/or cohesive conversations with caregivers; Brophy & Dunn, 2002). This diversity of problems prompted questions about causal directions.

To address this perennial problem of "chicken and egg", the Toddlers Up study was set up to examine relations between cognitive and social influences on younger children's development; age 2 was chosen as a likely lower limit for conducting many of the paradigms we had developed in the study of hard-to-manage preschoolers. People often use the phrase "terrible twos" to describe toddlers, because challenging behaviours are very commonplace in this age group (and so may even be seen as developmentally normative). Thus, although the London sample of preschoolers was selected on the basis of parent-rated symptoms of disruptive behaviour disorders, this strategy was unlikely to be successful for identifying an at-risk group of toddlers. Instead, we focused our efforts on maximizing the participation of low-income and/or teen-parent families, as (unlike other developmental disorders) conduct problems show a strong social gradient (Costello, Compton, Keeler, & Angold, 2003). Specifically, in our recruitment phase our research team made several visits to every mother–toddler group in each of the geographic areas in Cambridgeshire that fall into the most deprived national quartile (English Indices of Deprivation in 2000, 2004 and 2007, see http://www.communities.gov.uk/publications/communities/indicesdeprivation07). This strategy proved successful in that our core sample (additional children were recruited as friends at ages 4 and 6) showed clear social diversity. This was evident in terms of: *family structure* (25% were from lone-parent households; 43% had mothers who were teenagers at the birth of their first child); *family income* (25% of families were living below the poverty line, £12k, and a further 28% had incomes that were below the national median, £20k); and *parental education* (more than 50% of the mothers and fathers had left school at 16 with few or no educational qualifications). Full details of the participants' family backgrounds are provided in Appendix 1.

The first obvious difference between the Cambridge Toddlers Up study and the London hard-to-manage study is that the two samples are from geographically quite distinct areas. Thus, the children in the Cambridge Toddlers Up study were living in or around a prosperous small city in a rural area that is quite different from the London inner-city borough of Southwark, where most of the hard-to-manage preschoolers lived. Reflecting this geographical contrast, there was also a clear difference in ethnic diversity: unlike the hard-to-manage sample, which included at least as many Black children as White children, nearly all of the parents in the Toddlers Up study described themselves as White British. Another point of contrast was family size. Relatively few of the hard-to-manage preschoolers in the London study had siblings, and so it was difficult to assess how sibling interactions may contribute to children's development; one goal of the Toddlers Up study was therefore to maximize the number of participants with siblings. This made recruitment more time consuming (mothers are much less likely to attend toddler groups once they have more than one child), but we were able to ensure that 88% of the Toddlers Up study children had at least one sibling at the first time-point. These contrasts allowed us to test the generalizability of earlier findings from the London hard-to-manage study. To this end, we attempted, as far as possible, to use similar measures in the two studies. Below, our observational and experimental cognitive measures are summarized briefly, as a familiarity with the tasks and procedures used in the study will help the reader to understand the findings presented in this book (more details are given in Appendices 2 and 3).

Recruiting toddlers enabled us to observe family interactions at multiple time-points (at ages 2, 3 and 6 – as children get older conducting observational home visits becomes more challenging, both because older children are more aware of the camera and because they spend less time in close proximity to other family members). As in the London study, we observed the children both at home (with mothers, siblings and in unstructured evening meal-time interactions) and at school (in dyadic free play and structured play with a best friend – at ages 4 and 6). The Toddlers Up study also included lab visits that, at ages 2 and 3, involved mother–child pairs filmed interacting as separate dyads and together. At age 6, lab visits involved filming two same-sex triads of children: (i) in dyadic interactions, with the third child joining the play in a "peer entry" task; and (ii) as a group of six children both watching a professional magic show and having a tea party.

The number and diversity of observations made at each time-point brought a number of benefits. For example, combining observations made on different days/places/times of day maximizes reliability by reducing effects of day-to-day variability. Conversely, comparing equivalent observations at different time-points enables one to assess both developmental change and stability of individual differences. In addition, comparing measures of children in equivalent situations with different social partners (e.g., sibling vs. friend) provides valuable information on partner effects, while comparing measures of children in contrasting situations with the same social partner provides valuable information on context effects. Moreover, gathering longitudinal data on children's interactions with different partners allows the relative independence and interplay of predictive effects to be assessed. Finally, some of the observations made in the Toddlers Up study were also quite novel, enabling us to address new questions. For example, by bringing together two same-sex triads of 6-year-old unfamiliar peers, the lab tea parties provided an opportunity to examine whether individual differences in social understanding predicted variation in how children interact with members of their "in-group" (i.e., their triad) *versus* members of an "out-group", and so enabled us to bring together key paradigms used by developmental and social psychologists (see Chapter 7).

Observational measures

Many of the observations carried out in the Toddlers Up study focused on children's interactions with other children. Figure 0.1, which shows a pair of friends from the Toddlers Up study playing together at ages 4 and 6, provides a nice illustration of both developmental continuity and change in these interactions. At both time-points it was evident that the children were good friends; they were also recognizably the same children (note, for example, the similarity in the girl's expression of laughter at ages 3 and 6). However, by age 6, the friends' interactions had also changed, becoming more formal and grown up. The same developmental continuity and change can be seen in the video images from parallel observations of mothers and children interacting (see Figures 5.1 and 5.2 in Chapter 5). At age 6, we also filmed the children interacting with unfamiliar peers (see Figures 8.1–8.3 in Chapter 8). A summary of all the observations in the study, with details of the coding systems used, is provided in Appendix 2.

Figure 0.1 Elizabeth playing with her friend David, at age 3 and at age 6.

Experimental tasks

Chapter 1 presents an overview of developmental milestones in children's social understanding, from infancy to school age, framed within a theoretical perspective that highlights: (i) both continuity and change in children's understanding; and (ii) the importance of individual differences in this domain. This extended view of development in social understanding contrasts with early theoretical accounts, which highlighted a narrow preschool period (between 3 and 5 years) as a time of near universal dramatic progress in children's understanding of mind, such that only children with autism were thought to show significant delay in acquiring an understanding of others as agents with beliefs, desires and intentions (Baron-Cohen, Leslie, & Frith, 1985). Both the sheer magnitude of conceptual change attributed to typically developing preschoolers and the deficits displayed by children with autism (which appeared independent of general language delays) fuelled intense research interest in this area, as described earlier. As a result, there are now a large number of experimental tasks available for assessing children's understanding of mind. The tasks chosen for the Toddlers Up study were, as indicated above, partly chosen to allow us to test the generalizability of our earlier findings; because this earlier London study involved "hard-to-manage" children with limited attentional spans, these tasks have also been selected as being fun and engaging for children to complete. For illustrative purposes, three of the social-understanding tasks are illustrated below (two further tasks, used to tap into children's planning and self-regulatory skills, are shown in Chapter 2).

Figure 0.2 shows my two older children, Alistair and Elora (who at the time were aged 5 and 2), playing the Penny Hiding game: note Alistair's delight at

Figure 0.2 Alistair and Elora play the Penny Hiding game.

being able to deceive his little sister; note also her look of rapt concentration. In the Toddlers Up study, each child played this game with a researcher, who first modelled how to hide the penny three times, and then asked the child to have a go: on each of three trials, one point was given for each of three measures of deceptive ability – hiding both hands behind one's back, bringing both hands forward closed, and keeping the penny out of view.

Figure 0.3 shows some of the puppets used in the emotion understanding task administered at ages 2 and 3 in the Toddlers Up study. Children were first asked to choose the right face for when the puppet was feeling happy/sad/angry/scared, then to label the faces verbally, and then to choose the appropriate face for each of a set of stories involving unambiguous and ambiguous scenarios. The unambiguous scenarios were situations in which all children would be expected to feel the same way (e.g., happy to be offered an ice-cream, sad to fall over). The ambiguous vignettes were administered at age 3 after interviewing the mother about the child's likely response to a scenario. For example, if the mother reported that a big friendly dog would be likely to evoke a fearful response from her child, the researcher enacted being happy to see a big friendly dog; thus to pass these stories the children could not simply project their own emotional responses to specific situations, but needed to demonstrate affective perspective taking.

Figure 0.3 The Denham Puppets task.

In later chapters, I describe latent variable analyses of the stability of individual differences in false-belief understanding from ages 3 to 6. To orient the reader, the indicators for this latent variable are briefly described here. At age 3, indicators for false-belief understanding included scores for: (i) predicting and explaining a false belief in a standard object transfer task (in which one character – Noddy – places miniature cutlery in a drawer and then leaves the scene while another character – Big Ears – moves the cutlery to a pot; on Noddy's return, children are asked to predict where he will look for the cutlery, and to explain why he will look there); (ii) predicting another's false belief in a peep-through picture book task (described below); (iii) recalling own false belief in a deceptive contents task (an egg box that contained a toy character); and (iv) distinguishing between appearance and reality (a realistic looking egg that was actually made of plaster). At age 6, indicators for false-belief understanding included scores for: (i) an explanation version of the classic "Sally Anne" object transfer paradigm (in which one doll – Sally – puts a ball into a basket and then leaves the scene while another doll – Anne – moves the ball into a box; on Sally's return children were asked to explain why she looks in the basket); (ii) predicting another's false belief in a peep-through picture book task (with a picture that looked like an orange, but turned out to be a sun); (iii) predicting false belief in two belief–desire reasoning tasks (involving a nice or a nasty surprise); (iv) predicting and explaining a character's emotion based on a false belief in the same two belief–desire reasoning tasks; and (v) predicting and explaining a character's second-order false belief (i.e., a mistaken belief about a belief) in two stories involving either the transfer of chocolate by a character who didn't know his sister was watching from a window, or a mother's birthday gift of a puppy to her son, whom she thought was expecting a less exciting gift.

Part I

Cognitive perspectives on social understanding

1 Milestones in social understanding – from infancy to school age

Research on children's cognitive development has, for many decades, been heavily influenced by Jean Piaget's constructivist account of how children come to understand the world around them (e.g., Piaget, 1926). In turn, as noted by Russell (1996), Piaget was heavily influenced by the eighteenth-century German philosopher Immanuel Kant, such that much of his empirical work focused on children's mastery of abstract scientific concepts of time, number, order and transformation. Indeed, Piaget often referred to children as "little scientists" exploring and experimenting with the physical world around them (for parents, one familiar example is the way in which babies enjoy games of dropping things and watching them fall). Building on this metaphor, research over the past thirty years has revealed the extent to which young children can also be viewed as "little psychologists", intently interested in understanding causal relations within their social worlds (J. Dunn, 1995). In particular, three decades of research have revealed that young children have a much more sophisticated understanding of their social worlds than Piaget suspected, such that by late preschool most children appear able to explain, predict, and interpret actions and speech by attributing mental states – such as beliefs, desires, intentions and emotions – to oneself and to other people (see Wellman, Cross, & Watson, 2001, for a meta-analytic review).

These abilities were first described as reflecting a "theory of mind" by Premack and Woodruff (1978), in a study of chimpanzees learning to impute desires or intentions to others in order to make inferences about behaviour. According to these authors, this system for imputing mental states is a "theory", because it is used to make predictions from unobservable (mental) states. However, other theorists (e.g., Dennett, 1978; Harman, 1978) argued that the attribution of belief (rather than desire or intention) is the litmus test for a theory of mind, because beliefs are only in the running for the truth, such that one can pit against each other belief- *versus* reality-based predictions about behaviour. In other words, understanding how someone with a mistaken (i.e., false) belief about a situation will behave is the *sine qua non* of having a theory of mind. This view led to an intense research focus on preschool-aged children's performance on false-belief tasks, discussed later in this chapter. Over time, however, researchers have adopted broader definitions of "theory of mind" leading to expansions in both the constructs encompassed by this term and the developmental scope of this research field.

As a result, the term "theory of mind" means quite different things to different research groups (which is another reason for preferring the more inclusive term "social understanding"). For example, one theoretical camp highlights the parallel between the development of scientific theories and children's developing understanding of mental states. According to this "theory-theory" view, theory of mind is a domain-specific and cohesive set of mental-state concepts employed to explain and predict behaviour, which is reorganized over time when faced with counter-evidence to its predictions (e.g., Gopnik & Wellman, 1994). In contrast, simulation-theorists (e.g., Harris, 1992) have argued that mental-state concepts are not theoretical postulates but are derived from experience, while modularity-theorists (e.g., Baron-Cohen, 1995; Leslie, 1994) have argued that the theory is an innate system that develops via a process of neurological maturation.

Cutting across the above camps, however, is a growing recognition of the importance of adopting a developmental framework that recognizes both changes and continuities across different stages of children's social understanding. For example, Tager-Flusberg and Sullivan (2000) have proposed that distinct social-perceptual and social-cognitive subsystems underpin early versus later developing theory of mind. Various other researchers (e.g., Dienes & Perner, 1999; U. Frith, 2004; Hughes, 2005; Karmiloff-Smith, 1992) have made similar distinctions between intuitive and reflective social understanding. Social intuition refers to a set of socioperceptual skills that make immediate online appraisals of people's mental states from information conveyed in facial expressions, gestures, movements and vocal tone (Tager-Flusberg, 2001). This provides implicit social "know how" within the mental domain from as early as infancy (Hughes et al., 2005). By contrast, reflective social cognition begins to develop in the toddler years and entails an explicit conceptual domain involving a set of interconnected principles about how the mind works (Hughes et al., 2005).

Two strands of evidence support this distinction between intuitive and reflective components of theory of mind. First, the corresponding social-perceptual and social-cognitive processes appear to depend on two distinct neurological substrates (e.g., Saxe & Powell, 2006) and show differential impairment/sparing in different populations (U. Frith, 2004; Tager-Flusberg & Sullivan, 2000). Second, the relative salience of genetic *versus* environmental influences on individual differences in children's understanding of mind appears to shift with development. Specifically, findings from twin studies suggest that genetic influences on individual differences in children's understanding of mind are moderate to strong in toddlerhood and the early preschool years (Hughes & Cutting, 1999; Ronald, Happé, Hughes, & Plomin, 2005) but much weaker in late preschool/early school age (Hughes et al., 2005). At the same time, there is also evidence that, in typical development, these two components show developmental continuity from infancy to age 4 (e.g., Wellman, Lopez-Duran, LaBounty, & Hamilton, 2008; Wellman, Phillips, Dunphy-Lelii, & LaLonde, 2004).

This chapter is devoted to summarizing key milestones in social understanding from infancy through to the transition to school. This summary is based on a chapter in the forthcoming *Oxford Handbook of Developmental Psychology*

(Astington & Hughes, in press), which considers four distinct stages: (i) infants' understanding of attention and intention; (ii) toddlers' intuitive awareness of world-inconsistent goals; (iii) preschoolers' ability to reflect on their own or others' mistaken beliefs; and (iv) school-aged children's ability to engage in recursive reasoning and adopt an interpretative model of the mind.

The first of these stages is summarized only briefly, as it is beyond the scope of this book. To make up for this, I shall illustrate the next three stages by using conversational excerpts gathered in home visits to one of the Toddlers Up families, in which the study child (whom we shall call "Angus") is the youngest of three children. At the first visit, "Angus" is 2½ years old, his sister "Sasha" is 4½ years old and his brother "Lucas" is 8 years old. The second home visit took place 12 months later, and the third home visit took place a further 3 years later.

Understanding of attention and intention in infancy

Even before birth, babies are immersed in social information. For example, after five months in the womb the auditory system is almost fully developed, leaving four months for learning about the mother's voice. As a result, from the first few hours of life infants show a clear preference for their mother's voice (Mehler et al., 1988) and stronger brain responses to natural speech than to speech signals with impoverished prosody (Sambeth, Ruohio, Alku, Fellman, & Huotilainen, 2008). These preferences facilitate engagement and interaction, from which infants continue to learn about their social worlds. Although most research on this topic has focused on mother–infant interactions, a quick glance through any family photo album will illustrate the size and variety of many babies' social networks. Overleaf are just a few examples from my niece Misha's baby album at 10 weeks' old – with just some of the people with whom she has regular (i.e., daily, weekly or fortnightly) contact.

The first chief milestone in the journey towards a fully fledged theory of mind is the ability to recognize goals in others' actions. There is now good evidence that infants master this "teleological reasoning" in the first year of life (Woodward, 2003) and behave in ways that suggest an awareness of others' perceptions and desires. For example, when given the chance to play with three different toys before receiving an ambiguous request for a toy from an adult who has seen just two of the toys, 12-month-olds typically offer the particular toy the adult had not previously seen (Tomasello & Haberl, 2003).

Other researchers have argued that infants' own experiences of goal-directed action facilitate mental-state awareness even earlier in life. For example, giving 3-month-old infants Velcro mittens with which to retrieve objects led to increased sensitivity to an adult's goal, as indexed by longer looking times on the first habituation trial (Sommerville, Woodward, & Needham, 2005). Interestingly, however, this facilitatory effect of first-person experiences of agency may in turn depend on maternal affective mirroring, as mothers who show low levels of attunement into their infants' smiles, vocalizations, facial expressions and gazes typically have infants who find it difficult to coordinate attention, or to use emotional cues to

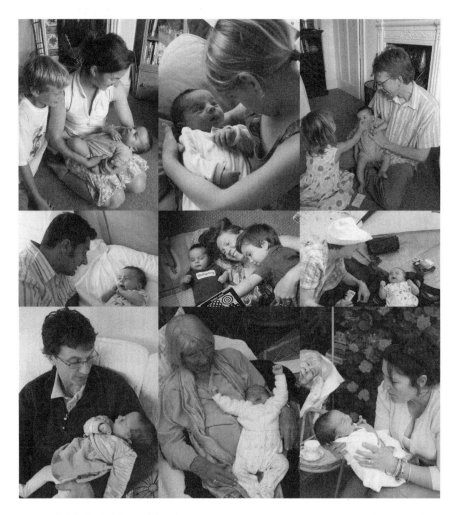

Figure 1.1 Baby Misha and family.

predict action (Legerstee & Varghese, 2001). These findings echo Reddy and Trevarthen's (2004) description of emotions as "intensely shared, because it is in the nature and function of emotions to stir up sympathetic responses in others". Thus, highlighting second-person (rather than first-person) knowledge, Reddy (2008) has argued that, rather than "discovering" attention between 9 and 12 months of age, infants begin life immersed in the emotional experience of being the object of attention. The pleasure of these interactions motivates further engagements that expand their awareness of the different kinds of objects of others' attention. In addition, caregiver–infant games of teasing and mucking about (e.g., peek-a-boo, tickling, bouncing, blowing raspberries) provide emotionally rewarding and fertile contexts for expanding infants' awareness of intentions. The argument is therefore that infants learn about intentions from the first person (feeling the shape of an action in one's own body) and from the second person (feeling actions directed at self and in response to self) long before they begin to adopt a third-person perspective towards others and themselves.

At least two interesting conclusions emerge from Reddy's account. First, the emotional acts typically described as self-conscious (e.g., showing off, displays of pride, embarrassment or coyness) precede rather than result from a concept of self, which typically emerges at about 18 months of age (e.g., as evident in toddlers of this age touching their own noses when presented with a mirror showing their reflection with a rouge mark on the nose (Amsterdam, 1972). That is, these emotional acts (of showing off or coyness, etc.) are rooted in perceptions of the other's attention and emotion, rather than in thoughts about the self, and so might be better renamed "other-conscious emotions". Second, children with autism pass the mirror test by the appropriate developmental age but appear to lack this experiential base of the first- and second-person views, in that they fail to display self/other-conscious emotions (see Hobson, Chidambi, Lee, & Meyer, 2006, for similar results and conclusions). If this is the case, interventions that provide alternative means of engaging infants in dyadic interactions may well prove useful for children with autism; interestingly, recent studies with robots provide some empirical support for this proposal (Bird, Leighton, Press, & Heyes, 2007; Robins, Dautenhahn, Boekhorst, & Billard, 2005).

Toddlers understand world-inconsistent goals

For many researchers, the first and most important milestone in children's understanding of mind is the ability to recognize goals that are at odds with real-world situations – as illustrated so wonderfully by toddlers when they first begin to engage in pretend play – that is, between the ages of 18 months and 2 years (Leslie, 1987). Early forms of pretend play are typically "solo" episodes that are quite brief, nicely illustrated by Angus at the first visit, playing with the lid from a jar of Marmite (a very British sandwich spread made of yeast extract). Note that in this and all other conversational excerpts in this book, *X/Y*: denotes *X* speaking to *Y*.

Angus/Mother: I'm putting this on my head.
Mother/Angus: That's not a hat, is it?
Angus/Mother: Yes, it is. My hat.
Mother/Angus: It's a Marmite pot lid. You'll get Marmite in your hair. [*smiles*]
                  [*Sasha giggles*]
Mother/Sasha: He thinks he's got a hat on, Sasha. How many pieces of toast do
                  you want – two or one?

At 2½ years of age, however, Angus is also capable of joining his older sister in more complex and extended shared pretend-play narratives:

Sasha/Angus:	[*pause*] you haven't got the picnic blanket.
	[*Angus looks at Sasha then begins packing the basket*]
Sasha/Angus:	What about in this lovely shade? [*pretend voice*]
Angus/Sasha:	Yeah. Put them away. Put them back.
Sasha/Angus:	There, there we are [*pause*]. Now we can have a proper picnic [*pause*]. Let's put all the food here. Oh, lovely bread. [*pretending to eat*]
Angus/Sasha:	I got more bread.
	[*Angus puts a toy crisp on the mat for Sasha*]
Sasha/Angus:	Oh, crisp! [*delighted tone, pretending to eat*]
Angus/Sasha:	More crisps [*pause*]. More bread. And dat. Do you want those?
Sasha/Angus:	Oh melon, I love melon.
Angus/Sasha:	More crips. More crips. See these, for me.
	[*Sasha reaches into the basket. Angus takes out a pear that comes apart*]
Angus/Sasha:	I chopped this up, in half, I'm going to cut this up. You want piece?

After a few more minutes of this pretend narrative, the children pack away the toy picnic and find some toy handcuffs, which leads to a swift change of plot:

Angus/Sasha:	Is that going in there?
Sasha/Angus:	And we do need some handcuffs if there's a robber coming we need to put some handcuffs on him, and tell the police. But we'd really like to [*speech unintelligible; puts handcuffs on herself*]
Angus/Sasha:	Yeah, oh. Baby put way! Baby took them [*pause*] I'm going to get the robber. I tread on him, I already did.
Sasha/Angus:	Oh no, where are the keys?
Angus/Sasha:	I tread on them.
Sasha/Angus:	Now a robber has got me now.
Angus/Sasha:	What?
Sasha/Angus:	The robber has got me now.
Angus/Sasha:	What?
Sasha/Angus:	The robber stole the handcuffs and now I can't get out.
	[*Angus looks worried, then smiles and goes to Sasha*]
Angus/Sasha:	I can help you, I can help you.
Sasha/Angus:	I think I've done it.

As the above excerpt illustrates, engaging in pretend play also depends on the ability to plan and control actions, and to adjust flexibly to shifts in topic. For example, helped by external props such as toy handcuffs, Angus is clearly able to follow his sister Sasha as she switches the theme of pretence from picnic to cops and robbers; later, when Sasha introduces a twist to the tale by making the fictional robber put the handcuffs on her, Angus has a little more difficulty, looking worried for a few moments before coming to her rescue.

Removing these performance factors (involving "executive functions", discussed in Chapter 2) may reveal mental-state awareness even in much younger children. For example, Onishi and Baillargeon (2005) modified the standard object transfer paradigm used to test preschoolers' false-belief understanding to include two distinct conditions (true- *vs.* false-belief, in which the protagonist did/did not witness the object transfer), each with two distinct endings (the protagonist reached into the original box, or into the other box, where the object really was). From previous research we know that infants tend to look longer at surprising events (e.g., Jeffrey & Cohen, 1971), and so Onishi and Baillargeon (2005) were able to use looking times to index these 15-month-olds' expectations. In the false-belief condition, these toddlers showed longer looking times when the protagonist reached into the box that currently hid the object, but in the true-belief condition they showed the opposite pattern. That is, 15-month-olds' looking times reflected the violation of an expectation based on the pro-tagonist's belief states rather than the actual location of the object. Using a similar paradigm to assess toddlers' understanding of pretence, Onishi, Baillargeon, and Leslie (2007) reported that 15-month-olds (who are not yet displaying pretend play themselves) appear surprised (i.e., look longer) when an adult shows inconsistent pretend action sequences (e.g., pretends to pour a liquid into one cup and then pretends to drink from another cup). Building on the above findings, Song, Onishi, Baillargeon, and Fisher (2008) have shown that 18-month-olds understand that an agent's false belief can be corrected by an informative communication (The ball is in the cup!) though not by a non-informative communication (I like the cup!). That is, by 18 months of age children appear able not only to attribute a false belief to another, but also to recognize that beliefs are changed in response to appropriate communication.

However, these studies have been criticized on a number of grounds: for example, ambiguity in interpretation of the results due to the limited number of familiarization trials, or the possibility that looking times may reflect other perceptual variables that vary between familiarization and test events (Cohen, 2004; Sirois & Jackson, 2007). This criticism, coupled with the striking contrast with 3-year-olds' failure on standard false-belief tasks, has led to several challenges. One alternative account is that the looking-times measure reflects infants' ability to attribute ignorance rather than a specific false belief to an agent (Southgate, Senju, & Csibra, 2007). Logically, ignorance should lead to chance performance, but in reality young children expect ignorant agents to get the answer wrong (Ruffman, 1996; but see Friedman & Petrashek, 2009, for a counterview). Thus it is possible that the 15-month-olds in Onishi and Baillargeon's (2005) study may have looked longer in the incongruent condition simply because they did not expect an ignorant agent to find the object.

If looking times are too indirect, are there other nonverbal means of assessing false-belief attribution in very young children? To address this challenge, Southgate et al. (2007) used an eye-tracker to measure anticipatory looking in 25-month-olds as they watched actions on a computer monitor. The question is, in anticipating a protagonist's return to search for an object that has been moved from one location to another, will 25 month olds look towards the entry point by the new location where the object actually is, or towards the entry point by the old location where the protagonist last saw it? Some time ago, Clements and Perner (1994) showed that from 2 years 11 months children's anticipatory looking indicated false-belief understanding. In the Southgate et al. study, the object disappeared from the scene, and rather than using Clement and Perner's verbal prompt ("I wonder where he's going to look?") familiarization trials involving a light/sound cue were included to elicit anticipatory looking. In addition, numerous controls were adopted to ensure that the 25-month-old children were not simply responding to low-level cues (e.g., the object's actual or last location) and the eye-tracker (unlike Clement and Perner's video data) gave detailed information about where the children looked, which included their careful monitoring of the protagonist's eye gaze. Southgate et al.'s (2007) results indicate that 25-month-olds show an implicit understanding of others' false beliefs.

Toddlers' sensitivity to others' mental perspectives is also seen in their ability to distinguish between intention and action, to respond differentially to others' emotions, and to respond to desires different from their own. Experimental evidence also shows that, from as early as 18 months of age, toddlers watching an adult fail in their attempt to perform a task and then, given the opportunity to imitate, will perform the intended action rather than copy the movements that led to failure (Meltzoff, 1995). That is, children this age can recognize intention in behaviour; they also know that trying is not the same as pretending (H. Rakoczy, Tomasello, & Striano, 2004) and can recognize desire in behaviour. For example, if an adult shows pleasure toward one food and disgust toward another, 18-month-olds understand that they should give the adult the food toward which she or he showed pleasure, even if they themselves prefer the other food (Repacholi & Gopnik, 1997). This awareness of the subjectivity of tastes was also demonstrated by Angus during the first home visit, when he was playing with his sister Sasha.

Sasha/Angus: Oh, I love dinosaurs.
Angus/Sasha: I don't like dinors.
Sasha/Angus: I like dinosaurs.
Angus/Sasha: I don't like that much. I don't like dinors.

At this age toddlers also appear able to take another person's perspective into account when regulating their behaviour in response to the other's expressed emotion; for example, if one adult expressed anger towards another adult for acting on an object, 18-month-olds only avoided acting on the object if the person who had previously displayed anger could see them (Repacholi & Meltzoff, 2007).

Thus, in various ways, by 18 months of age children show considerable ability to take others' mental perspectives into account, as evidenced by their understanding of pretend, desire, intention, emotion, and their implicit understanding of actions guided by false beliefs. For caregivers these findings may come as no surprise – after all, even before the age of 12 months, babies show amusement when others engage in pretend acts (e.g., making animal noises, or pretending to gobble baby up), at this age babies also make great efforts to communicate what they want when a parent appears to misunderstand them (Lock, 1980). Interestingly, this observation provides a valuable pointer towards the ontogeny of social understanding: what babies know about others' minds may well be rooted in their experience of social interactions with caregivers and others close to them. That is, rather than (or perhaps as well as) emerging from the use of language as a symbolic tool, such knowledge may be shaped by social interactions from the very beginning of life. For example, Lillard and Witherington (2004) have shown that caregivers provide numerous cues that help infants recognize the distinction between pretend and real-life events. In their elegantly simple study, caregivers were filmed engaging with their 18-month-old toddlers in real versus pretend snack scenarios. Interestingly, caregivers did not use mental-state terms (e.g., "pretend") more often during the imagined snack, but they did talk more about their "actions" (drinking, eating); caregivers also showed much higher rates of smiling, eye-contact and amusing sound effects during the imaginary snack than during the real snack. Each of these features of caregivers' interactions was associated with increased toddler understanding of the pretend situation. As we shall see later, these results also anticipate the findings from our transcript-based analyses of home-based interactions between 2-year-olds and their caregivers, in which conversational "connectedness" (i.e., semantic relatedness of speech to the previous turn – a linguistic equivalent of establishing eye contact) predicted improvements in children's performance on theory-of-mind tasks between the ages of 2 and 4 years (Ensor & Hughes, 2008), or even 2 to 6 years (Ensor, 2009). Indeed, this quality of connectedness is clearly evident in the conversations between Angus and Sasha noted earlier, and continues to be apparent at the third home visit, when Angus (now 6) and his sister, playing with a Playmobil zoo-set, show an impressive ability to build on each other's ideas for fantasy play, perhaps because they share a sense of humour that has a distinctly scatological flavour…

Angus/Sasha:	This is mine! Yes, fight between you and me. [*pretend gorilla voice*]
Sasha/Angus:	OK. Don't kill the lions. [*pause*] No that, that one bites him. [*making lion bite Angus's gorilla*]
Angus/Sasha:	He dead, now this one chomps him.
Sasha/Angus:	Look now they eat him. Look he's eating him, don't.
Angus/Sasha:	Bottom's the best bit. [*both laugh*]
Angus/Sasha:	The elephants need to have a big space.
Sasha/Angus:	Elephant. Little baby one.
Angus/Sasha:	This is to clean it, clean out the elephant poo. [*holding toy broom*]
Sasha/Angus:	Oh look at the baby, [*pause*] the baby. There's the man, go in there. He's cleaning up the poo? No he's going to clean up the poo.
Angus/Sasha:	He's the poo cleaner.
Sasha/Angus:	Elephant poo. Man that's a big one! [*both laugh*]

Preschoolers show a representational understanding of mental states

The results from the experimental toddler studies outlined in the section above have generated tremendous interest, not least because, for a long time, the general view was that false-belief understanding served as a hallmark for a representational theory of mind, and was indexed by success on a standard object-transfer task, typically achieved by children around 4 years of age. This object-transfer task does, however, require children to follow a rather complicated story narrative and attribute beliefs to dolls and so a second task was designed to reduce these demands. In this "unexpected-contents" task (Perner, Leekam, & Wimmer, 1987), children are: shown a prototypical box (e.g., a familiar candy box); asked what they think is inside (candy); allowed to discover its unexpected contents (e.g., pencils); and then asked either (i) what another person, who had not seen inside the box, would think was inside it; or even (ii) what they themselves had thought was inside the box, before they opened it (Gopnik & Astington, 1988). For either of these two test questions, the modal response from 3-year-olds was "pencils", but "candy" from 4- and 5-year-olds. In other words, 3-year-olds found it as difficult to remember their own previous false belief as to predict another person's false belief. Evidence from a separate study (Flavell, Green, & Flavell, 1986) showed that 3-year-olds found it equally difficult to recognize that objects can be misleading in their appearance (e.g., a candle that looks like an apple, or a sponge that looks like a rock).

Once again, however, direct observations demonstrate that in real life at least some 3-year-olds have a clear understanding of the difference between appearance and reality. Take, for example, the following brief excerpt from one of our study children (whom we'll call "Jimmy"), filmed at home at age 3. He is setting the table for dinner, and humming to himself.

Mother/Jimmy:	What are you drinking for tea Jimmy?
Jimmy/Mother:	I'm drinking Shrek blood.
Mother/Jimmy:	Shrek blood? Okay! [*smiles*]
Jimmy [*to self*]:	Shrek, Shrek, Shrek blood! [*waving dinner knife around*]

Of course, Jimmy doesn't really expect to drink Shrek blood – this is his playful way of asking for blackcurrant juice; because he knows that his mother will understand his request, he is able to enliven the task of preparing things for dinner. Thus this excerpt both illustrates 3-year-old Jimmy's understanding of the appearance–reality distinction and highlights the social benefits of conversational partners who can connect with one's ideas and interests – this is a theme that will be developed in Chapter 4.

In experimental situations, however, the findings remain remarkably robust even when specific task demands are manipulated in a variety of ways (see Wellman et al., 2001, for a meta-analytic review). In short, between the ages of 3 and 5 years, children consistently show a marked improvement in their performance on these object-transfer/unexpected-contents false-belief tasks and unexpected-identity tasks. This is interesting, because the failure of 3-year-olds on these types of task contrasts sharply with 15-month-olds' abilities to take others' mental perspectives into account, as described in the previous section. So, why do 3-year-olds answer incorrectly in a verbal false-belief test while infants correctly anticipate the actor's behaviour in a nonverbal test? In fact, 3-year-olds also fail some nonverbal tests (J. W. Astington & Baird, 2005), so that the contrast is perhaps better expressed as direct versus indirect tests of false-belief understanding (Perner, 2009).

For some researchers (e.g., Csibra & Southgate, 2006; Leslie, 2005; Leslie, Friedman, & German, 2004; Southgate et al., 2007), these early findings from preschoolers are simply rendered invalid by the more recent findings from 15-month-olds. In other words, peripheral task demands (e.g., on language skills, planning and the ability to inhibit prepotent responses based on children's true beliefs) mask 3-year-old children's competence on the standard object-transfer false-belief task (e.g., Leslie, German, & Polizzi, 2005). Other researchers (e.g., Perner & Ruffman, 2005) defend the earlier findings and explain the recent findings without assuming that infants have knowledge about the mind. One suggestion is that during the familiarization phase of the task activation of neurons in the prefrontal cortex creates an association between the actor, object and location, such that a consistent test combination (i.e., in the true-belief condition) will require less processing than an inconsistent test combination (in the false-belief condition) that requires a new association to be formed. As a result, there is no need to invoke attribution of beliefs to explain why "looking times" are longer for false-belief than for true-belief conditions. Alternatively, they argue that the infants' behaviour can be explained on the basis of behavioural rules to which any added assumption of mentalistic understanding adds nothing in explanatory power or theoretical parsimony (Povinelli & Vonk, 2004). Admittedly, 4-year-olds' performance on the standard false-belief tasks can be explained in the same way but 4-year-olds can also respond flexibly in non-standard situations (e.g., tasks that involve more than two hiding places) that cannot easily be explained by behavioural rules (Perner, 2009).

Perhaps, however, there is no fundamental conflict: while toddlers clearly show an intuitive understanding of mind, it is only considerably later in development that children show a reflective understanding of mind. Moreover, this reflective understanding is probably only gradually acquired, as shown by 3-year-olds' success on some manipulations used in the false-belief tasks – for example, in object-transfer tasks that include a deceptive motive for moving the object, or that decrease the object's salience by removing it from the scene (Wellman et al., 2001). Three-year-olds also appear to understand false beliefs in word-learning tasks (Carpenter, Call, & Tomasello, 2002; Happé & Loth, 2002): that is, when acquiring a novel word for an unfamiliar object they take account of a person's false belief in a situation where the object was moved while the person was off the scene.

Note also that once children acquire representational false-belief understanding at the end of the preschool years, they soon recognize the emotional consequences of a person's holding a false belief – for example, if someone is misinformed about a situation, they may feel happy because they think they are getting what they want, even though they may be sad after they discover the true state of affairs (Harris, Johnson, Hutton, Andrews, & Cooke, 1989). Children of this age also appreciate the distinction between real and apparent emotion: that is, they recognize that a person may dissemble, displaying a facial expression different from their real feelings, in order to avoid being teased or to protect someone else's feelings (Harris & Gross, 1988).

If we accept the idea that an early intuitive understanding of false belief in infancy and toddlerhood gives rise to reflective understanding later in the preschool years, then an urgent question is: how does this come about? This question has been addressed from two distinct perspectives, which focus on: (i) developmentally synchronous improvements in other cognitive domains, including young children's language abilities and "executive functions" (i.e., their ability to adopt flexible, goal-directed thinking); and (ii) children's close family relationships as a source of learning about the mind.

Adopting the first of these two perspectives, it seems most likely that language plays an important role in children's growing ability to reflect on mental states. Language development in the second and third year brings about dramatic transformations in children's abilities not only to reflect on the world around them, but also to engage in conversations about things out of sight. As a result, children's mental horizons expand rapidly; rather than being captive in the here and now, children can think about past events and make plans for the future. The conversational excerpt below, which shows a mother reading at home to her blond 6-year-old son, with a dark-haired younger son hovering near them, is a good example of this. See page 92 (Figures 5.1 and 5.2) for the pictures that accompany this excerpt:

Mother: I can remember something you didn't like about school [*shakes cuddly toy elephant*]. Who didn't come to school with you?
Child: Ellie.
Mother: How did that make you feel? Can you remember?
Child: Sad.
Mother: You didn't like Ellie not going to school with you. Do you remember what we did at the beginning? Can you remember what we used to do?
Child: Yes, took him on the bike and once I dropped him and Tusha got her for me.
Mother: Yeah and then what did we do with Ellie? Did she go into school with you?
Child: No.
Mother: She came back home again didn't she? [*C nods*] Do you still miss Ellie at school?
Child: No.
Mother: Not at all? [*C shakes head*] He's just a home elephant.
Child: Sometimes when I feel [*pause*] sometimes I do really want him like if I hurt myself.
Mother: Mm. So, what do you do when you're at school and you haven't got Ellie?
Child: There's a very nice monkey I like.

Mother: Have you got a monkey in your classroom? You're allowed to cuddle it when you need a cuddle?

Child: [*Nods*] Also sometimes if I'm tired. Once George was really tired and he had to go home, they cuddled up on the sofa with a small blanket and he cuddled Percy.

Mother: Ah, that's quite nice. Who's Percy?

Child: That's the dog.

This excerpt illustrates the vividness of children's memories (e.g., "Yes, took him on the bike and once I dropped him and Tusha got her for me.") and demonstrates this 6-year-old's ability both to generate a plan B when a habitual object of comfort is unavailable ("Sometimes I do really want him like if I hurt myself." [*Question*:] "So what do you do when you're at school and you haven't got Ellie?" [*Answer*:] "There's a very nice monkey I like.") and to show flexibility in problem solving ("Once George was really tired and he had to go home, they cuddled up on the sofa with a small blanket and he cuddled Percy." [*a toy dog*]).

Thus language development emerges hand in hand with advances in young children's executive control (i.e., their ability to inhibit prepotent responses and to engage in flexible and goal-directed acts) as well as with children's growing understanding of mind. Alongside this developmental synchrony between these three domains (of language, executive control and social understanding) are significant, independent and asymmetric associations between individual differences in each domain. Specifically, individual differences in language skills and executive control each predict improvements in children's performance on explicit theory-of-mind tasks (e.g., Hughes & Ensor, 2007a). These predictive relationships are discussed at length in Chapters 2 and 3.

At the heart of the second, sociocultural, perspective is the proposal that children's close relationships serve as developmental wellsprings for their growing social understanding. Multiple processes are likely to underpin associations between children's social experiences and their ability to reflect on mental states. These include both direct effects (e.g., via conversations that highlight differences in points of view) and indirect effects (e.g., as a result of the need to understand and so control negative emotions). These proposals are discussed fully in Chapters 4, 5 and 6.

School-aged children show a recursive and interpretative understanding of mental states

As outlined above, studies of preschoolers' understanding of the representational nature of mental states have used tasks that focus on false beliefs about real situations. But social understanding encompasses an awareness not just of how mental states govern people's interactions with the physical world (e.g., where they will look for an object that has been moved in their absence), but also of social interactions within human relationships. For this, one needs to think about one's own and others' mental states in relation to each other. In the early school years children become aware that people have beliefs about the content of others' minds (e.g., about what others think or want) and recognize that these beliefs may be different or wrong. Take, for example, this conversation between Angus and his mother, filmed at home when he was 6 years old. They are discussing one of a set of three short stories provided by the research team and designed to elicit adult–child conversations about negative emotions and ambiguous intentions (Root & Jenkins, 2005).

Mother: Look, that's the end of the story – So I wonder what happened to Max's car? Where do you think the car might've gone to?

Angus: I think Max's friend might've tooken it with him, 'cause he liked the Batmobile so much.

Mother: Yes [*pause*] I wonder if somebody had taken the car. What do you think? [*pause*] What other things might've happened to the car?

Angus: Might've got [*pause*] some [*pause*] might've got put into the closet next to the gym?

Mother: That's true. It could've been put away with all the school toys, couldn't it, by mistake? [*Angus nods*] Yeah. Or maybe another teacher might've put it in a special safe place and forgotten to tell him. [*Angus nods*] But anyway, what do you think Max's friend, Peter, was thinking about the Batmobile car when he saw it?

Angus: I think he was thinking, I really want that, my birthday is ages away so I just wanna take it today and bring it back tomorrow.

Mother: Yes, that's quite possible, isn't it? 'Cause if it was a really long time 'til your birthday and you really, really loved something, then you might think that it would be really nice just to have it just for a little while, wouldn't you? [*Angus nods*] Do you think that if you saw a friend's toy, like say somebody brought a really, really, really nice – I don't know what – I know – say, like, your friend had Heelies and they put them somewhere. Do you think that it would be really nice to borrow them, and try them on, and play with them? [*Angus nods*] Do you? And, anyway, so, how do you think someone feels when they see something and they really want it and it belongs to somebody else, it's not theirs?

Angus: They think, I'll just take it for a little while and he won't notice.

Mother: Yes, that's right. And how do you think Max felt when he was standing by his cubby, here, look, can you see that, that funny – ?

Angus: He was sad.

Mother: Yes, very sad. Because he's put his Batmobile there, hasn't he? And now it's not there. He's very sad, isn't he? And when you read a story like this [*pause*]

Angus: Yes [*pause*]

Mother: I think that it would be good to feel sorry for Max 'cause Max has lost his toy, hasn't he? [*Angus nods*] And what do you think about Peter?

Angus: I think he's a very naughty boy.

Mother: And what do you think he's thinking? If he has taken it, which we don't know if he has, do we, 'cause it could've got put somewhere else by accident.
Angus: Yeah.
Mother: But if he has taken it, what do you think he's thinking? Do you think he thinks he's naughty?
Angus: No.
Mother: No?
Angus: He thinks that he will get away with it.

At least two points about this conversation deserve note. First, Angus's mother is doing a wonderful job of encouraging him to reflect on other people's thoughts, feelings and motives, as well as on the range of possible explanations of how the toy car got lost. Second, 6-year-old Angus is clearly able to represent another person's belief about someone else's beliefs: "They think, I'll just take it for a little while and he won't notice. ... He thinks that he will get away with it." Such beliefs about other mental states are referred to as second-order mental states (see S. Miller, 2009, for a recent review).

Perner and Wimmer (1985) showed that, in experimental situations, children start to demonstrate an ability to represent and reason from second-order beliefs: "X believes that Y believes that p" from around 7 to 8 years of age. A simplified task (Sullivan, Zaitchik, & Tager-Flusberg, 1994), with probe questions giving corrective feedback and a memory aid just before the test question, scaffolded 5- and 6-year-olds' performance, but even without these aids a simplified storyline showed genuine second-order belief attribution by 7 years of age (Astington, Pelletier, & Homer, 2002). Somewhat earlier, children acquire the ability to understand second-order representations involving desires and intentions, such as understanding that someone wants to make another person believe something (Leekam, 1991). Somewhat later, children acquire the ability to deal with third-order representations involving beliefs, desires, intentions and attitudes (Filippova & Astington, 2008).

What do these cognitive advances mean for children's social interactions with other people? Astington and colleagues have, over a number of years, investigated this issue and concluded that this kind of recursive ability underlies age-related increases across the school years in children's use of complex language, particularly indirect speech acts, such as irony and metaphor. Indirect speech is defined by a contrast between what is actually said and what is meant (a very British example would be the expression "Shall I put the kettle on?" which means "Have you got time for a cup of tea and a chat?"). Another, less domestic example of indirect speech is verbal irony, when someone says something that is false but does not intend the listener to believe it to be true, but rather to recognize the falsity and interpret the statement as funny or sarcastic (Filippova & Astington, 2008). Likewise, metaphors are not intended as statements to be literally interpreted but are used to create poetic images (Winner, 1988).

Understanding recursive mental states also leads to an increasing sensitivity to the interpersonal dynamics of social situations. For example, during the school years children come to understand "white lies" where something untrue is said to protect a person's feelings (Talwar, Murphy, & Lee, 2007). They also recognize when someone has produced a "faux pas" and unintentionally revealed secret information or created hurt feelings (Baron-Cohen, O'Riordan, Stone, Jones, & Plaisted, 1999). As well, they can invent or select persuasive strategies, which require the manipulation of a person's mental states in order to get them to believe or do something (Bartsch & London, 2000; Bartsch, London, & Campbell, 2007).

Social understanding in school-aged children is characterized not only by the ability to understand multiple embeddings in higher order mental states, but also by the recognition of interpretive diversity (i.e., the understanding that two people may make legitimate but different interpretations of the same external stimulus). This ability is correlated with the development of second-order false-belief understanding and also appears around 7 years of age (Comay, 2009). Interestingly, at this age, children also understand the dynamic nature of mental activity of the mind. In particular, while preschoolers can report the content of their mental states it is not until the early school years that children become aware of the stream of consciousness that fills the waking mind (Flavell, Green, & Flavell, 1995).

Compared with the plethora of studies that focus on preschoolers, later normative developments in children's social understanding have received much less research attention. However, a number of measures of advanced social understanding have been developed for research on clinical groups (e.g., adolescents with autism spectrum disorders and adults with schizophrenia; see Sprong, Schothorst, Vos, Hox, & Van Engeland, 2007, for a meta-analytic review). These include two vignette-based tasks: the Strange Stories (Happé, 1994) and the Hinting task (Corcoran, 2003). In the Strange Stories task, individuals are presented with scenarios in which a protagonist says something that is not literally true (e.g., white lie, bluff, double bluff, sarcasm, joke) and asked to explain why s/he said this. In the Hinting task, story characters make oblique remarks and individuals are asked to explain their underlying intentions (e.g., a request for help). Both of these tasks therefore tap understanding of the distinction between literal and intended meaning. However, conclusions from studies involving these tasks are constrained by the lack of published data on either their psychometric properties or normative age-related improvements.

Chapter summary

The aim of this chapter was to provide a theoretical and empirical context for the rest of the book, using conversational excerpts from the Toddlers Up study to illustrate the sophistication of children's social understanding. Importantly, this chapter presented a developmental view of theory of mind, in which early intuitive awareness of self and others gives rise to explicit, reflective understanding. By mapping out developmental changes from infancy through to school age this chapter also highlighted the expansion of research horizons beyond their original narrow focus on preschoolers' false-belief comprehension to encompass multiple milestones over an extended developmental period. Importantly, the later developing explicit theory of mind does not replace the former but both together underpin self-reflection and social understanding from childhood to adulthood. This framework is consonant with others' views, including the family resemblance of distinctions cited in the introduction to the chapter. Moreover, the framework has proved useful for some time now. For example, Tomasello, Kruger, and Ratner (1993) argued for a developmental progression in cultural learning, from imitative learning, to instructed learning, to collaborative learning. Imitative learning involves joint attention, which requires understanding the other as an intentional agent. In contrast with the later two levels, it is not dependent on language and in that sense is "intuitive". Instructed learning is reflective and collaborative learning is recursively reflective – that is, the other is understood *as* a reflective agent. In general, this framework provides a fertile foundation for research and may help lay to rest the fruitless, either/or arguments the field has seen between so-called "boosters" and "scoffers" (Chandler, Fritz, & Hala, 1989) who advocate either rich or lean interpretations of behaviour. This framework acknowledges the authentic nature of infants' social skills while still allocating tremendous importance to the changes in self-reflection and social understanding that occur through early and later childhood.

2 Executive functions and children's understanding of mind

As any parent will know, the first years of a child's life are a time of dramatic changes across many fronts. These include cognitive milestones (e.g., in language or memory), behavioural milestones (e.g., physical coordination, emotional regulation) and social milestones (e.g., compliance with social norms). What is not yet known is whether these dramatic changes are interconnected, and, if so, how? In this chapter I address this question by focusing on one current hot topic for research: the associations between children's understanding of mind and their "executive functions". In the clinical literature, the term "executive functions" is also often used as a shorthand for the functions of the prefrontal cortex; note, however, that the neural substrate for executive functions also includes subcortical structures (e.g., the basal ganglia). In cognitive psychology, "executive functions" is used as an umbrella term to refer to the set of higher order processes (e.g., inhibitory control and working memory) that underpin flexible goal-directed behaviour.

Figures 2.1 and 2.2 show just two of the battery of tasks used in the Toddlers Up study to assess young children's executive functions (a further task, shown in Figure 2.3, is described later in this chapter). In the "Spin the Pots" task, shown in Figure 2.1, children are invited to search for each of 6 stickers hidden in the 8 boxes (to do this efficiently, they must hold in mind which boxes have already been opened). Figure 2.2 shows the materials for the "Baby Stroop" task, in which children are invited to play a topsy-turvy game in which they must say "Mummy's" when they are shown the baby cup or spoon and "Baby's" when they are shown the grown-up cup or spoon (to do this, children must inhibit responding with the more habitual labels for each object).

This chapter addresses several questions about how individual differences in early executive functions might contribute to individual differences in children's understanding of mind. First, the origins of research into this topic are outlined, along with subsequent theoretical developments. Next, two key predictions from this proposal are considered: (i) do early individual differences in executive functions predict later individual differences in social understanding (and, if so, is this association asymmetric or bi-directional?); and (ii) is the link between executive functions and social understanding independent of common associations with background factors, such as verbal ability or family background? Next, I briefly

Figure 2.1 The Spin the Pots task.

Figure 2.2 The Baby Stroop task.

discuss findings that cast light on whether the link between executive functions and social understanding should be viewed as general or specific in nature. Finally, I address the issue of universality, by examining whether the link between executive functions and social understanding holds up for atypical groups (e.g., children with autism or attention deficit hyperactivity disorder, ADHD) and for typically developing children from different cultures.

Why might executive functions matter for children's understanding of mind?

The first clue that success on false-belief tasks (often thought of as the "litmus test" for theory of mind) may depend on more than children's mentalizing ability came from the finding that children with autism's widespread failure on such tasks (e.g., Baron-Cohen et al., 1985) is often accompanied by failure on tests of executive function (e.g., Ozonoff, Pennington, & Rogers, 1991). This finding lent weight to the view that success on false-belief tasks depends not just on children's ability to attribute mental states to others, but also on their ability to track complex sequences of events and to suppress responses based on their own correct (and therefore doubly salient) knowledge of a situation (Moses, 2001a). In addition, children's everyday experiences are much more likely to involve true rather than false beliefs. Each of these factors makes the false-belief task a very conservative test of children's mentalizing skills. Thus, children may fail on the false-belief task, not because they lack an understanding of mind, but because they lack the higher order control needed to *express* this understanding (Moses, 2001a).

Concerns about the impure nature of false-belief tasks were amplified by reports of perseverative errors by both 3-year-olds and children with autism during tests using a "deception" paradigm known as the Windows task (Hughes & Russell, 1993; Russell, Mauthner, Sharpe, & Tidswell, 1991). In this task, children were first trained to understand that a sweet placed in one of two opaque boxes could be won by leading a competitor towards the empty box; in the test phase, the opaque boxes were replaced by boxes with windows, so that the children could see exactly which box contained the sweet. Despite being clearly motivated to win the sweets, 3-year-olds and children with autism showed a "visual capture" error, repeatedly pointing to the baited box often for as many as 20 trials.

In my PhD work (conducted under Jim Russell's supervision) I designed an apparatus, later dubbed the "detour reaching box" (shown in Figure 2.3), that, by removing all elements of deception from the Windows task, provided a means of testing the strength of the perseverative "visual capture" error shown by 3-year-olds and children with autism. The design for this box was inspired by childhood memories of an exhibit at the Science Museum in London: a large round table with a golden ball at the centre that "magically" disappeared into a hole as soon as anyone reached out to grasp it. In the detour reaching box, an attractive marble is positioned on a platform inside the box such that it can be seen through a Perspex window with a round hole (big enough for a hand to reach through). Just behind the window is a small infra-red circuit; in addition, the marble rests on a platform that includes a trapdoor that is activated when this infra-red circuit is broken. Thus, as soon as the child reaches into the box (or pokes any object through the window) the marble drops through the trapdoor and out of sight. At the front of the box are two lights, one orange and one green. Children are given a few attempts at retrieving the marble via a direct reach and then shown two alternative solutions. In the first of these (signalled by the orange light being illuminated) children can turn a knob on the right-hand side of the box in order to knock the marble down a chute. This "knob route" can be blocked by throwing a bolt; this action extinguishes the orange light and activates a green light, which signals the second alternative "switch route". In this route, children can retrieve the marble by flicking a switch on the left-hand side of the box before reaching in through the hole in the window.

Figure 2.3 The detour reaching box.

Interestingly, 3-year-olds and children with autism on this task showed no diffi-culty with the "knob route" but made lots of perseverative errors on the "switch route", just as they had in the Windows task (Hughes & Russell, 1993). These perseverative errors (i.e., repeatedly making a direct reach for the sweet in the Windows task, or for the marble in the detour-reaching task) were very striking and echoed the "A not B" error shown by babies on Piaget's Object Permanence task (Piaget, 1952). In this task, 5-month-olds can see that an object has moved from location A to location B, but often persist in searching for it in its original location; by 8 months most babies are able to search correctly at the new location. Originally, Piaget had interpreted younger infants' failure on this task as indi-cating a lack of object permanence, thus confirming his theory of infantile egocen-tricity. (Note that this term refers to a view of the world in which self and other are not conceptually distinct, rather than to any kind of infant "selfishness".) Early researchers who used this paradigm supported this view (e.g., Harris, 1975), but later studies (in which infants' perceptual understanding was assessed via looking times rather than physical reaches) demonstrated that infants display object permanence from as early as 4 months of age (e.g., Baillargeon, Spelke, & Wasserman, 1985).

Further studies replicated Baillargeon's findings, but also confirmed Piaget's original finding of search errors by young infants on the A not B task. In a review of this work, Munakata, McClelland, Johnson, and Siegler (1997) argued that infants younger than 8 months have the object permanence principle but lack means–ends abilities. Crucial to this conclusion were findings from lesion studies of rhesus monkeys, which demonstrated that the dorsolateral prefrontal cortex is vital for success on the A not B task, such that improvements on this task between the ages of 7½ and 12 months in human infants probably reflect maturation of this region (Diamond, 1988; Diamond & Goldman-Rakic, 1989). Importantly, as noted by Diamond and Goldman-Rakic (1989), success on the A not B task marks the development of the ability to hold a goal in mind without external cues, and to use that remembered goal to guide behaviour despite the pull of previous rein-forcement (or salient perceptual triggers) to act otherwise. In short, success on the A not B task is a very early manifestation of infants' growing cognitive flexibility and volitional control.

Building on these findings, Russell (1996) developed a theoretical perspective in which deficits in executive control among children with autism underpinned not only the *expression* but also the *emergence* of their understanding of mind (cf. also Moses, 2001a). Specifically, Russell (1996) argued that children's devel-oping concepts of volition (or intention) depend crucially on their direct first-hand experience of goal-directed volitional control. Support for this executive account of children with autism's failure on false-belief tasks came from two studies (conducted independently in the USA and in the UK), which showed that children with autism performed very poorly on standard neuropsychological assessments of executive control (Hughes, Russell, & Robbins, 1994; Ozonoff et al., 1991). Specifically, both studies demonstrated striking deficits in children with autism's performance on tests of attentional set shifting (the Wisconsin Card Sort Test and the Intra-Dimensional Extra-Dimensional Shift Test) and tests of planning (the Tower of Hanoi and the Tower of London). Likewise, in a more recent study Pellicano (2007) confirmed a significant association between theory of mind and executive-functions among young children with autism (mean age = 5½ years) and shown that, consistent with Russell's (1996) model, dissociations were found in one direction only: impaired theory of mind coupled with intact executive functions. However, the acid test for any cognitive account of autism must be how well that account can explain the nature and severity of symptoms in autism. In one of the few studies to address this question (using a sample of school-aged verbal children with autism), Joseph and Tager-Flusberg (2004) found that, beyond effects of verbal ability, individual differences in both theory of mind and executive functions predicted communication symptoms, but neither theory of mind nor executive functions predicted unique variance in social interaction deficits or repetitive ritualistic behaviours. In many ways, then, the causes of autism remain elusive. Note also that, echoing the shift from polemical debate to integrative models described in Chapter 1, Russell's account of the role of executive functions in children's understanding of mind has changed over the last decade or so, such that it now complements rather than challenges nativist or theory–theory models. Specifically, Russell's current view (personal communication, March 2010) is that the growth of executive functions in the preschool years helps explain how children *make use* of their early intuitive understanding of mind.

For the purposes of this chapter, however, it is worth noting that Russell's (1996) executive account of deficits in social understanding among children with autism also leads to two testable predictions with regard to typically developing children. The first of these is that early individual differences in executive control should predict later individual differences in children's understanding of mind. The second is that this predictive relationship should be much stronger than its reverse (i.e., early individual differences in children's understanding of mind should not predict later individual differences in children's performances on tests of executive control). Before reviewing the evidence for each of these predictions, it is worth noting that the link between theory of mind and executive functions may be neuro-anatomical rather than psychological. That is, theory of mind and executive-functions skills may depend upon functionally independent systems that happen to share a common neural substrate (as illustrated in Figure 3.1, p. 62): imaging studies show that neighbouring regions of the prefrontal cortex are activated in adults completing either theory-of-mind tasks (Alexander, Benson, & Stuss, 1989; C. Frith & Frith, 1999; Sabbagh & Taylor, 2000) or executive-functions tasks (Duncan, 2005; Rabbitt, 1997). Investigating this possibility requires addressing a whole field of research in the neurosciences and is beyond the scope of this chapter; for the interested reader, several recent reviews are available (e.g., Perner & Aichhorn, 2008; Perner, Aichhorn, Kronbichler, Staffen, & Ladurner, 2006).

Does early executive function predict later social understanding (or vice versa)?

Early executive accounts of children's developing understanding of mind hinged on two lines of evidence. First, improvements in these two distinct aspects of children's cognition show clear developmental synchrony; in particular, the preschool years are characterized by dramatic age-related improvements in both theory of mind (Wellman et al., 2001) and executive functions (Carlson, 2005; Gerstadt, Hong, & Diamond, 1994; Kochanska, Murray, & Harlan, 2000; Zelazo, Frye, & Rapus, 1996). Second, as detailed later in this chapter, there is a robust correlation between individual differences in preschoolers' performances on theory of mind and executive-functions tasks (which, as discussed in the next section, remains significant when common effects of verbal ability and family background are taken into account). However, these cross-sectional findings are silent on the issue of causal direction and, indeed, some theorists have argued that theory-of-mind skills underpin success on executive-functions tasks. For example, the meta-representational ability needed to pass theory-of-mind tasks (e.g., to recognize the fallible and subjective nature of beliefs) may enable children to "tag" a prepotent response as "maladaptive" such that it can be suppressed (Carruthers, 1996; Perner, 1998; Perner, Lang, & Kloo, 2002).

Longitudinal data are needed to assess this issue of causal direction. In the first study to address this challenge, Hughes (1998b) gave theory of mind and executive-functions task batteries to 50 children seen at ages 4 and 5: age-4 executive functions predicted age-5 theory of mind, even with initial theory of mind controlled; however there was no independent relationship between age-4 theory of mind and age-5 executive functions. The same asymmetric association was also found in a study of 81 children followed from ages 2 to 3 (Carlson, Mandell, & Williams, 2004). In addition, two micro-genetic studies have also demonstrated that most children succeeded at executive-inhibition tasks before having a good understanding of false beliefs (Flynn, 2007; Flynn, O'Malley, & Wood, 2004). These findings converge in suggesting that the capacity to engage in goal-directed acts (and to inhibit stimulus-driven responses) precedes and/or promotes children's ability to reflect on such goal-directed behaviour (cf. Russell, 1996). Support for this conclusion comes from the findings that theory-of-mind performance improves when demands for resisting a prepotent response on a theory-of-mind task are removed (Carlson, Moses, & Hix, 1998; Hala & Russell, 2001) and worsens when these demands are increased (Leslie & Polizzi, 1998). That said, each of the above studies involved relatively short time-spans (13 months or less) and included children from rather homogeneous family backgrounds. As a result, it is not clear to what extent the asymmetric association between early executive functions and later theory of mind can be generalized to more diverse samples or longer time-scales. In addition, a recent training study has shown less clear-cut results: children's performance on tests of both executive functions (the Dimensional Change Card Sort) and theory of mind (false-belief comprehension) improved following training in either domain (Kloo & Perner, 2003), indicating a bi-directional or reciprocal relationship between theory of mind and executive functions.

The Toddlers Up study enabled us to extend the developmental span of this previous research, by following up a socially diverse sample of 122 children who completed comprehensive batteries of theory of mind and executive-functions tasks at age 2, at age 3 and again at age 4 (Hughes & Ensor, 2007a). In total, of six separate analyses conducted to assess relations between theory of mind and executive functions across these three time-points (± controlling for initial domain performance), five supported predictive relations between executive functions and later theory of mind, but only two supported predictive relations between theory of mind and later executive functions. Thus, although the Toddlers Up study provides partial support for the proposal that success on executive-functions tasks depends on children's theory-of-mind skills, it provides stronger evidence for the view that children's success on theory-of-mind tasks depends on their emerging executive-functions skills.

Does the link between theory of mind and executive functions reflect common effects of a third factor?

The studies described above addressed the question of causal direction for the association between executive functions and theory of mind; however, it is also worth considering whether this association can be explained in terms of a third factor. Frye, Zelazo, and Palfai (1995) were the first to articulate this possibility, proposing that age-related changes in the complexity of children's reasoning underpinned improvements in both theory of mind and executive-functions tasks. Specifically, in a set of three experiments, Frye et al. (1995) showed that the ability to use embedded "if–then" rules could account for advances between 3 and 5 years of age in children's understanding of both physical causality and mental states, as well as in their ability to switch between sorting rules. This proposal was later formalized as a theory of cognitive complexity and control (e.g., Müller, Zelazo, & Imrisek, 2005; Zelazo & Frye, 1998) and bears more than a passing resemblance to the proposal that syntactic complexity (specifically, mastery of embedded complements) underpins children's success on false-belief tasks (P. de Villiers, 2005). Empirically, associations between verbal ability, executive functions and theory of mind are widely documented (e.g., Happé, 1995; Hughes & Ensor, 2005, 2007a; Milligan, Astington, & Dack, 2007). That said, most of the studies that report an association between false-belief performance and executive functions controlled for co-varying effects of verbal ability. Thus, although individual differences in verbal ability are known to make a substantial contribution to individual differences in each domain, when these effects are partialled out, there remains a significant independent association between executive functions and false-belief performance.

Another background factor that may contribute to the association between executive functions and theory of mind is socioeconomic status. This proposal has received much less attention, perhaps because most studies in this field have involved socioeconomically homogeneous (predominantly middle-class) samples. Yet socioeconomic status is a robust predictor of cognitive performance (Bradley & Corwyn, 2002) and so may eclipse any association between individual cognitive domains. Indeed, studies that have included more diverse and representative samples demonstrate that there are important associations between individual differences in family socioeconomic status and in children's performance on false-belief tasks (Cole & Mitchell, 1998; Cutting & Dunn, 1999; Holmes, Black, & Miller, 1996).

More recently, collaborative work with colleagues at the Institute of Psychiatry gave me the opportunity to explore this association between socioeconomic status and false-belief performance in a large-scale twin study. This study (led by Terri Moffitt and Avshalom Caspi) involved a socially diverse sample of 1116 same-sex pairs of 5-year-old twins, selected from a representative British cohort of more than 10,000 twins (Plomin & Dale, 2000). My first step was to bring together a battery of theory-of-mind tests that showed good test–retest reliability and were developmentally appropriate for 5-year-olds (Hughes et al., 2000a). Next, the children were all individually tested during home visits conducted by pairs of researchers (one child tester and one mother interviewer, who also kept the co-twin and other siblings occupied during the test session). Model-fitting analyses (comparing the similarity in performances of identical *versus* fraternal co-twins) showed that 20% of variation in the children's false-belief scores was explained by shared environmental influences that also contributed to variation in verbal ability (Hughes et al., 2005). Previous studies have shown clear contrasts in how parents of different socioeconomic status speak to their children; for example, low-income families typically show low levels of both overall talk and child-directed talk (Hart & Risley, 1995; Hoff, 2003). By demonstrating overlapping environmental influences on verbal ability and false-belief understanding, the results from this twin study suggest that contrasts in family talk may also contribute to variation in children's social understanding (see Chapter 4).

Turning to executive functions, several recent studies (e.g., Ardila, Rosselli, Matute, & Guajardo, 2005; Hughes & Ensor, 2005; Mezzacappa, 2004; Noble, McCandliss, & Farah, 2007) have demonstrated that individual differences in family socioeconomic status explain significant variation in children's performance on executive-function tasks. However, as noted earlier, very few investigations into relations between executive functions and false-belief performance have involved children from a variety of socioeconomic backgrounds. The Toddlers Up study is one exception to this rule. In this sample, individual differences in social disadvantage predicted significant variance in both social understanding and executive functions at the initial age-2 time-point, and at follow-up time-points at ages 3 and 4 (Hughes & Ensor, 2005, 2007a). In addition, latent variable growth modelling showed that between the ages of 4 and 6 (i.e., across the transition to school) children from disadvantaged families failed to catch up with children from more affluent families in their performance on executive-function tasks (Hughes, Ensor, Wilson, & Graham, 2010b). However, social disadvantage did not contribute to the association between executive functions and social understanding

(Hughes & Ensor, 2007a). That is, the association between these domains appears independent from background effects of both verbal ability and family socioeconomic status.

Is the link between executive functions and social understanding general or specific?

As noted earlier, the term executive function is widely used as an umbrella term that encompasses the set of higher order processes that underpin flexible, goal-directed actions. This consensus masks a number of controversies, not least of which concerns the extent to which executive function is a unitary versus fractionated construct. One advantage of the fractionated model is that it avoids the philosophical problem of the homunculus or "ghost in the machine" (Ryle, 1949). That is, as neatly expressed by Shallice and Burgess (1991), it is possible to think of the executive system not as a miniature engineer supervising lower level brain functions, but8 as an automated tool-box of distinct functions that together enable flexible goal-directed actions. The disadvantage of this fractionated approach, however, is the loss of parsimony: for example, how many different processes should be distinguished, and why? Given these theoretical problems, it is no wonder that many researchers have adopted an empirical approach to resolving the structure of executive functions.

In particular, several studies have adopted a factor-analytic approach to examining the structure of executive functions. Factor analysis allows one to investigate whether performance on several different tasks can be represented by one or several latent common factors (Wiebe, Espy, & Charak, 2008). Early studies using exploratory factor analysis (EFA) and principal components analysis (PCA) provided evidence from adults, school-aged children and preschoolers for a multi-factor solution for executive functions. However, the conclusions that can be drawn from EFA and PCA are limited, for two reasons. First, while these techniques provide a useful way of representing observed data, they cannot be used to test theory-driven models. Second, to maximize the interpretability of their findings, most of these early studies applied varimax rotation in order to achieve uncorrelated factors. As a result, the findings are sample-specific and difficult to replicate (Gorsuch, 1997). More recently, as software packages have become more advanced, researchers have begun to use more sophisticated methods of structural equation modelling. In a pioneering study of this kind, Miyake and colleagues (Miyake et al., 2000) gave a battery of executive-functions tasks to undergraduates and subjected the data to confirmatory factor analysis (CFA), a latent-variable approach that not only avoids many of the problems of EFA but also brings a number of advantages, chief of which is a means of evaluating how well different hypothesis-driven models fit the data (for more advantages of CFA, see Chapter 3, p. 63). In line with the conclusions from earlier studies using EFA (e.g., Hughes, 1998a; Welsh, Pennington, & Groisser, 1991), their CFA results indicated three key aspects of executive functions: planning/ working memory; attentional flexibility; and inhibitory control.

Building on this three-factor solution, several studies have attempted to refine our understanding of the nature of the association between executive functions and social understanding by examining whether individual differences in any specific factor (planning/working memory; attentional flexibility; and inhibitory control) show particularly strong links with individual differences in social understanding. In one of my London studies, I found that each factor showed specific links with distinct aspects of social understanding: thus inhibitory control appeared closely associated with children's deceptive skills, while working memory appeared closely associated with false-belief performance (Hughes, 1998a). Other studies (e.g., Keenan, Olson, & Marini, 1998) have also reported particularly close ties between working memory scores and false-belief performance. In contrast, the work of Carlson and colleagues indicates that inhibitory control predicts false-belief performance, even when individual differences in working memory and planning are taken into account (Carlson, Moses, & Breton, 2002). Interestingly, this association appears highly specific: success on false-belief tasks is unrelated to children's abilities to delay or withhold a response, but strongly related to children's abilities to inhibit a prepotent response in order to execute a different response (Carlson et al., 2002).

In short, opinions on which aspects of executive functions are most closely associated with individual differences in theory-of-mind performance are rather divided. One reason for this may be that improvements in children's understanding of mind involve a series of distinct achievements, such that different elements of executive functions may be particularly important for specific milestones. For example, as discussed in Chapter 1, several recent theorists have distinguished between the developmental processes that underpin "implicit" "on-line" or "intuitive" mentalizing and those required for more explicit or formal "off-line" mental-state reasoning (e.g., Apperly, Samson, & Humphreys, 2009; de Vignemont, 2009). This model of dual processes goes some way to explaining why young children can show quite sophisticated mentalizing skills in their everyday interactions and yet fail experimental false-belief tasks. It may also be helpful for clarifying the exact nature of links between theory of mind and executive functions: for example, Tager-Flusberg (2001) has proposed that early onset "socioperceptual" skills (aka intuitive mentalizing) depend on modular cognitive processes, whereas later-onset "sociocognitive" skills (aka off-line mental-state reasoning) depend on other aspects of cognition, and, in particular, language and executive functions. Although this proposal has yet to be tested formally, it does resonate with one of the themes developed in Chapter 1, namely that development in social understanding is characterized by an increase in recursive reflective awareness, such that by school age, children can understand not only multiple embeddings in higher order mental states, but also recognize that two people may make legitimate but different (and possibly even competing) interpretations of the same external stimulus.

In other words, it seems likely that a simple distinction between on-line and off-line theory of mind is too simple, as each of these is likely to be a multi-faceted construct. For example, as summarized above (and described more fully in Chapter 1), researchers often distinguish between children's "off-line" understanding of first-order and second-order false beliefs, although the nature of this distinction remains a topic of debate. In a recent review of this field, Miller (2009) noted that these two concepts can be viewed either as fundamentally different (in that second-order false-belief understanding involves recognizing that a belief can be a *target* of another's belief) or as differing only in complexity (i.e., number of elements to hold in mind). These two views lead to different predictions about which aspects of executive functions are likely to matter the most: the former highlights the importance of cognitive flexibility, while the latter highlights the importance of working memory. As a result, empirical study of the exact nature of links between theory of mind and executive functions may help refine theoretical accounts of the nature of each domain.

Links between executive functions and theory of mind in atypical groups

As outlined earlier, much of the impetus for research into links between theory of mind and executive functions came from studies of children with autism. Another useful approach may be to investigate relations between these constructs within typically developing children who have suffered a traumatic brain injury (TBI). Childhood TBI is known to be associated with deficits in several aspects of executive functions, including inhibitory control (e.g., Konrad, Gauggel, Manz, & Scholl, 2000) and working memory (e.g., Roncadin, Guger, Archibald, Barnes, & Dennis, 2004), as well as with deficits in several aspects of theory of mind, including understanding real versus deceptive emotions (Dennis, Barnes, Wilkinson, & Humphreys, 1998) or irony and empathy (Dennis, Purvis, Barnes, Wilkinson, & Winner, 2001). In a recent study of 43 school-aged children with TBI, Dennis and colleagues (Dennis, Agostino, Roncadin, & Levin, 2009) showed significant associations between executive functions and theory-of-mind deficits, and used path analysis to elucidate the nature of this association. Their findings support models of executive functions in which inhibitory control serves as a foundation for other executive functions, and in particular working memory (Barkley, 1997). Specifically, the relationship between impaired inhibitory control and theory of mind was mediated by impairments in working memory (Dennis et al., 2009). As these authors note, the findings from this TBI study offer some support to the "cognitive complexity and control" model (Frye et al., 1995) described in Chapter 1.

Recently, links between theory of mind and executive functions have also been studied in children for whom normal development has been disrupted not by TBI, but by environmental insult in the form of fetal exposure to toxic levels of alcohol, resulting in fetal alcohol spectrum disorder (FASD), which is characterized by a range of physical, cognitive, behavioural and/or learning deficits, as well as poor executive functioning and social skills. In this study, Rasmussen, Wyper, and Talwar (2009) compared theory-of-mind and executive-functions performance in 4- to 8-year-olds with FASD and controls and showed group differences in both mean scores (in the expected direction) and in the nature of relations between theory of mind and executive functions. Specifically, theory-of-mind performance was correlated with inhibitory control for the FASD group, but with visual-spatial working memory for the control group. This is (to my knowledge) the first study to examine links between theory of mind and executive functions in children with FASD and so the findings need to be replicated; however, they add to the emerging consensus that links between theory of mind and executive functions are robust, but complex and multi-faceted.

Finally, links between theory of mind and executive functions have also been studied among young children with behavioural problems, such as the participants in the London study of "hard-to-manage" preschoolers that, as described in the introduction, gave rise to the Cambridge Toddlers Up study. In this London study, 40 preschoolers with clinically significant parental ratings of conduct problems and/or hyperactivity were compared with 40 control children, matched for age, gender and school on a battery of tasks including tests of theory of mind, executive functions and emotion understanding. In all three cognitive domains, group differences were small but significant; in addition, among the hard-to-manage preschoolers there was a significant association between theory-of-mind and executive-functions performance (Hughes et al., 1998). In this paper, I argued that this link between theory of mind and executive functions suggests both direct and indirect links between executive dysfunction and disruptive behaviour. That is, children with poor executive functions may display disruptive behaviour simply because they fail to "look before they leap", or because their poor executive function constrains their emerging understanding of others, and so affects their ability to comply with social norms. Equally, however, given that these hard-to-manage preschoolers showed marked problems in their interactions with peers (Hughes et al., 2000b), one could argue that the link between executive functions and theory of mind is both direct (as suggested by Russell and others) and indirect. Specifically, executive-functions skills are likely to enhance children's ability to cooperate and engage in social interactions, such as shared pretend play, which in turn promote children's social understanding (Hughes, 2001).

Further findings from the Toddlers Up study

As noted previously, early findings from the Toddlers Up study demonstrate that predictive relations between executive function and later social understanding are significant between the ages of 2 and 4 (i.e., across a broader age-range and longer temporal span than in previous studies). More recent analyses from the study have helped shed light on the specificity and generality of relations between these domains.

First, findings from the Toddlers Up study suggest that different aspects of social understanding are associated with variation in executive function in different ways. In particular, ongoing analyses of data from the first three time-points of the study suggest that, between the ages of 2 and 4, early executive functions have direct effects on later false-belief understanding but at least partially socially mediated effects on later emotion understanding. These analyses were guided by Baron and Kenny's (1986) four criteria for mediation: namely that the independent variable (age-2 executive functions) should predict the mediator variable (age-3 problem behaviours); that both should predict the outcome (age-4 social understanding); and when entered simultaneously, the predictive effect of the independent variable should be attenuated, but the predictive effect of the mediator should remain significant (see Chapter 10 for a fuller discussion of mediation analyses). Our results suggested that executive-function performance at age 2 was a significant predictor of children's understanding of both emotion and false-belief at age 4; age-3 problem behaviour was only supported as a (partial) mediator of the relation between early executive function and later emotion understanding. This finding mirrors results from the London study of hard-to-manage preschoolers, which showed that displays of anger in dyadic play with a friend at age 4 were both related to deficits in executive functions and predicted poorer moral understanding at age 6 (Hughes & Dunn, 2000).

Second, latent growth models demonstrate that variation in children's gains in executive functions between the ages of 4 and 6 predicts variation in broader aspects of social understanding, including a latent variable for children's perceptions of their own academic competence (Hughes & Ensor, in press-a). This result builds on recent findings that highlight the importance of early executive functions for children's school readiness (C. Blair & Diamond, 2008; C. Blair & Peters, 2003; C. Blair & Razza, 2007) and, by focusing on children's own views of their success at school, takes the research field forward in an important new direction. In particular, developmental theorists have long argued that self-perceptions actively shape children's behaviour (e.g., Cicchetti, 1993; Rutter, 1989); this view is supported by evidence that positive self-perceptions predict favourable outcomes such as academic achievement (Marsh, Ellis, & Craven, 2002) and peer acceptance (Boivin & Bégin, 1989), while negative self-perceptions are associated with depression (e.g., Harter & Jackson, 1993) and peer rejection (Coplan, Findlay, & Nelson, 2004). Interestingly, the same latent growth models showed that gains in executive functions across the transition to school were unrelated to a latent variable for children's self-perceived social success (e.g., the number of friends they had). In addition, the relationship between gains in executive functions and children's self-perceived academic success remained significant when individual differences in verbal ability were taken into account. Each of these findings suggests that although executive functions may be related to multiple aspects of social understanding, the nature of these relationships is likely to be quite specific. Clearly, much more work is needed, both to replicate these findings and to elucidate the diverse processes that may underpin relations between executive functions and different aspects of social understanding.

In this section we have come a long way from the original simple question of whether the link between executive functions and theory of mind should be viewed as general or specific. In particular, the brief has been extended to include indirect as well as direct associations between these two domains; in addition, it is clear that the answer to this question varies from study to study, depending on the measures used and the nature of the sample. The next section builds on this point, to consider whether links between executive functions and theory of mind are equally apparent in children from different cultural backgrounds.

Cross-cultural perspectives on links between executive functions and social understanding

Although most studies of relations between executive functions and theory of mind have involved children in the USA and the UK, several studies provide equally robust evidence of an association between these domains in preschoolers from all over the globe, including Australia, New Zealand, China, Korea, Germany, Costa Rica and Cameroon (see Table 2.1). These findings are particularly interesting with regard to Chinese and Korean children, for whom an association between individual differences in false-belief understanding and executive functions (and, in particular, inhibitory control) appears alongside a developmental asynchrony between these two domains. That is, unlike Western children who typically show developmentally synchronous improvements in their performance on tests of both executive function and false-belief tasks, children in Confucian cultures (e.g., China and Korea) show high levels of self-control from an early age, but do not show a corresponding advantage on false-belief tasks.

Table 2.1 Studies of relations between executive functions and false-belief performance, by sample age and country

Age-range	Country	Reference
Toddlers	USA	Carlson, Mandell, & Williams, 2004
	UK	Hughes & Ensor, 2005, 2007a
Preschoolers	USA	Carlson, Mandell, & Williams, 2004
		Carlson & Moses, 2001
		Carlson, Moses, & Breton, 2002
		Carlson, Moses, & Claxton, 2004
		Frye, Zelazo, & Palfai, 1995
	UK	K. Cole & Mitchell, 2000
		Hughes, 1998a, 1998b
	Australia	McAlister & Peterson, 2007
	Austria	Perner & Lang, 2000
	Canada	Hala, Hug, & Henderson, 2003
		Hala & Russell, 2001
	Germany, Costa Rica, Cameroon	Chasiotis, Kiessling, Campos, & Hofer, 2006
	China, Korea, Japan	Lewis, Huang, & Rooksby, 2006
		Lewis et al., 2009
		Sabbagh, Xu, Carlson, Moses, & Lee, 2006
Kindergarten	USA	McGlamery, Ball, Henley, & Besozzi, 2007
School-age*	Canada, UK, USA	Charman, Carroll, & Sturge, 2001
		Fahie & Symons, 2003
		Speltz, Deklyen, Calderon, Greenberg, & Fisher, 1999

Note: *Samples with externalizing problems.

As a result, analyses of within-sample individual differences and comparisons of age-related changes suggest diverging conclusions: associations between individual differences in executive functions and false-belief performance appear relatively universal (but see below), whereas patterns of age-related changes in executive functions and false-belief performance appear culture specific. This apparent paradox can be interpreted in several ways. For example, as noted by Sabbagh and colleagues (Sabbagh, Xu, Carlson, Moses, & Lee, 2006), the one-child policy in China means that Chinese children have fewer opportunities for engaging in the kinds of child-like interactions (e.g., pretend play, conflictual exchanges, jokes, teasing and deception) that foster social understanding. The effects of these restricted opportunities run counter to potential benefits from accelerated executive-functions development, which may explain why Chinese children do not outperform Western children on tests of social understanding. However, data from a recent meta-analysis challenge this view, because children from Hong Kong (which does not have a one-child policy) performed less well on false-belief tasks than children from mainland China.

In addition, Lewis et al. (2009) have recently argued that the association between individual differences in executive functions and theory of mind does not extend to children from Confucian cultures. Their counter-findings emerged from four studies of children from China, Korea and Japan. The first study, set in Seoul, in Korea, showed ceiling effects on a range of executive-functions tasks (tapping working memory, inhibitory control and attentional set-switching) for *both* 3- and 4-year-olds; these findings were replicated in a second study, which also showed that: (i) British 3-year-olds performed significantly less well than British 4-year-olds on this task battery; and (ii) even the oldest British children performed less well than the youngest Korean children. Probably as a result of the ceiling effect in Korean children's executive-functions scores, this sample showed no significant association between executive functions and theory of mind. The third study compared British and Japanese children; here, the expected association between theory of mind and executive functions was found for both samples, but only remained significant in the British sample when effects of age and verbal ability were controlled (note, however, that the Japanese children in this study showed an extended age-range). Finally, a fourth study indicated no significant association between false-belief performance and executive functions in Chinese preschoolers.

Together, the above findings provide an interesting challenge for theorists aiming to explain the relationship between false-belief performance and executive functions and highlight the importance of methodological factors (e.g., sample characteristics and developmental sensitivity of tasks). As noted in Chapter 5 (in the discussion of links between false-belief performance and parenting in different cultures) one key step for future research is to assess how equivalent are the constructs being compared across cultures? This goal can be broken down into two steps. The first is to assess whether executive functions and false-belief performance measures in children from different cultures show conceptual and functional equivalence (i.e., do the measures have similar meaning and correlates across cultures?). The second is to capitalize on recent dramatic improvements in the accessibility of statistical model-fitting packages in order to test whether executive functions and false-belief performance measures in children from different cultures show operational and scalar equivalence (i.e., do test scores show similar loadings and intercepts?). A second useful direction for future research would be to adopt a more fine-grained analysis in order to establish whether the *nature* (as opposed to magnitude) of associations between executive functions and false-belief performance is similar across cultures.

Chapter summary

Building on the extended developmental framework set out in Chapter 1, the findings reported in the current chapter show that the long-established links between preschoolers' social understanding and executive-function skills are also evident across a broad developmental period and in a wide variety of cultural groups, but may differ in nature for children with distinct developmental disorders. This chapter began with an outline of the origins of research into links between executive functions and theory of mind, along with subsequent theoretical developments. The next section reviewed longitudinal findings in order to ascertain the direction and temporal reach of relations between executive functions and theory of mind. This was followed by a review of studies (involving both typically developing children and atypical groups) that address the nature of this relation between executive functions and theory of mind: does it vary with age, is it general or specific, direct or indirect? The final section addressed the issue of universality, by examining whether the link between executive functions and social understanding holds up for children from different cultures.

Overall, the findings presented in this chapter support four key conclusions. First, individual differences in children's social understanding show robust associations with individual differences in executive control across a wide age-range (from toddlerhood to early school age). This is all the more impressive because, as outlined in Chapter 1, this broad developmental period encompasses significant changes in the nature of social understanding.

Second, predictive relations between early executive functions and later theory of mind are, in general, stronger than predictive relations in the reverse direction and remain significant even over relatively extended periods of time. In addition, these predictive relations remain significant even when individual differences in verbal ability are taken into account – this is an important point because the emergence of executive function is closely entwined with developmental improvements in language skills and, as discussed in Chapter 3, language skills are also a strong independent predictor of individual differences in social understanding. Thus, early executive function and language ability appear to show both overlapping and independent associations with children's social understanding.

Third, results from the Toddlers Up study suggest that, between the ages of 2 and 4, early executive functions have direct effects on later false-belief understanding and at least partially socially mediated effects on later emotion understanding; in addition, individual differences in executive-functions *gains* between the ages of 4 and 6 predict individual differences in children's self-perceived academic competence. In other words, executive functions appear to be linked (via distinct mechanisms) with diverse aspects of children's social understanding. We will return to the interplay between cognitive and social influences on children's social understanding in the second part of this book (Chapters 4, 5 and 6).

Fourth, although an association between executive functions and theory of mind has been reported for a variety of different samples (including children with typical development from different cultures, children exposed to traumatic brain injury or toxic levels of alcohol during gestation, children with behavioural problems and children with autism), the nature of this association is difficult to pin down, and may well be different for distinct groups of children. In the next chapter we shall find similar evidence for moderation effects on the association between language and social understanding.

3 Language and theory of mind: Cognitive perspectives

In the introduction to their edited volume *Why Language Matters for Theory of Mind* Astington and Baird (2005) begin at the beginning – with a discussion of what is meant both by "theory of mind" and by "language". As they note, the term "theory of mind" entered the developmental literature via two different routes, as it was used by Wellman (1979) to refer to children's conception of human cognition at around the same time as Premack and Woodruff's (1978) landmark study, in which the same phrase was used to ask whether chimpanzees were able to attribute mental states in order to predict and explain human behaviour. Despite this apparent convergence, the term "theory of mind" has provoked sustained controversy. At the most fundamental level, some researchers (e.g., Hobson, 1991; Nelson, Plesa, & Henseler, 1998) have argued that invoking the metaphor of a theory leads to an arid and impoverished view of how children make sense of their social worlds. Nevertheless, the term "theory of mind" has gained support, perhaps because it offers a useful versatility. That is, "theory of mind" can be used to refer to simple infant interfacing of minds, or to complex adult understandings, or to anything in between (A. Lillard, 1997). This versatility can, of course, also be a problem – Astington (1998) described it as a Humpty Dumpty word: " 'When *I* use a word', Humpty Dumpty said in rather a scornful tone, 'it means just what I choose it to mean – neither more nor less' " (Carroll, 1872, p. 124).

From the viewpoint of this chapter, the multi-faceted nature of theory of mind is important, because it highlights the likelihood of complex and developmentally dynamic connections with language. This complexity is magnified by the fact that language is an even broader construct, with multiple distinctions to be made, within both structural and functional perspectives. In terms of *structures*, there is a basic distinction between *form* (phonology, morphology, syntax) and *meaning* (lexical and discourse semantics, which can each be divided into mentalistic and non-mentalistic categories). In terms of *functions*, there is a core distinction between (intra-individual) *representation* and (inter-individual) *communication*; there is also an important distinction within the latter between children's own language skills and their linguistic environment. As a result, there is potentially a kaleidoscope of different connections between theory of mind and language, particularly because development in each domain is characterized by striking individual differences.

Clearly, then, it is possible to study the links between language and theory of mind at many different levels. Given this complexity it is worth considering whether there is anything special about theory of mind that requires language, or anything special about language that allows theory of mind to develop (Astington & Baird, 2005). Indeed, researchers from many different theoretical camps argue that language has *no* special role to play in theory-of-mind development because: (i) theory of mind is an innate and modular system (Baron-Cohen, 1995; C. Frith & Frith, 2000; Leslie, 1994); or (ii) associations with verbal ability merely reflect peripheral task demands (Chandler et al., 1989; Lewis & Osborne, 1990); or (iii) language simply enables children to acquire domain-general cognitive operations (e.g., embedded reasoning; Zelazo, 1999); or (iv) language simply provides children with the database of information needed to construct a theory of mind (Gopnik & Wellman, 1994). In contrast, other theoretical camps view language as playing a fundamental role in the development of a theory of mind, again for a diversity of reasons: because theory of mind depends upon acquiring the semantics of mental-state terms (Bartsch & Wellman, 1995); because mastering the syntax of sentential complements provides children with the tools for representing false beliefs (J. de Villiers & de Villiers, 2000); because conversations provide children with access to, and a means of reflecting on, thoughts and feelings (J. Dunn, Brown, Slomkowski, Tesla, & Youngblade, 1991b); or because it is within Wittgensteinian language games that children collaborate in the co-construction of an understanding of mind (Montgomery, 2005; Nelson et al., 2003). Clearly, then, the relationship between theory of mind and language can be considered from both a cognitive and a social perspective. In this chapter we adopt a cognitive perspective to examine the relationship between language and theory of mind. The first section considers evidence from studies of typically developing children, using meta-analytic reviews to summarize the findings from the very large number of existing studies. This is followed by brief reviews of three interesting but as yet understudied research topics: cross-cultural contrasts, bilingualism and training studies. The second section considers the evidence from studies of clinical groups, such as children with hearing impairments, specific language impairments (SLI), autistic spectrum disorders (ASD) and William's syndrome. The third section provides an overview of recent research within the neurosciences that may illuminate the relationship between language and theory of mind. The chapter ends with some recent analyses from the Toddlers Up study, which apply latent variable analyses to examine predictive relations across the transition to primary school between individual differences in children's language ability and their social understanding. The next chapter adopts a social perspective, which emphasizes the pragmatic and dyadic aspects of conversation.

Making sense of links between individual differences in language and theory of mind

Most methods of testing children's understanding of mind require considerable verbal skills, raising the possibility that test performance merely reflects peripheral demands on language comprehension. As a result, researchers have generally included one index or more of language ability as a covariate, to exclude the possibility that test performance merely reflects language comprehension. Interestingly, the strength of the correlation between children's language skills and false-belief understanding varies widely across studies. One obvious explanation for this variability hinges on the fact that different research groups often favour slightly different theory-of-mind tasks and may also utilize different instruments to assess language. Meta-analysis offers a valuable means of exploring the effects of these measurement contrasts, in order to illuminate the exact nature of the relationship between children's language skills and false-belief understanding. Broadly speaking, two types of camp can be identified: in one, children's false-belief understanding is viewed as dependent on a specific aspect of language (such as syntax, semantics, etc.); in the other, the relationship between language and false-belief understanding is seen as general or multi-faceted.

The clearest example of a specific account is J. de Villiers and de Villiers' (2000) proposal that sentential complements provide children with the key to understanding false beliefs. This proposal extends Russell's (1996) proposal that predicting or explaining others' behaviour hinges on understanding propositional verbs (i.e., verbs that indicate a subject's propositional attitude towards the mental content); such verbs are often followed by a "that" clause (e.g., think that ..., hope that ...). Simply put, complements are grammatical objects of main sentences containing either untensed infinitives (e.g., *to have fun* is the object of the main sentence: "Harriet wanted to have fun") or tensed, sentential structures (e.g., *that she had fun* is the object of the main sentence: "Harriet said that she had fun"). Complements are commonly used to describe mental and communication activities and so are often embedded within verbs such as want, think and say. A key feature of embedded complements is that they can express either a true or a false proposition, without affecting the truth value of the sentence as a whole. Thus, mastery of embedded or sentential complements may be a vital foundation for false-belief comprehension. This proposal is fascinating and, if supported, offers clear guidance for developing interventions to promote children's social understanding. However, it may be that, as indicated earlier, language matters at many different levels, such that a narrow focus on a specific milestone (such as understanding sentential complements) is quite misleading. Moreover, this specific focus on complements has been challenged at both theoretical and empirical levels.

Theoretically, Perner and colleagues have reported that German children handle "want that"-complements much better than "think that"-complements (Perner, Sprung, Zauner, & Haider, 2003); this contrast highlights the importance of considering conceptual contrasts in the content of superficially similar utterances (see also the next chapter for a discussion of ontogenetic changes in the pragmatics of children's use of the term "want"). Empirically, Milligan, Astington, and Dack (2007) have addressed this issue of how the relationship between language and false-belief understanding should be characterized in a meta-analytic review of data from 104 studies ($n = 8891$), which all involved English-speaking children under the age of 7. The findings from their analyses can be summarized by three points.

First, *the relation between language and theory of mind is substantial*. In statistical terms, the overall correlation was significant and moderate to large in effect size ($r = .43$, indicating that 18% of the variance in false-belief understanding is shared with language). This contrasts with the much weaker effect size for gender reported in an earlier meta-analysis (Charman, Ruffman, & Clements, 2002). Indeed, further analyses of the subset of studies that reported age-partialled correlations showed that 10% of the variance in false-belief understanding was shared with language, even when striking age-related improvements were taken into account.

Second, analyses of the subset of studies that included longitudinal data indicated that, although significant in both directions, *predictive relations between early language and later false-belief understanding are stronger than relations in the reverse direction*. As Millington et al. (2007) note, this finding supports the view that language provides children with the resources required to represent and communicate about mistaken beliefs. Interestingly, although very few studies have examined linguistic contributions in social understanding in older children or adults, there is some evidence that language resources remain important. For example, language skills have been shown to predict the ease with which children progress from understanding actions based on false belief to understanding feelings based on false beliefs (de Rosnay, Pons, Harris, & Morrell, 2004). Likewise, as discussed in the section on deafness later in this chapter, the emergence of a sign language in Nicaragua has been linked to between-cohort contrasts in deaf adults' understanding of false belief (Pyers & Senghas, 2009).

Third, *the magnitude of the correlation between language and theory of mind differs strikingly across studies*, with shared variance estimates ranging from 0 to 77%. This variability could not be explained by differences in: (i) sample characteristics (e.g., proportion of boys, children's mean ages); (ii) study quality (sample size, use of control questions); or (iii) the type of false-belief task used (indicating that the association is not an artefact of task demands). However, the type of language measure used did explain some of this variability: studies that used receptive vocabulary to index children's language skills showed weaker effect sizes than studies that included general language measures. Studies that included sentential complements showed stronger effect sizes, but this contrast was not statistically significant. Overall, then, the existing empirical evidence appears to favour general rather than specific links between language and social understanding (see also Slade & Ruffman, 2005).

Convergent support for a general relationship between language and social understanding comes from a large-scale twin study, involving more than 1000 pairs of same-sex twins living in Britain (Hughes et al., 2005). In this study, both shared genes and shared environmental influences contributed significantly to the correlation between language and social understanding. In other words, external factors (relating to both nature and nurture) appear to have a common influence on language and social understanding and thus contribute to the association between these domains. We return to this point in the next chapter; for now, however, we turn our attention to three further key areas of research: (i) cross-cultural comparisons that address the issue of universality in children's developing social understanding; (ii) studies of bilingualism; and (iii) training studies that directly assess the functional influence of language on children's social understanding.

Cross-cultural contrasts

Until quite recently, studies of the relationship between language and theory of mind have focused almost exclusively on English. However, the conclusion that relations between language and theory of mind are general rather than specific is supported by evidence from two further studies that involved direct cross-cultural comparisons. In the first of these, Shatz, Diesendruck, Martinez-Beck, and Akar (2003) compared preschoolers speaking languages with explicit terms for false belief (Turkish and Puerto-Rican Spanish) with preschoolers speaking languages without explicit terms (Brazilian Portuguese and English) and found that between-culture effects of lexical explicitness were localized and relatively modest compared with more general effects related to children's socioeconomic status. In the second study, Cheung et al. (2004) reported that, for both English- and Cantonese-speaking 4-year-olds, associations between complement understanding and false-belief performance fell below signifi-cance once individual differences in general language comprehension were taken into account.

More recently, Liu, Wellman, Tardif, and Sabbagh (2008) conducted a second meta-analysis that included data from more than 3000 Chinese children and yielded two key findings. Specifically, alongside parallel developmental trajector-ies in false-belief performance for children in China and North America, Chinese children displayed a significant lag (of up to 2 years) in the timing of their devel-opment. Interestingly, this lag was unchanged by the presence of "think-falsely" verbs in Chinese languages (and in many Chinese false-belief tasks), supporting the idea that effects of language on children's growing social understanding are likely to be general rather than specific.

Upon closer inspection however, Liu et al.'s (2008) meta-analytic findings are rather puzzling. In particular, other studies have shown that Chinese children outperform their North American counterparts on tests of executive function (e.g., Sabbagh et al., 2006) and, as discussed in Chapter 2, executive function scores are a strong predictor of false-belief performance. In addition, Chinese adults have been found to show better perspective-taking skills than their North American counterparts (Wu & Keysar, 2007). For each of these reasons, compared with North American children, Chinese children might be expected to do better rather than worse on false-belief tasks. Given that having a sibling may fast-track a child's development in theory of mind (Perner, Ruffman, & Leekam, 1994), it is tempting to explain the lag in terms of China's one-child policy. However, the lowest performing cultural group in Liu et al.'s (2008) meta-analysis did not come from mainland China, but from Hong Kong, where children are more likely than their mainland counterparts to be Westernized, to have sibs and to be bilingual (another characteristic associated with gains in theory-of-mind development – see below). As a result, Liu et al. (2008) concluded that no single sociocultural or linguistic factor could provide a straightforward account of the pattern of differences obtained in their meta-analytic study. Instead, they suggested that a myriad of processes (both cognitive and social) jointly contribute to individual differences in children's developing understanding of mind.

Bilingualism

For children growing up as native speakers of more than one language, the role of language in the development of theory of mind may be particularly central. For example, by the age of 3, bilingual children are adept in addressing monolingual conversational partners in the appropriate language (Genesee, Nicoladis, & Paradis, 1995). This experience of language-switch situations could contribute to children's performance on false-belief tasks both directly and indirectly. Directly, such situations might enhance bilingual children's awareness of differences between their own and others' states of knowledge. Indirectly, gaining practice in controlling multiple languages could enhance these children's developing executive functions – preschool bilingual children do indeed outperform monolinguals on executive control tasks (Bialystok, 1999) – and this improved executive control might in turn enable them to succeed on theory-of-mind tasks (see Chapter 2). In a recent study, Kovács (2009) argued that the direct account leads to the prediction that any advantage for bilingual children will be restricted to situations that involve a language switch, while the indirect account leads to the prediction that bilingual children will show an advantage on any false-belief task that involves inhibiting maladaptive prepotent responses. Her results supported the indirect account: Romanian–Hungarian bilingual 3-year-olds performed similarly to their Romanian monolingual peers (matched for age, socioeconomic status and IQ) on control tasks, but showed superior performance on both a language-switch false-belief task *and* a standard false-belief task. In other words, for bilingual children at least, effects of language on false-belief performance appeared to be at least partially mediated by improvements in executive control.

Further evidence for an advantage in theory-of-mind development associated with bilingualism comes from a recent study of native signing deaf children attending schools with either a bilingual (i.e., sign and spoken) or monolingual (spoken only) language environment (Meristo et al., 2007), which is discussed later in this chapter (see also the final section on neurosciences). Note, however, that research on theory of mind and bilingualism is still in its infancy, and the findings may be more mixed than they appear at first glance; for example, unpublished studies by Perner and colleagues have failed to find any group differences (Perner, personal communication, 2009).

Training studies

Early training studies (e.g., Appleton & Reddy, 1996; Guajardo & Watson, 2002) showed that talking to children about characters in storybooks or videos who engage in tricks or other deceptive behaviour leads to improvements in false-belief performance, relative to untrained control groups. However, these early studies could not shed light on the exact mechanisms underlying this beneficial effect. More recent training studies have aimed to tease apart the effects of perspective taking, or mental-verb semantics, or complement syntax on false-belief performance. For example, Hale and Tager-Flusberg (2003) found that children's false-belief understanding improved when they were provided with overt evidence of falsity in statements (by training them to use false complement constructions with communication verbs). Similarly, in a study of German 3-year-olds (pre-screened as initially failing false-belief tasks), Lohmann and Tomasello (2003) found that although simple (non-conversational) exposure to deceptive objects (e.g., a pen that looked like a flower) had no effect on false-belief understanding, performance improved in three other training conditions: (i) conversation about deceptive objects that involved no sentential complements; (ii) training on the syntax of complementation (without the deceptive objects); and (iii), most clearly, conversations about deceptive objects that included the use of sentential complements. These findings suggest that dyadic conversation and individual mastery of complementation syntax each make independent contributions to the development of false-belief understanding.

Language and theory of mind in clinical populations

This section provides a brief review of the literature on language and theory of mind in three distinct atypical populations: children with marked hearing loss, children with specific language impairments and children with autism spectrum disorders.

Hearing loss

Research interest in the relation between language and theory of mind has been greatly fuelled by research on children with congenital hearing impairments (which occur in about 0.5–1 per 1000 births). Most (96%; Mitchell & Karchmer, 2004) of these deaf children are born to hearing parents (hereafter dubbed "DoH"), but a minority are born to deaf parents (hereafter dubbed "DoD") who are fluent signers. The significant contrast in the linguistic experiences of these two groups provides an intriguing natural experiment for studying the effects of language on children's understanding of mind. Several studies have shown that late-signing DoH children are profoundly delayed in their ability to understand false beliefs (e.g., J. de Villiers & de Villiers, 2000; Peterson & Siegal, 1995); strikingly, these delays are not found in DoD children (Schick, de Villiers, de Villiers, & Hoffmeister, 2007). Together, these findings highlight the importance of early exposure to language for children's developing understanding of mind (see Corina & Singleton, 2009, for a recent review).

Confirmation for this view comes from parallel findings of contrasts in false-belief comprehension and use of mental-state verbs between two cohorts of deaf adults in Nicaragua: the first cohort (mean age = 27 years) was exposed to a nascent form of Nicaraguan Sign Language (NSL) during childhood, whereas the second cohort (mean age = 18 years) were exposed to a later more developed form of NSL (Pyers & Senghas, 2009). Both cohorts attended the same school for the same number of years, and were taught by the same teachers using the same methods; even as adults they have similar-sized deaf social networks. At two time-points (24 months apart) they received a low-verbal false-belief task (that included "true belief" control conditions) and were assessed for their ability to produce mental-state verbs in response to video clips involving mistaken beliefs. Although almost a decade younger than cohort 1, individuals in cohort 2 produced more mental-state terms and were more likely to pass the false-belief task; in 6 of the 8 cases, mental-state talk preceded false-belief success (Pyers & Senghas, 2009).

A further recent extension to the early work on theory-of-mind development in deaf children comes from the study by Meristo et al. (2007), mentioned earlier. As well as replicating the delay in theory-of-mind success for DoH children in Italy, Estonia and Sweden, this research group found that DoD children attending bilingual schools (i.e., sign and spoken language) outperformed those attending monolingual (spoken language only) schools. This contrast within a group of DoD children is interesting and suggests that, above and beyond the improvements associated with mastery of syntactic complements associated with early language experience (cf. Schick et al., 2007), developments in children's understanding of mind may also relate to their continuing access to linguistically enriched environments, including school-based influences on these children's opportunities to engage in mental-state discourse. The results (discussed earlier) from the hearing bilingual children studied by Kovács (2009) suggest that the advantage of bilingualism in DoD children may be partially mediated by improvements in executive control; further work is needed to test this proposal.

Specific language impairment (SLI)

As noted by Bishop (2006), talking comes so naturally to most children that we rarely stop to marvel at the complexity of this achievement. And yet SLI, or delayed language acquisition in the absence of neurological, hearing or nonverbal impairments, affects about 7% of children (Tomblin et al., 1997); twin studies show that about half to three-quarters of the variance in SLI can be attributed to genetic factors (Bishop, 2002). Because an SLI is a general marker for language disorder, rather than a specific disorder or disease, the problems of children with SLI can be very diverse, ranging from difficulties in the production, recognition or ordering of speech sounds to problems understanding long or complex sentences.

The long-term outcomes associated with SLI are also quite varied, although literacy problems and difficulties with social interactions are typically quite persistent (e.g., Brinton & Fujiki, 1998; Redmond & Rice, 1998). Indeed, recent work suggests greater overlap between SLI and autism spectrum disorders (ASD) than traditionally thought. For example, Bishop and Norbury (2002) have reported pragmatic language impairments within both SLI and ASD. Similarly, Conti-Ramsden, Simkin, and Botting (2006) have reported an elevated incidence of ASD among adolescents with a history of SLI. These findings raise the possibility that deficits in social cognition (which were originally thought to be specific to children with ASD) might also be found in at least some children with SLI.

Interestingly, although early studies of school-aged children with SLI suggested age-appropriate performance on false-belief tasks (e.g., Leslie & Frith, 1988; Perner, Frith, Leslie, & Leekam, 1989; Ziatas, Durkin, & Pratt, 1998), or at least on low-verbal false-belief tasks (C. Miller, 2001), more recent studies do indeed indicate deficits in theory of mind among children with SLI. Specifically, studies of younger children's understanding of false belief have shown that SLI is associated with significant delays of about 12 to 18 months (e.g., Farrant, Fletcher, & Maybery, 2006), while for older children with SLI success on second-order false belief shows substantial delays of about 2 to 3 years (Farmer, 2000).

As argued by Bishop (2006), using SLI to tease apart the relationship between language and social cognition is complicated not only by the heterogeneity of SLI as a disorder, but by the fact that SLI appears to involve multiple cognitive deficits. This multiplicity of underlying deficits makes sense when one thinks about the remarkably robust nature of ordinary language acquisition: most children will learn to speak adequately, even if they are visually impaired or exposed to impoverished language input. In other words, to compromise language development, multiple domains must be affected. As a result, although studying theory-of-mind development in children with SLI might appear an obvious and simple approach to studying the role of language in children's developing social understanding, the true story is likely to be anything but simple.

Note also that the relationship between language and social understanding may be very different in adults and children with SLI. For example, although the studies discussed so far present a strong case for the importance of language (and perhaps particularly understanding the syntax of complements), at least two adult cases have been reported to show severe agrammatical aphasia alongside intact performance on theory-of-mind tasks (Varley & Siegal, 2000; Varley, Siegal, & Want, 2001). These case reports demonstrate that although grammar may be vital for configuring cognitive processes, once established these processes can operate without grammar.

Autism spectrum disorders (ASD)

Early studies of children with ASD showed links between deficits in theory of mind and in language and communication (U. Frith, Happé, & Siddons, 1994; Mundy, Sigman, & Kasari, 1990). According to the classic "theory-of-mind" hypothesis for autism, an innate impairment in a neural system dedicated to processing information about mental states provides a unified explanation for the deficits in social interaction, communication and pretend play that are a hallmark of ASD (e.g., Baron-Cohen, 1988). For example, with regard to language, an impaired understanding of mental states can explain a variety of problems, including impairments in conversational or narrative discourse and deficits in interpreting the intended meaning of non-literal statements. However, this hypothesis fails to explain why a "talented minority" of individuals with ASD – about 20% in the original study by Baron-Cohen and colleagues (Baron-Cohen et al., 1985) – succeed on false-belief tasks.

In response to this paradox, some researchers (e.g., Bowler, 1992; Happé, 1995) have argued that individuals with ASD who pass theory-of-mind tasks do so using compensatory, verbally mediated, "hacking-out" strategies. While pragmatic impairments in language use are universal in ASD, some individuals do develop rich vocabularies and speak in grammatically complex, even rather pedantically formal utterances. Hacking strategies may work in closed, structured situations (such as a forced-choice false-belief task) but are unlikely to be fruitful when faced with complex, real-life social situations. This contrast may explain why even individuals with ASD who reliably pass false-belief tasks display profound difficulties in their everyday social lives.

Early evidence for the argument that language may assist this talented minority of individuals with ASD to pass false-belief tasks came from the finding that children with ASD who passed false-belief tasks showed higher verbal mental ages and better pragmatic skills (Eisenmajer & Prior, 1991). Building upon this work, Happé (1995) pooled together data from a large number of studies in the UK and found that, for both typically developing preschoolers and children with ASD, vocabulary scores predicted false-belief success, even when effects of age were controlled. Around the same time, Tager-Flusberg and colleagues (Tager-Flusberg & Sullivan, 1994) compared the predictive value of different aspects of language performance (e.g., vocabulary vs. syntax) and found that syntactic development was a particularly strong predictor of false-belief success. The same research group later reported that mastery of complement syntax predicts theory-of-mind performance in older children and adolescents with ASD, but not in age- and language-matched participants with developmental delay (Tager-Flusberg, 2000; Tager-Flusberg & Joseph, 2005). More recently, Lind and Bowler (2009) have strengthened this finding, by demonstrating statistically that the syntax predicted performance on a location-change false-belief task more powerfully for ASD individuals than for controls.

From a clinical perspective, the above results are important because they offer an explanation for the finding that, among individuals with ASD, language is the key predictor of long-term cognitive, social and adaptive outcomes (Howlin, Mawhood, & Rutter, 2000; Mawhood, Howlin, & Rutter, 2000). Specifically, the results from the above studies indicate that, for individuals with ASD at least, language facilitates the development of social cognition. Viewed in detail, the findings from the above studies also provide important guidance for the development of intervention programmes. For example, Tager-Flusberg and Joseph (2005) reported that, whereas both cognitive and communication verbs predicted false-belief success in typically developing preschoolers, mastery of communication verbs was particularly important for children with ASD. Thus, through listening and talking about what people say, rather than what they think, children with ASD may recognize that what people say does not always match reality, and so come to achieve a representational understanding of others' minds.

Language, theory of mind and imaging research

Social phenomena cut a broad path through human experience; unsurprisingly, then, the neural systems that underpin social behaviours are multi-purpose and highly entwined with more basic sensory-perceptual, emotional, linguistic and cognitive components (Corina & Singleton, 2009). Broadly speaking, however, social processes involve two types of mental inferences: (i) those concerning goals and intentions (i.e., transitory states); and (ii) those that concern inferences about personality traits and social scripts (i.e., enduring characteristics). As summarized in Chapter 1, developmental research indicates that the first type of mental inference appears as early as infancy, whereas it is only in school age that children start to apply information about personality traits and social scripts to predict people's actions (Apperly et al., 2009; de Vignemont, 2009).

Interestingly, imaging studies indicate that two cortical regions (shown in Figure 3.1) are consistently activated in mental inference tasks. These are the right temporoparietal junction (TPJ) and the medial prefrontal cortex (mPFC). Findings from recent meta-analytic review of more than 100 functional magnetic resonance imaging (fMRI) studies of human social cognition indicate that these two regions correspond well with these two types of mental inferences (Van Overwalle, 2009). That is, the TPJ (which extends from the superior temporal sulcus, STS, to the inferior parietal lobe and is closely associated with the mirror neuron system) is consistently activated in tasks that require identifying goals or intentions, whereas neurons in the mPFC (which has extensive interconnections with the dorsolateral PFC, the anterior STS, the TPJ and other brain regions) are uniquely oriented to time and fire over extended periods of time and across events (e.g., Huey, Krueger, & Grafman, 2006), and so may serve in the integration of social information over time (i.e., via scripts or traits). In his meta-analysis, Van Overwalle (2009) concluded that the neural system that underpins social cognition starts with the more posterior TPJ, where immediate goals and desires are inferred, and progresses towards the more anterior mPFC, which is associated with explicit reasoning based on enduring personality traits or social scripts.

Note, however, that the above conclusions do not reduce to a modular perspective. For example, the TPJ is also activated by non-mentalistic tasks (e.g., the false-photo task) and by tests of basic attentional processes (e.g., the flanker task). In his meta-analysis, Van Overwalle (2009) referred to the TPJ as the "where-to" system (by analogy with the "where" system in the parietal lobe). In other words, the neural systems for mindreading are closely entwined with more basic cognitive systems. The neat division of labour between these two regions (TPJ and mPFC) may also be confounded by modality differences in the tasks used: tasks tapping goal-directed inferences typically involve visual presentations, whereas those that require more complex inferences about scripts or traits typically involve verbal presentations. Note, however, that performance on cartoon theory-of-mind tasks also activates the mPFC (Gallagher et al., 2000).

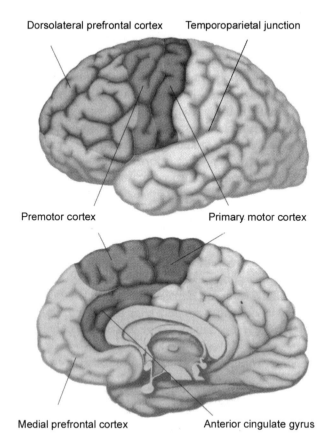

Dorsolateral prefrontal cortex   Temporoparietal junction

Premotor cortex   Primary motor cortex

Medial prefrontal cortex   Anterior cingulate gyrus

Figure 3.1 The temporoparietal junction (TPJ) and the medial prefrontal cortex (mPFC).

Returning to the relation between language and theory of mind, imaging studies of bilingual adults and children suggest that the neural base for theory of mind cannot be pre-specified in a genetic code awaiting maturation (Perner & Aichhorn, 2008). For example, in a series of studies involving monolingual and bilingual Japanese children and adults, Kobayashi, Glover, and Temple (2006, 2007, 2008) found that: (i) for adults, processing of theory-of-mind tasks is associated with distinct regions of brain activity in Japanese and in English; and (ii), for children, processing of theory-of-mind tasks is associated with diffuse and overlapping brain activity in these two languages. Together, these results suggest both developmental specialization and linguistic/cultural variation in the neural substrates that are activated during theory-of-mind tasks.

Predictive relations between language and false-belief understanding in the Toddlers Up study: A latent variable approach

In their meta-analysis, Milligan et al. (2007) commented on the scarcity of longitudinal studies of relationships between language and false-belief understanding. Supporting this view, a recent literature search (using Scopus) produced 1699 hits for articles reporting findings from studies that included false-belief tasks, but only 16 of these studies (i.e., < 1%) assessed false-belief understanding at more than one time-point. In terms of their temporal span, only 2 of these 16 studies (Hughes & Ensor, 2007a; Lockl & Schneider, 2007) involved an interval of at least 24 months. In terms of their *developmental span*, all 16 studies involved children aged 5 or younger. As a result, it is not yet known whether preschoolers who perform poorly on false-belief tasks continue to lag behind following the transition to school.

From a methodological perspective, a key issue of concern is the test–retest reliability of experimental tasks. Early studies suggested that the test–retest reliability of false-belief tasks was, at best, relatively modest (e.g., Charman & Campbell, 1997; Mayes, Klin, Tercyak, Cicchetti, & Cohen, 1996). However, later work (e.g., Hughes et al., 2005) showed that these tasks show good test–retest reliability, especially when aggregate scores were used to index individual differences (Hughes et al., 2000a). Unfortunately, however, the conventional methods of computing aggregate scores (e.g., summing scores across individual tasks) used by Hughes et al. (2005) do not address the problem of measurement error. As a result, it is not clear whether the "reliability" of these aggregate scores merely reflects stable individual differences in the extent to which children are affected by peripheral task demands (e.g., for verbal comprehension, memory, inhibition of prepotent but maladaptive responses).

Fortunately, it is possible to address this issue by using a latent variable approach, such as confirmatory factor analysis (CFA), to provide an accurate representation of the underlying latent construct. CFA also offers a number of other advantages, including: (i) the use of multiple-fit indices (to test how well the data fit the theoretical model); (ii) the opportunity to specify *a priori* which task measures share common demands; (iii) the potential to test whether the same model can be applied equally well to different subgroups (e.g., girls *vs.* boys); and (iv) the facility to combine CFA results with path analyses (by specifying correlations and regressions between latent variables). Coupled with the recent advances in statistical software (e.g., MPlus) that have dramatically increased the accessibility of CFA, these advantages provide a powerful motivation for applying CFA within studies of children's understanding of mind.

Recently, we have applied a CFA to false-belief data gathered at ages 3 and 6 from 115 children in the Toddlers Up study in order to assess the stability (and equivalence) of individual differences in false-belief comprehension across this three-year period (Hughes & Ensor, in press-b). The indicators of false-belief understanding at each of these time-points were outlined in the introductory chapter (see p. 11). Children's centile scores on standardized language assessments – the British Abilities Scale (Elliott, Murray, & Pearson, 1983) at age 3 and the British Picture Vocabulary Scale (L. Dunn, 1997) at age 6 – were used to indicate individual differences in children's verbal ability. Briefly, our model showed a good fit, and when the significant covariance between false-belief performance and language scores at ages 3 and 6 was taken into account, individual differences in both verbal ability and false-belief understanding showed significant stability. Interestingly, consistent with the meta-analytic findings reported by Milligan et al. (2007), although the longitudinal association between language and theory of mind was significant in both directions, the effect was stronger from age-3 language to age-6 false-belief understanding (standardized parameter estimate = .56) than from age-3 false-belief understanding to age-6 language (standardized parameter estimate = .26).

These results add to the existing literature in several ways. As noted earlier, nearly all the reports of associations between language and false-belief understanding come from cross-sectional studies; moreover, the three-year interval between time-points is not only longer than in any previous longitudinal study, but also straddles the transition to school. This is important, because starting school provides children with all sorts of new opportunities for expanding their social and linguistic horizons (e.g., making friends, interacting with teachers, learning to read). Demonstrating that language ability at age 3 predicts almost a third of the variance in children's false-belief understanding at age 6 is therefore a significant achievement. Finally, adopting a latent variable approach enables effects of peripheral task demands to be partitioned out, such that the association between language and false-belief performance cannot be attributed to common effects of measurement error, such as individual differences in children's attention or compliance. Moreover, our analyses also revealed predictive associations between children's false-belief understanding at age 3 and the quality of their discourse with friends at age 6 (these findings are discussed in Chapter 8). In the next chapter, we turn to social perspectives on the links between language and false-belief understanding, with a special focus on conversations between mothers and children.

Chapter summary

It is difficult to do justice to the wealth of cognitive research on links between children's language skills and social understanding within a single chapter. My aim was therefore more modest: to give the reader a sense of the diversity of conceptual and empirical approaches that exist within this field. Thus this chapter can be seen as a language-based parallel to the previous chapter on executive function; in particular, both chapters highlight the developmental breadth, strength and multiplicity of relations with social understanding. This diversity reflects the fact that both language and social understanding are multi-faceted constructs, such that many different types of relation between these domains are possible, making specific links less likely than general associations. Meta-analytic findings highlight this point. Specifically, although the overall association between language and false-belief performance appears quite robust (with language skills explaining 10% of variation in false-belief scores, even when age-related improvements are taken into account), it differs in magnitude strikingly across studies (explained variance estimates range from 0 to 77%), with more general measures of language ability producing stronger results. That said, more work is clearly needed to establish fully the specificity/generality of links between these domains; in particular, adopting a developmental perspective that differentiates between different kinds of social understanding (e.g., intuitive vs. reflective; or on-line vs. off-line) highlights the potential value of a conceptual reorganization that allows for finer grained analyses of the links between language and social understanding.

Cross-cultural work, studies of bilingualism and training studies all provide converging support for the multiplicity and generality of associations between language and social understanding among typically developing children. Research with distinct clinical groups (children with hearing impairments, SLI and ASD) also suggests a multiplicity of relations between language and social understanding. For example, studies of children with hearing impairments demonstrate that, across a wide developmental period, the richness of their linguistic environments (e.g., presence within the family, the school or the broader community of conversational partners who are fluent in sign language) is a key predictor of their understanding of other minds. Interestingly, although SLI is strongly heritable, studies of social understanding among children with SLI have yet to consider whether impoverished linguistic environments contribute to deficits in social understanding. Research in this field has, however, led to two important conclusions. These concern the need to recognize: (i) the overlap in sociocognitive deficits shown by children with SLI and children with ASD; and (ii) the importance of adopting a developmental approach: grammar may be vital for forming a representational understanding of mind, but, once established, processes of mindreading can operate without grammar. Finally, results from the growing number of imaging studies shed some light on the multiplicity of relations between language and social understanding. Specifically, meta-analyses of data from imaging studies indicate that two distinct cortical regions are consistently activated in two different types of mental inference task: the TPJ is activated by tasks that involve processing information about people's goals and intentions (i.e., transitory states), while the mPFC is activated in tasks that involve inferences about personality traits and social scripts (i.e., enduring characteristics). More work is needed to establish whether maturation of these distinct regions helps explain the sequence of developmental milestones in social understanding outlined in Chapter 1. Importantly, however, at least three points preclude inferences about modularity of cognitive architecture: (i) the TPJ is also activated by non-mentalistic tasks; (ii) there are significant contrasts in the verbal load of tasks that typically activate TPJ versus mPFC regions; and (iii) imaging results from studies of children are typically much more diffuse than those obtained in studies of adults. Finally, recent latent variable analyses from the Toddlers Up study strengthen and extend the conclusions reached in Milligan et al.'s (2007) meta-analysis. Specifically, with effects of measurement error partitioned out, relations between language and false-belief understanding are significant in both directions, but stronger from early language to later false-belief understanding than in the reverse direction, such that individual differences in language ability at age 3 predict almost a third of the variance in false-belief understanding at age 6.

Part II

Social influences on children's understanding of mind

4 Language and theory of mind: Social perspectives

In Chapter 3, individual differences in children's social understanding were considered in relation to variation in their own language skills (e.g., richness of vocabulary and syntactical complexity). The first half of this chapter shifts the focus towards variation in children's linguistic environments, with an emphasis on pragmatic and iconic functions of language. In particular, three distinct theoretical proposals will be considered. The first of these is Katherine Nelson's (2005) proposal that specific forms of conversation help children enter into a "community of minds", of which a prime example is parents' and children's shared talk about past events. The second proposal comes from Nancy Budwig (2002) who highlighted the importance of considering iconic features (e.g., variations in the volume or length of a sound that indicate an emotional state) as these anchor language within speech acts and so are pivotal to the construction of meaning. The third proposal comes from Paul Harris and Melissa Koenig (2006) who argued that children's ability to trust in the testimonies offered by their conversational partners is an important moderator of the relationship between conversational exposure to talk about the mind and developments in children's social understanding.

The second half of this chapter turns to the importance of recognizing that children's conversations are usually with people with whom they share a close relationship. This raises questions about whether links between family talk and children's social understanding actually reflect individual differences in relationship quality, or by other family characteristics (e.g., security of attachment, family socioeconomic status and maternal sensitivity); note that this issue is also addressed (more broadly) in Chapter 5. The current chapter includes an assessment of the independence of family talk as a predictor of children's social understanding. Most studies in this field have focused on maternal talk about inner states (thoughts, feelings, desires). However, the findings from the few studies that have examined quality as well as content in maternal talk indicate that *how* mothers talk to their children really matters. Our next question is therefore whether content and quality interact as predictors of children's social understanding. In other words, is maternal talk about inner states particularly helpful when it occurs within particular kinds of conversations? Finally, a relationship perspective leads to the prediction that, compared with conversations with mothers, conversations with other family members (e.g., siblings) might contribute to children's social understanding in distinct ways. These two proposals appear commonsensical, but have rarely been tested directly. Note that sibling conversations are considered in detail in Chapter 6.

Three distinct social perspectives on why language matters for social understanding

In Chapter 1, we noted that many theorists consider the term "theory of mind" to be misleadingly arid, in that it minimizes the importance of cultural conceptions of mind, and presents the child as a solitary scientific thinker. Building on her earlier work (e.g., Nelson et al., 2003), Nelson (2005) offers an alternative metaphor.

1 Children "enter into the community of minds"

Keywords here are "minds" (plural, rather than singular) and "community" (to incorporate the myriad sources of beliefs, reasons for doubting beliefs, beliefs that are commonly shared, or widely viewed as wrong, or held to be true, or to be immoral).

According to Nelson and colleagues, entry into this community of minds depends upon children's ability to talk about things that interest other members of the community (that is, things that are "on their minds"). Early milestones, such as shared attention, attributing intentions and word learning, lead children towards the community of minds but do not constitute participation in this community. However, beyond learning the language of the mind (e.g., "he thinks that's a good idea"), children also need to understand that the propositions that follow these words represent others' points of view (see also P. de Villiers, 2005). Achieving this understanding depends on access to particular types of narrative discourse, such as narratives that involve the language of consciousness (Bruner, 1985), which is concerned with beliefs, thoughts, motives, goals and emotions. Stories are a fertile context for such language (e.g., Dyer, Shatz, & Wellman, 2000), and also require children to represent in their minds a reality that differs from the known present reality. But conversations about past events (e.g., Nelson & Fivush, 2004) also provide a powerful key, as illustrated by a conversation recorded during a home visit to a Toddlers Up study child (Angus), which takes place between the mother and Angus's older brother, "Lucas" (then aged 8). The mother's opening gambit makes it clear that she is revisiting a conversation about an amusing event at school that she and Lucas have enjoyed previously:

Mother: Has anyone been getting up to mischief today Lucas? Any good stories? Anybody put the shower on your clothes today? [*smiles*]
Lucas: No, not today. [*positive tone*]
Mother: So, has anyone got to the bottom of what happened then?
Lucas: Probably, but I haven't heard.

Mother:	Okay, so they haven't expelled any third formers yet then?
Lucas:	Nobody's been expelled, but they're in deep trouble.
Mother:	Deep trouble.
Lucas:	Strangely, the teacher didn't even know where the switch was, Mr Mason [*pause*]
Mother:	Didn't even know where the shower switch was?
Lucas:	Yes.
Mother:	So he couldn't turn it off? [*disbelief and amusement*]
Lucas:	Yes. Me and Richard had to go in there with our clothes on. [*positive tone*]
Mother:	[*Laughs*] Getting soaked. Oh no. Who was in the changing room? I bet everyone was really laughing. What did Douglas say? [*positive tone*]
Lucas:	Soaked.
Mother:	He got soaked. I bet he thought that was hilarious, didn't he? [*smiling*]

This conversation neatly illustrates how references to mental states can be indirect rather than explicit: "So, has anyone got to the bottom of what happened then?" (i.e., does anybody know what happened?) "Probably, but I haven't heard" (i.e., someone else probably knows, but not me). It is also a wonderful example of co-construction of a story narrative, via inferences that also help to embellish the story. For example, when Lucas indicates that he doesn't know who the culprits were, the mother says: "Okay, so they haven't expelled any third formers yet then?". Through this comment the mother is implicitly expressing her belief that Lucas would have heard if there had been any expulsions; the comment also brings drama to the narrative, which Lucas picks up on, by saying, "Nobody's been expelled, but they're in deep trouble". Likewise, the mother adds coherence to the storyline by building on Lucas's comment that the teacher, Mr Mason, didn't know where the switch was, adding, "So he couldn't turn it off?"; she also adds emotional colour to the anecdote by saying: "I bet everyone was really laughing ... I bet he thought that was hilarious, didn't he?". In short, the mother does a marvellous job of coaching her son in the art of spinning a yarn that is full of suspense, drama and humour.

Later on in this chapter the reader will find another mother–child conversation about an event in the past (a boat trip). This second conversation illustrates another key feature of such shared stories about past events: namely that when the central characters are the children themselves or their loved ones, differences in points of view are made salient.

2 Iconic aspects of language help children represent reality in different ways

The second proposal comes from Nancy Budwig (2002) who argued that, beyond its symbolic functions (whether at the level of the lexicon, or syntax, or pragmatics), language can be seen as iconic and/or indexical. Like pragmatic accounts, indexical approaches centre on the communicative functions of language. However, whereas pragmatic accounts focus on how language is acquired through games and practice, an indexical account treats language as contributing to the interpretation and construction of context (cf. Duranti, 2006). Linguistic indices include onomatopoeia, or variations in the volume or length of a sound that indicate an emotional state. Two particular features of these indices enable children to represent reality in new ways. The first is the emphasis they provide on the relationship between the object and its linguistic referent. The second is the fact that linguistic indices are used variably in different situations and so, by becoming associated with these situations, play a pivotal role in the construction of meaning. That is, in everyday conversations we frequently use language to describe and reflect on our social and cultural worlds.

Budwig (2002) illustrated this point with findings from a detailed longitudinal study of toddlers' use of the desire term "want", which appeared with equal frequency at 18 months and at 30 months, but with different functions: 18-month-olds use "want" to elicit caregivers' instrumental assistance in obtaining desired objects but, from about 24 months, shift to using "want" to elicit caregivers' sanction for desired acts. As Budwig puts it: "the children have a burgeoning awareness that desire alone is not enough to motivate human action [but] ... have come to realize the social connectedness of action as well" (Budwig, 2002, p. 73). This work also suggested interesting similarities and differences between children and caregivers' use of desire terms. For example, children and caregivers show similar frequencies of reference to desires (which, for both partners, are nearly always a reference to the *child's* desire). However, for children, desire talk occurs largely within action assertions, whereas caregivers typically refer to desires within inquiries, permission requests and clarifications.

Developmental changes in *how* children use mental-state terms are not restricted to the early stages of language acquisition, as similar findings have emerged from within the Toddlers Up study, in an analysis that focused on 57 siblings (aged between 3 and 6 years) filmed playing with the target children at the first two time-points, 12 months apart (Hughes, Marks, Ensor, & Lecce, in press). Specifically, although the mean frequency of children's references to inner states (beliefs, feelings, desires) did not increase over time, there was a significant increase in the proportion of references to inner states that occurred within children's explanations. Below are a couple of examples, taken from the second time-point, when the study child was aged 3. In the first example, the study child is a girl (whom we'll call Bethan), and the sibling is her brother ("Andy"), who was almost 10 at the time of this visit:

Andy/Bethan:	Are these scary things Bethan?
Bethan/Andy:	Yeah.
Andy/Bethan:	No they're not they're monkeys, look he's laughing. Is this a scary thing? [*pause*] These are old bears Bethan.
Bethan/Andy:	A bear?
Andy/Bethan:	Yeah there's old bear and there's brown one [*speech unintelligible*]. Are these scary things?

Bethan/Andy:	Nah.
Andy/Bethan:	Who are they then?
Bethan/Andy:	Panda.
Andy/Bethan:	No, that's a panda [*pointing to another toy*], I think this is a panda, that's a panda. These are, um, koala bears, I think.
Bethan/Andy:	Lala bear.

This excerpt is part of an extended conversation in which Bethan and Andy have been playing with a large assortment of plastic animals, sorting them into "scary" and "not scary". Andy first offers Bethan the explanatory principle that animals are not scary if they are laughing, and then explains why he thinks a particular bear is not a panda, by pointing out the contrast with another bear he recognizes as a panda. Thus both explanations serve to highlight the importance of paying close attention to how things look. The second example comes from a family in which the study child is a boy (whom we'll call Dorian), who has a 5-year-old older sister ("Anna"). At the start of this excerpt the older sibling's explanation again highlights the importance of noting just how things look:

Anna/Dorian:	I think they might be real handcuffs. [*pause*] 'Cos I've seen real handcuffs that look just the same as this, real handcuffs.
Dorian/Anna:	Can you get you. [*picking up another pair of handcuffs*]
Anna/Dorian:	Handcuffs can put you in prison. Put your hands in there. [*Dorian picks up the wand, making it make a noise*]
Anna/Dorian:	Dore, I'm the fairy remember. [*trying to lay claim to wand*]
Dorian/Anna:	I want that wand, and I'm going to be Buzz Lightyear.
Anna/Dorian:	And I'm going to have some big fluffy wings.
Dorian/Anna:	This is for Buzz Lightyear. [*holds up the light sabre*]
Anna/Dorian:	I know, you can be Buzz Lightyear. And I came to save you?
Dorian/Anna:	No, no, Buzz Lightyear can't get catched. He's too [*pause*]
Anna/Dorian:	What?
Dorian/Anna:	Well, I don't want to be pretended to be catched.

Anna then tries to explain why she should have the wand, but gives in graciously when her little brother mirrors her claim. Later in the excerpt, 3-year-old Dorian has difficulty in finding a "within-script" explanation for why Buzz Lightyear can't be caught, before using mental-state terms to explain that he himself doesn't want to play at being caught. Together, these excerpts illustrate the way in which developmental connections between language and theory of mind can be characterized not just by the acquisition of new forms or functions (e.g., acquisition of inner-state terms, or emergence of communication through language), but also by important changes in how these forms and functions are related. These findings have clear implications for research: rather than simply considering age of onset researchers need to examine age-related changes in the relationship between form and function.

3 Learning from conversations depends on children's trust in testimony

The third proposal comes from Paul Harris (e.g., Harris & Koenig, 2006), who approaches the issue of conversational influences on children's understanding of mind (or, indeed, of any unobservable entity) by highlighting the importance of developments in children's trust in testimony. Specifically, Harris begins by arguing that Piaget's constructivist account of how children build up an understanding of their world from first-hand observations and physical enquiries applies equally to how children build an increasingly systematic and coherent understanding of unobservable processes (including mental states) by reflecting upon the (often implicit and incomplete) information they receive during conversations with others, and especially parents. Take, for example, another conversation recorded during a Toddlers Up home visit to Angus and his family. This time the mother is talking to his sister, Sasha (then aged 5), as she picks up a piece of paper with which the children have been playing:

Mother/Sasha: Sasha, look at this piece of paper. Look. Who made all those holes in it? Do you think a little insect has been nibbling it, or a slug or something? What do you think?
Sasha/Mother: We did it.
Mother/Sasha: What, the holes?
Sasha/Mother: Mmm.
Mother/Sasha: How did you make those funny holes?
Sasha/Mother: We folded it and then we ripped a bit.
Mother/Sasha: Did you? [*mock surprise and serious voice*]

From the mother's facial expression during this exchange, it is clear that she did not really believe that a little creature had created the holes in the paper – but is rather offering this as a playful suggestion; later, when her daughter Sasha fails to go along with this flight of fancy but instead explains that she and her brother made the holes, the mother's simple question, "Did you?" (delivered in a tone of feigned surprise) highlights the possibility of tricking somebody. Of course, we don't know how much of this particular conversation will have stayed in Sasha's mind, but it seems likely that repeated exposure to playful exchanges of this type would encourage children to have a go at pulling someone's leg, and so enter a new world of entertainment through deception.

In his commentary on Michelle Chouinard's (2007) monograph on children's questions (based on the CHILDES conversational database), Harris (2007) offers a further insight into how parent–child dialogues can foster children's understanding of mental states (and other unobservable entities). Specifically, Harris draws attention to the importance of episodes in which children display a "passage of intellectual search", by tenaciously questioning their parents until they are satisfied with the explanations they receive. This point is very similar to the argument (discussed in more detail later in this chapter) that references to mental states are only likely to promote children's awareness of minds when they occur within connected discourse, that is, conversations that relate directly to whatever it is that is on the child's mind at the time (Ensor & Hughes, 2008). Previous studies (e.g., Hart & Risley, 1992; McCarthy, 1930; Tizard & Hughes, 1984) have shown that there are strong socioeconomic-status-related contrasts in the frequency with which children engage in such tenacious curiosity-based questioning. Although it seems likely that these contrasts in children's ability or willingness to question their conversational partners contribute to socioeconomic-status-related differences in children's social understanding (e.g., Cutting & Dunn, 1999; Hughes et al., 2005), this proposal has yet to be tested empirically.

However, the central thesis of Harris's argument concerns children's trust in the accuracy and superior knowledge of their informants. Without this trust, children would not be able to assimilate material gleaned from conversations into their concepts of unobservable entities (such as mental states). This trust may explain why parent–child dialogues appear so special. That is, just as parents' emotional availability leads to affective attachments, their intellectual availability can lead to epistemic attachments. Support for this idea comes from a recent study of 6-year-olds (Corriveau et al., 2009), which demonstrated that securely attached children selectively favoured mothers' testimony in ambiguous situations, while insecurely attached children did not appear sensitive to ambiguity but instead showed a blanket preference for testimony from either strangers (in the case of avoidant children) or mothers (in the case of resistant children). These contrasts offer an explanation for the cognitive advantages enjoyed by securely attached children. That is, unlike avoidant children (who lack epistemic trust in their caregivers) or resistant children (who are overcredulous in their trust), securely attached children can evaluate when they should or should not trust in the information provided by caregivers (see Chapter 5 for more details).

Relationship perspective on links between discourse and social understanding

The results described above indicate that secure attachments may serve to strengthen the links between family conversations and children's cognitive development, a finding that brings us neatly to the relationship perspective that is the second theme of this chapter. For many researchers who examine the links between discourse and children's social understanding from a relationship perspective, the set of longitudinal studies carried out by Judy Dunn and her colleagues (in Cambridge, UK, in Pennsylvania in the USA and, later on, in London, UK) are of seminal importance.

Understanding emotion

Almost 20 years ago, Dunn and colleagues reported that 3-year-olds whose families often talked about feelings outperformed their peers on tests of emotion recognition and perspective taking at age 6; strikingly, this association remained significant when individual differences in both children's verbal ability and overall frequencies of family talk were taken into account (J. Dunn et al., 1991a). Convergent findings from several other independent studies (e.g., J. Cassidy, Parke, Butkovsky, & Braungart, 1992; Denham & Kochanoff, 2002; Denham, Zoller, & Couchod, 1994; J. Dunn, Bretherton, & Munn, 1987), including a study of low-income children (Garner, Jones, Gaddy, & Rennie, 1997), highlight family discourse (and maternal discourse in particular) as a key predictor of young children's understanding of emotions.

That said, the predictive relationship between early maternal talk and children's later emotion understanding is open to a number of alternative interpretations. In particular, individual differences in attachment security in toddlerhood also predict children's emotion understanding at age 6 (e.g., Laible & Thompson, 1998), raising the possibility that attachment processes underpin both early maternal talk about feelings and children's subsequent emotion understanding. To address this issue, de Rosnay and Harris (2005) assessed maternal discourse for a sample of 75 preschoolers (aged 4½ to 6 years) who, as infants, had completed the strange situation assessment of attachment. Their findings demonstrated that mothers' talk about inner states predicted children's emotion understanding, even when attachment status (as well as other possible confounds, such as child sex, verbal ability, number of older siblings and socioeconomic status) was controlled.

Understanding false belief

Parallel findings have emerged with regard to children's understanding of (false) beliefs. For example, in a longitudinal study of 82 mothers and their 2- to 4-year-olds (filmed in a picture book task at three time-points over a year), maternal talk about mental states consistently predicted children's later false-belief performance, even when child's age, language ability, mental-state talk and earlier false-belief perform-ance, as well as mother's education and other types of mother utterances, were all taken into account (Ruffman, Slade, & Crowe, 2002). Note also that this association was not reciprocal – early false-belief performance did not predict mothers' later mental-state reference. Several other studies (e.g., Adrián, Clemente, & Villanueva, 2007; Adrián, Clemente, Villanueva, & Rieffe, 2005) have reported significant asso-ciations between maternal talk and children's false-belief comprehension, but there is growing consensus that we need to go beyond simple overall frequencies of maternal references to mental states in order to elucidate the processes through which maternal talk scaffolds children's awareness of mental states.

From predictors to processes

While the above examples highlight the limitations of a narrow focus on explicit mental-state reference, there are quite pragmatic reasons (e.g., the need to ensure reliability of coding) for this focus. Taking research forwards to elucidate the processes through which maternal mental-state talk scaffolds children's aware-ness of mental states requires addressing a number of rather different challenges. One such challenge is the need to establish the specificity of relations between maternal mental-state talk and children's social understanding. Typically, studies that involve the picture-book paradigm have reported that individual differences in the *overall* frequencies of maternal mental-state reference are what matter (e.g., Adrián et al., 2005; Ruffman et al., 2002). However, studies that adopt lengthier home-based observations suggest quite specific links between children's exposure to and engagement in mental-state talk. For example, in a longitudinal study by Jenny Jenkins and colleagues (Jenkins, Turrell, Kogushi, Lollis, & Ross, 2003), 37 families with 2- and 4-year-old children were each observed for six 90-minute home visits. Their analyses showed that family talk about cognitive and emotional states at the first time-point predicted changes (over two years) in the younger child's talk about cognitive and emotional states, respectively. Similarly, analyses of naturalistic interactions during home visits for the Toddlers Up sample also point to specific rather than general links.

For example, analyses of mother–child interactions at age 2 led to three key findings, reported by Ensor and Hughes (2008). First, mothers referred to thoughts and desires much more often within connected turns (i.e., speech turns that were semantically related to the child's previous turn) than within other types of turn (e.g., successful or unsuccessful bid for attention). Second, mothers' connected talk and children's talk about thoughts or desires each independently predicted children's social understanding at age 4, even when verbal ability at age 4 and social understanding at age 2 were taken into account. Third, the strongest predictor of age-4 social understanding was mothers' connected talk about thoughts and desires.

Refining and extending the above findings, Ensor (2009) has examined mother–child conversations at ages 2 and 6 in relation to performances at age 6 on tests of social understanding (first- and second-order false belief, mixed emotions). Again, three key findings emerged from this second study. First, individual differences in maternal connected talk about thoughts, beliefs and knowledge were stable across this four-year period (i.e., from when the child was aged 2 to aged 6). Second, variation in maternal connected cognitive talk (but not connected desire talk) showed significant concurrent associations with individual differences in children's understanding of both false belief and emotion. Third, 2-year-olds whose mothers engaged in frequent connected cognitive talk outperformed their peers on the social-understanding tasks administered at age 6; this predictive relationship remained significant when social understanding at age 2 was taken into account and was particularly strong when mothers increased their connected cognitive talk as their children matured and developed.

Further support for adopting a fine-grained perspective comes from a study by Elizabeth Meins and colleagues (Meins et al., 2002), who coded mothers' free play with their 6-month-old infants (*n* = 57) in terms of both the frequency and appropriateness of maternal talk about mental states and found that early *and appropriate* maternal talk about inner states (but not attachment security) independently predicted variance in children's false-belief performance at age 4.

A third challenge is the need to minimize child-driven effects, in order to ensure that predictive relations do not simply reflect underlying continuities in child characteristics. Although Ruffman et al. (2002) found that early false-belief performance did not predict mothers' later mental-state talk, it would be premature to conclude that child-driven effects are negligible, because most mothers monitor their children's interests, and adjust their talk accordingly. However, at least two studies have minimized this problem, by sampling maternal talk *about* (rather than with) their children. The findings from these studies indicate that, even in the child's absence, the frequency of mothers' references to mental states predicts children's later understanding of emotion (de Rosnay & Harris, 2005), while mothers' self-reported preferences for elaborated, explanatory talk about the mental states is a key predictor of children's later understanding of false belief (Peterson & Slaughter, 2003).

The findings from Peterson and Slaughter's (2003) study, described above, indicate a fourth and important challenge: the need to distinguish between mental-state reference *per se*, and the kinds of speech within which mental-state references are likely to appear. That is, frequent maternal mental-state reference may predict children's later false-belief performance simply because it is a good proxy index of the extent to which mothers: (i) use elaborated discourse with their children; (ii) draw children's attention to events involving different points of view; or (iii) adjust their talk to their children's interests or attentional focus. Take, for example, the conversational excerpts, provided in Chapter 1, from Toddlers Up study child "Angus" and his family. When interacting with 8-year-old Lucas, or with Angus at age 6, the mother shows an impressive ability to engage in elaborated discourse that helps draw her sons' attention to differences in points of view. Equally, in a conversation recorded when Angus was just 3 years old, the mother proves adept at building on Angus and his sister Sasha's current fascination with the toy handcuffs provided by the research team. Just before she speaks, a police siren can be heard in the background.

Mother: There you are. The police are coming. They saw you with those handcuffs and they said, "Who's stolen my handcuffs?"

Through this comment, the mother is playfully suggesting that the police know that the children have possession of police property, are not happy about this and intend to come and arrest them – a complex web of mental states that is made accessible to 3-year-old Angus because it connects so well with the theme of the children's own pretend play of just minutes before.

More formal recent empirical work also provides support for the proposal that frequencies of maternal mental-state talk are a good proxy index of the extent to which mothers use speech turns that: (i) involve elaborated discourse; (ii) highlight differences in points of view; or (iii) tune into children's interests or attentional focus. First, in their study of mothers' conversations about a past event with their 4-year-old children ($n = 76$), Ontai and Thompson (2008) found that maternal conversational elaboration but *not* maternal mental-state reference (or children's attachment security) independently predicted children's performance on false-belief tasks. Second, in a study involving 70 mothers and their 3- to 5-year-old children, mothers' talk during shared reading of a picture book (chosen to include false-belief elements), Turnbull, Carpendale, and Racine (2008) found that the correlation between maternal mental-state reference and children's false-belief performance fell below significance once mothers' non-explicit talk about the false-belief elements of the picture book was taken into account. Third, transcript-based analyses of naturalistic home-based observations for 120 of the 2-year-olds in the Toddlers Up study demonstrated that only maternal mental-state references that appeared within connected turns (i.e., maternal speech turns that were semantically directly related to the child's previous utterance) independently predicted children's social understanding at ages 3 and 4; moreover, overall frequencies of maternal connected talk also independently predicted children's later social understanding (Ensor & Hughes, 2008).

Together, the above findings highlight the need for a broader and more contextualized approach within research on sociolinguistic influences on children's developing understanding of mind. At a theoretical level, several researchers have responded to this challenge by drawing on Wittgenstein's (1958) private language argument to propose that learning about the mind is not simply a matter of mapping words onto private mental entities, but a much wider endeavour that involves understanding and talking about human activity and social exchanges in psychological terms (e.g., Carpendale & Lewis, 2004; Montgomery, 2005). For example, Montgomery (2005) has proposed that the meaning of mental-state terms emerges from their pragmatic functions, rather than from word-referent relations. As a result, private experiences of internal sensations (e.g., pain, pleasure, desire) become imbued with meaning through shared interactions across a variety of social contexts.

Montgomery's (2005) proposal builds on early linguistic work (e.g., Austin, 1962) that ordered words and sentences on a continuum from descriptive (e.g., a red ball) to performative (e.g., I promise …) and is based on the premise that mental-state words fall at the performative end of the spectrum. This point is wonderfully illustrated by the variety of pragmatic functions served by maternal inner-state talk in the following 5-minute excerpt from a mother and a 3-year-old child in the Toddlers Up study (whom we'll call Henry, and we'll call his older sister Maisy). (Noise from the washing machine makes some of the speech (denoted - - -) unintelligible.)

Henry/Mother:	Want cheesy beans! [*tearful*]
Mother/Henry:	Yeah you want cheesy beans, I know you do. [*Henry hits mother on leg*] No Henry, right. Don't hit me Henry, doesn't do any good does it? Hey Henry, Henry, Henry, Henry. Do you know where we're going this afternoon? Do you know where we're going? We're going on a river boat [- - -]. Did you know that?
Henry/Mother:	[- - -] river boat.
Mother/Henry:	A big river boat, isn't it? [- - -] Did I show it to you? It's got the same name as you, it's called Henrietta, it's a Henrietta not a Henry. [*Henry starts crying again*]
Henry/Mother:	Where, where we [*pause*]

Maisy/Mother:	Mum, Mummy. [*running back in kitchen*]
Mother/Maisy:	Maisy.
Maisy/Mother:	Is, is, where is the boat taking us?
Mother/Maisy:	Well, it's just taking us for a ride up the river, but not very far.
Henry/Mother:	Where, where we [*pause*]
Mother/Maisy:	Up to where the cows are, you know where the cows are in the river part? Up to there, and then it's gonna turn round and come back, come back again.
Maisy/Mother:	[*Bring us?*] home?
Mother/Maisy:	Well, back to were we, we get on it, because we're gonna get on it near the swimming pool. You know where the swimming pool is? [*Maisy nods*] Yeah, well we'll get on it there, and then, takes us up the river towards the cows, and then back again.
Henry [to self]:	Oh, oh, oh, no! [*jumping around and out of room*]
Henry/Mother:	Mummy, [- - -] get out there?
Mother/Henry:	Are we going to what? Get out of the boat? Uh, I don't know Henry, maybe.
Henry/Mother:	Well I want to, how can we get out?
Mother/Henry:	Of the boat? [*Henry nods*] Well it's very easy you just climb on it and then when you, when you stop you climb off it. You'll see, when we go you'll see.
Henry/Mother:	Well I'm still scared.
Mother/Henry:	I'll come with you, you won't have to be scared.
Henry/Mother:	Not on handle.
Mother/Henry:	What handle Henry?
Henry/Mother:	The, the, the, the, the one when, when there's a [- - -], up on the pavement.
Mother/Henry:	What pavement?
Henry/Mother:	The, when we get out.
Mother/Henry:	Yeah, we'll get out and I'll hold you, and if you're scared in any way I'll hold you, but there's no need to be scared is there? You've been [*pause*]
Henry/Mother:	What if it, what if ducks will eat me? [- - -]
Mother/Henry:	Ducks will eat you? [*Henry nods*] I don't think so Henry. [*laughing*] They've never eaten you before have they? They've only eaten the bread you've given them. They don't normally eat little boys, well they don't ever eat little boys.
Henry/Mother:	But these, but but [- - -] scared. [- - -]
Mother/Henry:	Scared of what, ducks?
Henry/Mother:	No these little rivers.
Mother/Henry:	Oh, little boys are scared of rivers. Well that's a good thing really because you, if you fell into the river it wouldn't be good, but you won't fall in, because if you're careful and stay with

	Mummy you won't fall into the river. You hold Mummy's hand when she tells you to, okay?
Henry/Mother:	[- - -] the ladder.
Mother/Henry:	Yeah, with a ladder yeah. We'll probably get in with a ladder and then get out [- - -], you'll be alright Henry truly.
Henry/Mother:	I'm worried.
Mother/Henry:	Well, if you're worried Daddy's just rung up and said he'd like to come, so if you're worried you can hang on to Daddy as well. You will have fun I promise you.
Henry/Mother:	No I don't wanna go on the boat.
Mother/Henry:	You don't want to go on the boat? [*Henry shakes head*]
Henry/Mother:	I want to walk.
Mother/Henry:	You want to walk?
Henry/Mother:	Yeah.
Mother/Henry:	Okay then.
Henry/Mother:	Not on the boat.
Mother/Henry:	Alright darling, you don't wanna go you don't have to.
Henry/Mother:	Don't wanna go.
Mother/Henry:	Alright sweetheart. You've been on a very big boat, do you remember we went on a very big boat when we went to France?
Mother/Maisy:	Do you remember that Maisy?
Maisy/Mother:	Yeah.
Mother/Henry:	And then you loved it, and you looked at the seagulls didn't you? And you waved to the people in the, on the um, on the jetty bit, the bit that sticks out. You were very happy on that boat Henry.

Just prior to this conversation, Henry had become very upset, because having been offered cheesy beans for lunch (his favourite), his mother then discovered that there were no more cheesy beans in the house. This upset may be one reason why Henry uses several mental-state terms (e.g., *I want*, *I'm scared*, *I'm worried*). Each time, his mother echoes his sentiments. These phatic speech turns are used to demonstrate that she is listening to him, cares about his feelings and wants to reassure him (e.g., "… if you're worried you can hang on to Daddy as well"). Early on in the conversation, the mother also questions her child with a repeated "*do you know* …*?*". Here again, the mother's mental-state talk serves a pragmatic function: she is trying to distract Henry, who is venting his frustration about the lack of cheesy beans by hitting her. Next, the mother twice uses the phrase "*you know*" when addressing her daughter Maisy. In these speech turns the mother is attempting to align her daughter's point of view with her own, by clarifying the details of the afternoon family boat trip in order to ensure that Maisy knows their planned destination. Then, she turns her attention back to Henry and uses "*I don't know* … *maybe*" to indicate her lack of certainty about the exact details of their excursion; pragmatically, this turn also serves to avoid a conflict, as it seems probable that they won't be getting out of the boat, as Henry hopes. Shortly after, the mother uses inner-state talk ("You'll see, when we go you'll see") to help Henry understand that once he is at the boat he'll have a more informed view on how to get off it again. Next she uses inner-state talk to indicate that while there's no need to be afraid of ducks ("They don't normally eat little boys"), it makes sense to be aware of the perils of drowning ("...little boys are scared of rivers. Well that's a good thing really ..."). Then she uses inner-state talk in much the same way as a cognitive-behavioural therapist would, to reduce her son's fears by reminding him of a previous and very positive experience on a boat ("You've been on a very big boat, do you remember we went on a very big boat when we went to France?"). Note here that the mother draws Henry's sister Maisy into the conversation, consolidating this shared memory of a positive event (perhaps in order to foster anticipation and enjoyment of the boat trip planned for that afternoon). Finally, Henry's mother elaborates on this earlier experience, emphasizing how much pleasure it had given him ("And then you loved it, and you looked at the seagulls didn't you?").

On video, the persistence and versatility of this mother's efforts to reassure Henry are all the more impressive, as it reveals that throughout this conversation she is also sorting out laundry, getting a meal ready and balancing Henry (dressed up as a cat) on her knee! In other words, the above conversational excerpt neatly demonstrates the myriad of cognitive and affective processes that are likely to underpin the positive impact of maternal inner-state talk on children's development, such that it makes no sense to single out any one particular process as pivotal. The transcript also provides an excellent example for Dunn's (1994) argument that the kind of discourse that can promote children's social understanding is most likely to appear *within certain sorts of relationships* – in this case, the mother's sensitivity to her son's feelings and her ability to reassure him by drawing on shared positive experiences all point to a very warm and supportive child–caregiver relationship.

Relationships, however, involve two people, and there is now considerable evidence that children exert a powerful influence on their parents (e.g., Burke, Pardini, & Loeber, 2008; Gross, Shaw, & Moilanen, 2008; Larsson, Viding, & Rijsdijk, 2008; Pardini, Fite, & Burke, 2008). With regard to parent–child conversations, at least two studies have shown that child characteristics often constrain opportunities for connected discourse. For example, one finding to emerge from the London study of hard-to-manage preschoolers that motivated the Cambridge Toddlers Up study was that mothers of "hard-to-manage" preschoolers engaged their children in fewer connected conversations (Brophy & Dunn, 2002). Similarly, in another study that involved a reminiscing task, Deborah Laible (2004) reported that mothers elaborated more often if they perceived their child as self-regulated and attentive, but less often if they perceived their child as active in temperament. Another 5-minute excerpt from a different family in the Toddlers Up study illustrates this contrast. It provides a good counterpoint to the earlier example, because once again it begins with a child (here, called "Marie") who is frustrated because she cannot have what she wanted for supper (in this case, frozen peas – which have just been tipped by the mother into a pan of boiling water, and so can now only be eaten hot). This time there are two older siblings present, "Tilly" and "Peter".

Mother/Marie:	Do you want some peas and quiche? [*points at a pan*] Are you going to help me? [*She goes back to serving out the dinner with Marie still in her arms. She takes a pan off the hob and drains it at the sink. Marie is still crying into her mother's shoulder but not as loudly*]
Mother/Marie:	Would you like some quiche? [*kisses Marie's forehead*] [*Marie is still crying. Mother looks at her*]
Mother/Marie:	Would you like some? Are you going to be okay? [*Marie looks up but is still crying. Mother puts Marie down and talks to Peter who is back in view*]
Mother/Peter:	Can you bring the plates across, Peter? [*Peter leaves the room. Marie is crying loudly next to her mother*]
Tilly [*to self*]:	A de a de a de. [*quite loudly out of view*] [*Peter returns carrying plates, which he puts down on the worktop. Marie is crying loudly, but stops briefly and looks down at the floor*]
Marie:	No! [*loudly and stamps her foot, looks back up and starts crying again*]
Mother/Peter:	Peter, how much quiche would you like?
Peter/Mother:	[*Quite*] a lot.
Mother/Peter:	Okay.
Mother/Peter:	Darling, can you get some knives out? Peter? [*Marie reaches for the empty packet of frozen peas on the worktop, still crying*]
Mother/Marie:	No, no, no. [*moves the packet away from Marie*]
Mother/Peter:	Peter. [*Marie lies down on the floor.*]
Peter/Mother:	Yes.
Mother/Peter:	Can you get some knives out? [*Peter goes to a drawer. Marie is lying on the floor crying loudly still and still holding her teddy*]
Mother/Tilly:	Tilly, Tilly?
Tilly/Mother:	Yeah.
Mother/Tilly:	Could you give Marie a cuddle? [*Tilly walks over to Marie who rolls away from her*]
Tilly/Mother:	No she won't let me. [*walks out of view*] [*Tilly walks back, holding cutlery*]
Mother/Peter:	Do you want [*speech unintelligible*] that. [*can't hear as Marie is still crying. Tilly walks back into view and crouches to pick up something small off the floor*]
Tilly/Peter:	Peter, I've found one of your things. [*stands up and gives something to Peter who puts it in his pocket. Marie has stopped crying but is still lying on the floor*]
Mother/Marie:	Hey babs are you hungry? Are you a hungry girl?
Peter/Tilly:	Tilly?

Tilly/Peter:	Yeah?
	[*Peter gives Tilly a knife and fork*]
Mother/Tilly:	Tilly, would you like some quiche?
Tilly/Mother:	Yeah.
Mother/Tilly:	Would you like some peas?
Tilly/Mother:	Yeah, yeah.
	[*Marie is curled up face down on the floor and starts crying again*]
Tilly [*to self*]:	Oooh oooh. Er er er. Yeah, yeah. Er er err. Yeah, yeah. [*still in quiet sing-song voice*]
	[*Mother is dishing out food and Marie is still curled up on the floor crying*]
Tilly [*to self*]:	Yummee yum yum yummee. [*runs out of view*]
Mother/Tilly:	There's yours there [*speech unintelligible*] sitting here
	[*Marie stops crying for a couple of seconds and sniffs*]
Mother/Marie:	Marie, do you want to [*speech unintelligible*]
	[*Marie glances round and starts crying loudly again. Mother comes into the kitchen, picks Marie up and kisses the top of her head*]
Mother/Marie:	Shhh sshhh sshhh. [*softly*] Marie, would you like some water?
	[*Mother goes to carry Marie out of the room but Marie leans over pointing at the floor. Mother picks up her teddy and walks out of view carrying Marie, who is still crying loudly*]

The conversation between Henry and his mother succeeds in cheering him up and provides an opportunity for all kinds of meetings of minds and points of view. In contrast, the 5-minute excerpt given above ends with Marie still crying loudly, even though her mother has given her kisses and cuddles, has remained calm and made several attempts to offer her something to eat or drink. The striking contrast between these two conversations can be interpreted in many different ways, relating to possible contrasts in family background and child characteristics, as well as in parenting style. Note, however, that any differences between the two families in socioeconomic background favour Marie's family, and so are unlikely to explain the contrast between these two family conversations. Might the differences therefore reflect contrasts between the children; in other words, is Henry much more malleable and easygoing than Marie? In fact, on the Strengths and Difficulties Questionnaire (SDQ), both mothers rated their child as in the clinical range for conduct problems; likewise, one year later both children received the same (subclinical) "total difficulty" SDQ score from teachers. This leaves us with contrasts in the mothers' speech, which illustrate the power of conversation to distract children, by leading them away from the here and now (with its frustrating lack of cheesy beans or frozen peas) to other, brighter, worlds that can be evoked both by reminiscing about past events and by making plans for future events.

Temporally dynamic perspective on mother–child talk and social understanding

Of course, the two example conversations described above provide only a snap-shot view of mother–child interactions. Indeed, the calm and matter of fact way in which Marie's family reacted to her crying indicates that such displays of distress are relatively frequent, and perhaps they have all learned that the most effective strategy is simply to allow her to calm down by herself. In fact, a home visit 3 years later (when Marie was 6) confirms this view. She and her mother are reading a picture book that the research team had provided, that included a set of vignettes involving ambiguous events, in which one character's actions upset another character. Here's what Marie's mother says in response to a story about a boy and a girl who have had an argument; later on, the boy jumps out from behind a bush, as a result the girl falls off her bicycle.

Mother: OK, so what should you do if you are cross with someone and you have a fight? How do you how do you sort it out?

Marie: I think I would say sorry and shake hands and have one big hug.

Mother: You'd say sorry, that's good. Ah, OK, but do you think it's a good idea that Sam jumped out in front of her? [*Marie shakes her head*] So, if you're feeling cross and upset with someone, what do you [*pause*]

Marie: Definitely if you're on a bike, very, very, very dangerous.

Mother: I know.

Mother: So, what would be a better thing to do if you were upset with someone?

Marie: Say sorry.

Mother: Well, supposing they had been rude to you, is it better to get even?

Marie: What do you mean?

Mother: Well, is it better to hurt them back? If you're feeling upset with someone.

Marie: No.

Mother: No, it isn't, is it? So what would be a better thing to do?

Marie: I don't know.

Mother: It's a difficult question. Sometimes just waiting to let the anger pass.

Marie: Shake hands, have a hug and say sorry.

Mother: OK. Well done darling. Give me a cuddle.

Interestingly, in the context of this shared picture-book reading (again, filmed at home at age 6), Henry is much less engaged than Marie, and he and his mother fail to connect in the same way as they had during the visit three years earlier. Here's the parallel extract from their visit, when they are reading the same story about the bicycle fall.

Mother: Why do you think she fell off? My thought – Do you want my thought?

Henry: Because, um, Sam jumped out and it made her run into a bush.

Mother: Yeah. What do you think Maggie would've thought after she'd fallen off? Henry?

Henry: Angry.

Mother: Angry. With who? With [*pause*]

Henry: Sam.

Mother: With Sam. So, she was angry with him the day before. [*pause*] Do you think he might've done it on purpose?

              [*Henry talks into a cushion, so response is inaudible*]

Mother: Talk properly. Henry. Henry! We're nearly finished here. Turn round.

Henry: I think he done it on purpose.

Mother: You think he done it on purpose. Why do you think he did it on purpose?

Henry: I don't know. [*pause*]

              [*Henry is talking into cushion again*]

Mother: Henry, turn round.

Henry: [*Speech unintelligible*]

Mother: What?

Henry: [*Speech unintelligible*]

Mother: They're angry with each other. Can you sit round properly, please? And talk sensibly to me. 'Cause they were angry with each other? But when you're angry with people, what do you do?

              [*Henry doesn't respond*]

Mother: Henry?

Henry: Go to my room.

Mother: You go to your room, yeah. But if you were angry with somebody in particular, do you not sometimes try to annoy them a little bit?

Henry: No.

Mother: No? Come and sit back down. Come on.

So, at age 6, the contrast between the conversations Henry and Marie have with their mothers appears to have reversed. This shift points to two important lessons for research. The first of these is the importance of adopting a longitudinal approach within research: occasional highs and lows are much less likely to influence children's development than sustained patterns of positive or negative interaction. The second is the need to consider contextual effects. As children grow up, tasks and games administered at previous time-points may be developmentally inappropriate, but unless the observational context is held constant, conclusions about developmental change are difficult to reach.

Another important challenge for researchers is the need to consider both mean age-related changes and individual differences in children's trajectories. Fortunately, recent technological advances have dramatically increased the accessibility of statistical modelling techniques (e.g., latent growth curve modelling – LGM). Building on these new opportunities, this chapter ends with three findings from recent analyses that applied LGM to data on mother–child talk collected at ages 2 and 6 in the Toddlers Up study. These findings make a significant contribution to the field in that they bring a developmental perspective to bear on the question of how mother–child talk contributes to children's growing understanding of mind.

Specifically, LGM analyses established a good model fit for a latent variable that tapped both the frequency and quality (i.e., rates of cognitive references within connected turns) for mother–child talk at ages 2 and 6 (Ensor, 2009). As expected, initial levels of mother–child talk were higher for children with more educated mothers and for verbally able children. On average, mother–child talk increased significantly across time-points; however, alongside this mean increase there were also significant individual differences both in initial levels of mother–child talk and in changes over time. While most mother–child dyads showed a moderate increase over time in the frequency and quality of their conversations, this increase was dramatic for some dyads, whereas for others, mother–child talk actually decreased over time. Moreover, these individual differences in trajectories predicted children's performances on the social-understanding tasks administered at age 6: a rise in maternal talk predicted good social understanding at age 6. These findings highlight the importance of adopting a long-lens view on mother–child interactions, to capture individual differences in *trajectories*. One possible interpretation is that positive trajectories in the quantity and quality of mother–child interactions foster children's positive attitudes towards new relationships at school (e.g., with friends, peers and teachers) that, in turn, foster opportunities for children to deepen their understanding of mind and emotion. We will return to this proposal in Chapter 8.

Chapter summary

As a counterpart to the previous chapter's focus on children's own language skills, this chapter examined links between social understanding and children's linguistic environments. At the start of this chapter, three distinct theoretical perspectives on what kinds of conversations are likely to foster children's social understanding were outlined. These highlighted: (i) co-constructed narratives (e.g., shared talk about past events, such as the hilarious soaking of boys in a school changing room); (ii) pragmatic and iconic features that give speech meaning (in developmentally sensitive ways – so that phrases such as "*I want* ..." can mean quite different things when coming from a younger or an older child); and (iii) conversations with individuals whom children trust as reliable and accurate informants. The first of these perspectives connects with a theme from Chapter 3, and highlights the extent to which parents (and other competent social partners, such as older siblings) can scaffold children's storytelling abilities (which in turn may influence their ability to understand complex social narratives). The second perspective connects with the developmental theme developed in Chapter 1, and highlights the importance of attending to age-related increases in the pragmatic sophistication of children's references to mental states. The third perspective (which highlights trust) connects with the next chapter on parenting, in which individual differences in attachment security appear significant for children's developing social understanding. Each of these perspectives points to the need to move away from simple questions of quantity or content of family talk to consider the *quality* of family talk (e.g., the extent to which conversations highlight differences in points of view, or connect with the child's point of view). The conversational examples given in this chapter highlight both the myriad of cognitive and affective processes that contribute to the success of a conversation, and the importance of adopting a long-term perspective in which conversational trajectories eclipse snapshot measures as predictors of children's developing social understanding.

5 Parenting and children's social understanding

The childhood shews the man, As morning shews the day.

As this quote from Milton's *Paradise Regained* (Milton, 1671) indicates, ideas of how children should be socialized to flourish as adults have a long history. However, scientific studies of parenting only began in the twentieth century and have, since then, shown three major shifts (Maccoby, 1992). The first is a move from grand theories (such as behaviourism or psychoanalytic theory) to the development of distinct theories for different aspects of development (e.g., language acquisition or attachment). The second is a shift from *tabula rasa* models in which the child is viewed as a blank slate, to be moulded by experience, to models that recognize that, from as early as infancy, children have a powerful influence on their caregivers. The third is an increase in model complexity to include mediating processes and moderating factors that help to explain individual differences in outcomes.

To avoid overlap with Chapter 4, this chapter does not include a section on parent–child conversations, even though talk is a key medium for parental influences. Instead, this chapter begins with a historical overview of ideas about optimal parenting, which highlights positive emotion and parental perspective-taking skills as key ingredients for promoting children's compliance with societal norms (by fostering their understanding of others). Next the chapter presents three aspects of research that directly consider relations between individual differences in parenting (or parental attributes) and individual differences in children's social understanding. These three strands include: attachment research; studies that consider the impact of depression in caregivers; and studies that adopt a cross-cultural approach to examining the influence of parenting.

From history to current practice

Historically, parenting studies have focused on aggression, perhaps as a legacy of early psychoanalytic work, which both portrayed aggression as a core intrapsychic force that parents must channel into acceptable behaviour, and underscored the importance of children's experiences of conflict as they come to fear the loss of parental nurturance.

More recent support for this view comes from a meta-analysis of attachment research ($n = 734$) that shows a significant predictive relationship between disorganized attachment in infancy and aggression in school-aged children (Van IJzendoorn, Schuengel, & Bakermans-Kranenburg, 1999). Despite this emphasis on aggression, many of the empirical findings are relevant to our current focus on children's developing understanding of minds. For example, micro-analytic studies of mother–child interactions conducted in the 1970s resulted in a shift in attention from individuals to dyads, with an emergent focus on shared understandings, joint attention, awareness of each others' intentions and shared emotional states (Trevarthen & Hubley, 1978). Building on this work, Bowlby's (1982) account of "goal-directed partnerships" between caregivers and toddlers in their fourth stage of attachment highlighted three components: social goals (e.g., affiliation/dominance), understanding others' intentions (i.e., mindreading) and communicating to clarify one's own intentions in order to repair misunderstandings. Similarly, as illustrated in Cairns' (1979) historical review of social learning theory, while Bandura's early work referred to imitation or mimicry, these terms were later replaced with the phrase "modelling" and, later, "psychological matching", each of which clearly depends on children's understanding of social behaviour (Bandura, Ross, & Ross, 1963). Moreover, research on the processes that influence children's internalization of societal norms consistently highlights the value of *other-oriented induction* (i.e., parental reminders to children of how their actions are likely to make others feel). For instance, while power-assertive methods often secure immediate compliance, other-oriented induction is much more effective in ensuring compliance when the parent is not present (e.g., Maccoby & Martin, 1983). Chapter 7 includes a discussion of how an awareness of others' thoughts and feelings may serve to minimize children's engagement in antisocial acts. One aim of this present chapter is to identify which elements of parenting are most likely to influence children's growing awareness of others' thoughts and feelings.

At a practical level, historical shifts in theoretical models of parental influence are important because they change our understanding of optimal parenting. Arguably, current views of good parenting can be boiled down to three features, which together illustrate the potential importance of parenting for children's social understanding. The first feature is a balance between freedom and control. As illustrated by an excerpt from the *Book of Proverbs* (22:6) "Train up a child in the way he should go; and when he is old, he will not depart from it", early advice to parents focused on control. The psychoanalytic movement saw a dramatic swing towards the advocacy of permissive parenting (e.g., Bettelheim, 1987). This was followed by Baumrind's seminal work of the ideal or "authoritative" parent as steering a middle ground between permissiveness and authoritarianism (e.g., Baumrind, 1971). This balanced approach seems commonsensical, but it is worth asking what underpins its success.

Research into what makes authoritative parenting work has led to a change in how we view the structure of parent–child interactions. Historically, these have been presented as highly vertical (i.e., involving an asymmetric balance of skills and power). However, although parents and children clearly contribute to their relationship with each other in very different ways, research findings suggest that, in Western society at least, a vertical structure is much more characteristic of suboptimal strategies of either authoritarian parenting (in which all power rests with the parent) or permissive parenting (in which power rests with the child) than of effective authoritative parenting, which typically involves a high level of mutuality (Lindsey, Mize, & Pettit, 1997). Another interesting finding is that authoritative parenting appears to work by enhancing children's openness to caregivers' efforts at socialization (e.g., by maximizing bi-directional communication; Darling & Steinberg, 1993). Thus, developing and sustaining positive communication about general issues (e.g., connected conversations about a topic of interest to the child, or shared memories of an enjoyable activity) bring not just immediate rewards (e.g., increasing a child's knowledge base) but also long-term benefits through increasing the child's openness to socialization. In other words, like gardeners, parents need to ensure that there is fertile ground. Interestingly, as we'll see later in this chapter, the connected caregiver–child conversations that promote children's openness to socialization also appear to contribute to children's understanding of mind (e.g., Ensor & Hughes, 2008). This raises the possibility that improvements in children's theory-of-mind skills may partially mediate the relationship between connected caregiver–child conversations and children's internalization of societal norms.

Each of these findings (i.e., the importance of horizontal and bi-directional interactions) leads to a second key element within successful parenting, which is reciprocity. That is, children with authoritative parents quickly understand that they are expected to behave in socially appropriate ways (insofar as they are able, of course!), but that equally they can expect considerable care and responsiveness from their parents. In other words, socialization requires not only connecting with children's emotional states and ways of thinking (such that one can adopt a child's momentary goals as one's own) but also an awareness of what is in the child's (and family's) long-term best interests. This requires effort and considerable meta-cognitive skill, as parents need to maintain multiple perspectives at the same time.

In addition, as Figures 5.1 and 5.2 illustrate, the need to juggle between competing demands increases dramatically when parents have more than one child. Specifically, these figures illustrate triadic interactions between a mother and her two sons, filmed in the lab when the study child was aged 3 and in the home at age 6. (As an aside, it is worth noting that the triadic interactions shown in Figure 5.1 are quite unusual, as all mothers with new babies were offered either a researcher as a "baby sitter" or a baby recliner, to enable them to engage in one-to-one play with their older child during the age-3 lab visits.) What is striking in Figure 5.1 is the skill with which this mother divides her attention between her two sons, such that even the challenge of a sudden topple from the baby does not rupture the positive story-based interaction. Interestingly, this mother showed the same impressive capacity for engaging both sons in a storybook task in a home visit conducted three years later (see Figure 5.2). (The reader might also be interested to note that the conversation that accompanies these home

Figure 5.1 Sophie reading and catching a baby.

Figure 5.2 Sophie reading and family talk about starting school.

visit pictures can be found in Chapter 1, p. 26, in an excerpt about shared memories of when the older son started school and did not want to be separated from his toy cuddly elephant, shown in the picture.) In sum, effective parenting involves both a propensity to attend to the child's own thoughts and feelings and a capacity to juggle between multiple goals. As a result, individual differences in both children's *and* parents' theory-of-mind skills are likely to predict socialization outcomes.

Last but not least is emotion. Emotions are the first language for parent–child communication (Fernald, 1993) and so provide a foundation for children's cognitive understanding of their relationships with caregivers. Moreover, as noted in an early and influential review (Dix, 1991), parenting involves more joy, affection, anger and worry than most other endeavours. Thus emotion is at the heart of both effective and ineffective parenting. We will return to the latter of these points later in this chapter. With regard to the former, positive emotions promote patient, sensitive and supportive parenting (and favourable child outcomes); moreover, instilling a positive mood is a powerful means of diffusing conflict and ensuring compliance (Lay, Waters, & Park, 1989). It is therefore no surprise that, as noted by Patterson (cited in Maccoby, 1992), exceptionally well-functioning families display high levels of humour. As humour often involves an array of mindreading skills (e.g., knowing how to surprise someone), this finding suggests yet another route through which good theory-of-mind skills (in both parents and children) are likely to promote effective socialization.

Attachment and social understanding

As noted above, emotions are the bedrock of communication with infants; thus variation in emotional quality of parent–infant interactions is likely to have a profound influence on children's social understanding. Support for this view comes from several different studies that report significant cross-sectional and longitudinal associations between attachment security and children's understanding of false-belief and/or emotion. Note, however, that, as summarized in Table 5.1, at least three studies report negative findings and a further three studies offer only qualified support for the posited link between attachment and false-belief comprehension. In contrast, although fewer studies have assessed attachment in relation to children's understanding of emotions, their results are more consistently positive. This contrast is interesting, and may help shed light on how this association between attachment and social understanding should be explained.

One obvious confounding factor is verbal ability, thus all the results presented in Table 5.1 are from analyses in which co-varying effects of verbal ability were controlled. Another trivial account is that, as noted by Fonagy and Target (1997), attachment security may simply be a good marker for generally positive and relaxed parental attitudes that fosters children's ability to engage with adult researchers and so perform well on experimental tasks. Alternatively, the "secure base" provided by the attachment figure may enable children to engage in a variety of social interactions that are likely to promote social understanding (e.g., shared pretend play, conversations about thoughts and feelings, interactions within peer groups). A third and stronger hypothesis is that psychological understanding emerges directly from within infants' and young children's interactions with caregivers. That is, "the social processes which accelerate the mentalizing quality of self-organization are the very same as those which ensure security of attachment" (Fonagy & Target, 1997, p. 687, cited in Carpendale & Lewis, 2006). For example, if maternal sensitivity involves a proclivity to think about (and talk to) the infant in psychological terms, this characteristic (dubbed "mind-mindedness") may both promote secure attachments and scaffold children's awareness of psychological states (Meins et al., 2002). If so, the empirical findings summarized in Table 5.1 suggest that this scaffolding may be more effective for children's understanding of emotions than of beliefs. This makes sense, given Dunn's seminal observational findings that highlighted the salience of emotions (and conflict) for children's discourse about causal events and different points of view (J. Dunn et al., 1991a, 1991b). In contrast, as discussed in Chapter 4, there is

Table 5.1 Summary of key findings on attachment and social understanding

Study	Age (years)	Social understanding measures	Link with false belief?	Link with emotion understanding?
Fonagy, Redfern, & Charman, 1977	3 to 6	Belief-based emotion	Yes (but note task also taps into emotion understanding)	Yes
Symons & Clark, 2000	2, 5*	False-belief location-change task using object and "mother"	Yes (for mother version only)	Not applicable
Meins, Fernyhough, Russell, & Clarke-Carter, 1998	1, 4 & 5*	Pretend play task, false belief and informational access	Yes	Not applicable
Steele, Steele, Croft, & Fonagy, 1999	1, 6*	Mixed emotions	Not applicable	Yes
Steele et al., 2002	1, 1.5, 11	Emotional dilemmas	Not applicable	Yes
McElwain & Volling, 2004	1 & 4*	False-belief task	Yes (if parental sensitivity high)	Not applicable
Repacholi & Trapolini, 2004	4 to 5	False belief, causes of emotion	Yes (especially in mother version)	Yes
Humfress et al., 2002	12	Strange stories	Yes	
Meins et al., 2002	6, 12, 45 & 48 months*	False-belief task	No (but positive results for maternal mind-mindedness)	Not applicable
Ontai & Thompson, 2002	3, 5*	False-belief task	No (but positive results for maternal elaboration)	Not applicable
Greig & Howe, 2001	3.5	False-belief and emotion-understanding tasks	No	Yes

Note: *Longitudinal study.

growing evidence that shared picture-book reading is a fertile context for conversations about mistaken beliefs. Thus parental style (e.g., mind-mindedness) may be especially important for children's understanding of emotional mental states, while parental practices (e.g., frequency of shared reading) may be particularly important for children's understanding of epistemic mental states.

Although this speculative hypothesis is likely to be difficult to test (in real life, parental style and parental practices are typically closely entwined), the idea that children's understanding of emotions and beliefs may have different correlates makes sense from a theoretical perspective, as there are many distinctions between these two types of mental states. In particular, emotions are feelings made up of physiological and psychological components and are viewed by appraisal theorists (e.g., Arnold & Gasson, 1954) as closely tied to the intentional states that accompany success or failure in achieving an aim or desire. Thus, emotion provides an evaluation of fulfilment/frustration of desires rather than of truth/falsity of beliefs. This is important as, from a philosophical point of view, beliefs and desires differ from each other in their "direction of fit" and conditions of satisfaction (Searle, 1983). Beliefs have a true/false satisfaction condition and a mind-to-world direction of fit; they accommodate themselves to the world. In contrast, desires have a fulfilled/frustrated satisfaction condition and a world-to-mind direction of fit; to be fulfilled the world must fit the desire.

Note also that the proposal that attachment is more salient for emotion understanding than false-belief understanding should be distinguished from a view of attachment as selectively influencing children's emotional (rather than cognitive) development. Indeed, this view is challenged both by Bowlby's own theoretical work (e.g., Bowlby, 1969) and by several empirical findings linking attachment security to cognitive milestones such as object permanence (Murray, 1992) and even reading ability (Bus & Van IJzendoorn, 1988). Most recently, Corriveau et al. (2009) have shown that secure attachment is associated with an enhanced ability to distinguish between adults as reliable or unreliable sources of knowledge. Specifically, securely attached children preferred to act on information provided by a caregiver than by a stranger when no external cues were available, but reversed this preference when there was reason to believe that the stranger was better informed than the caregiver; in contrast, children with avoidant attachment consistently preferred to act on information from the stranger, whereas children with resistant attachment preferred to act on information from the caregiver, even when it was clear that the stranger was better informed.

At this point it should be noted that emotion matters in two quite different ways: as a challenge, and as a resource. On the one hand, coping with feelings of distress or anger requires children both to identify and understand these emotions, and to draw on cognitive strategies for resolution and repair. On the other hand, as attachment theorists have argued, emotional connections enable children to draw meaning from their interactions with caregivers, such that sensitivity to the psychological states of their attachment figures plays a key role in promoting children's understanding of their own and others' psychological states (Steele, Steele, & Johansson, 2002). In turn, these emotional connections are, at least in part, made possible by caregivers' abilities to reflect on their own attachment relationships. Strikingly, Steele et al. (2002) reported a significant association between how pregnant women responded in adult attachment interviews about their own childhood and their children's responses to emotional dilemmas 11 years later. Also of note was the finding that children's responses to these dilemmas were associated with maternal concurrent beliefs about nurturance, but were unrelated to children's verbal IQ or security of infant attachment (to either mothers or fathers) or fathers' responses to the adult attachment interview. These results challenge "critical period" models of early interactions and instead support a model in which primary caregivers have an ongoing influence that involves processes beyond attachment security (e.g., family talk about feelings in the post-infancy years).

Interestingly, the only study to include adolescents reported associations between mentalizing and both verbal ability and attachment, but not parenting (Humfress, O'Connor, Slaughter, Target, & Fonagy, 2002). They offer two alternative accounts for this null finding. Either the parenting measure adopted in this study (a questionnaire for adolescents) was insufficiently sensitive, or the lack of relationship is genuine. If so, the authors suggest that, among older children at least, peer relationships are most closely associated with mentalizing skills. This proposal is discussed in more detail in Chapter 8.

Finally, it is worth noting that recent years have seen an exciting integration of attachment research with studies of genetic influence. For example, Caspers and colleagues (Caspers et al., 2009) have shown that individuals who carry the (less efficient) short allele of the serotonin transporter promoter gene (5-*HTTLPR*) are at elevated risk for unresolved attachment. Serotonin is a major neurotransmitter involved in emotional regulation in response to stressful life events. In a very highly cited paper, Caspi and colleagues (Caspi et al., 2003) reported that individuals with the short allele of 5-*HTTLPR* show more severe depression in response to life stress. In other words, genetic factors may be pivotal to responses that theorists have previously viewed as environmentally driven. Equally, however, Kochanska, Philibert, and Barry (2009) have shown that, among children who carried a short allele of 5-*HTTLPR*, those who were insecurely attached developed poor regulatory capacities, whereas those who were securely attached performed as well as those who were homozygotic for the long allele. That is, a secure attachment relationship can serve as a protective factor in the presence of a risk conferred by a genotype. This evidence for an interaction between attachment relationships and genetic factors opens up an exciting new panoply of research questions about the processes that underpin predictive effects of individual differences in children's attachment relationships.

Caregiver depression, family relationships and social understanding

All caregivers experience (and occasionally express) negative emotions; this is particularly true for caregivers with young children, for whom challenging behaviours (e.g., non-compliance or tantrums) are so common as to be developmentally normative (hence terms such as the "terrible twos"). Indeed, the incidence of depression is elevated among mothers of young children: Mclennan, Kotelchuck, and Cho (2001) found that, of a national sample of 7537 mothers in the USA, 24% reported clinically significant levels of depressive symptoms when their toddlers were 17 months old, with this proportion dropping to 17% when their children were 35 months old. (In comparison with these national figures, maternal depression in the Toddlers Up study appeared remarkably stable, with around a quarter of the mothers reporting clinically significant levels of depression when their children were aged 2, 3, 4 and 6.) Given this elevated incidence, it is important to note that research on "distressed families" (characterized by chronic and intensely negative parental emotion) has shown that negative emotion adversely affects parenting in several ways, including a bias towards negative appraisals and disruption of parental attention, monitoring and problem solving (e.g., Dix, 1991). However, as Dix and Meunier (2009) concluded from their recent review of 152 studies, the strength and nature of links between maternal depression and poor parental competence vary widely, reflecting individual differences in contextual factors (e.g., social disadvantage, social support, marital conflict and father involvement) and in the severity/duration of depressive symptoms.

Similarly, findings from recent longitudinal studies indicate that variation in parenting competence can strengthen or attenuate the relationship between maternal depression and child outcomes. For example, the predictive (negative) relation between early maternal depression and children's social acceptance at age 5 appears to be increased when children also experienced high levels of maternal negativity (Maughan, Cicchetti, Toth, & Rogosch, 2007). Conversely, findings from a study that followed children from toddlerhood to the early teen years indicate that both current and long-term consequences of maternal depression are diminished when depressed mothers are affectionate and responsive to their toddlers (Leckman-Westin, Cohen, & Stueve, 2009). Furthermore, results from a recent randomized controlled trial indicate that treatment that is effective at reducing post-natal depression is not sufficient to improve the developing mother–child relationship (Forman et al., 2007). This suggests that interventions should adopt a dual focus on caregiver depression and the caregiver–infant relationship.

Other factors, such as gender and family circumstances, also moderate the impact of caregiver depression on children. For example, in one of the first studies to examine the association between caregiver depression and children's problem behaviours using a multi-informant prospective longitudinal design, Sinclair and Murray (1998) noted that associations between post-natal/recent maternal depression and child problem behaviours were particularly strong for boys and for children from low-income families. A similar gender contrast has also been reported in a more recent study in which 3-month-olds were filmed in the Still Face paradigm (in which mothers are instructed to play with their infants, and then assume a still face for a minute before attempting to reconnect with their infant). In this study by Weinberg, Olson, Beeghly, and Tronick (2006), difficult interactions during the reunion phase were particularly evident among male infants of depressed mothers.

In another recent study that also included fathers, Cummings, Keller, and Davies (2005) reported differential relationships between mothers and daughters and fathers and sons. In particular, maternal dysphoria (i.e., depression or discontent) was related to peer exclusion more strongly in girls than in boys, while paternal dysphoria was (negatively) related to prosocial behaviour more strongly in boys than for girls. This study also showed significant associations between parental dysphoria and diverse aspects of family functioning, including marital conflict/insecurity, reduced parental warmth and increased psychological control; interestingly, negative marital relations (rather than negative parenting) partially mediated the association between parental dysphoria and adverse child outcomes. This is important, as about 25 years of research has shown that the transition to parenthood predicts a marked deterioration in the quality of couples' relationships (see Bateman & Bharj, 2009, for a recent review).

Taken together, these findings indicate that interventions with depressed mothers should include strategies for supporting not only the mother–infant relationship (as suggested above) but also mothers' relationships with their partners. Moreover, focusing on the relationship between the parents is also likely to have a powerful positive effect on *fathers'* engagement with their children; findings from a recent American randomized control trial involving low-income families offer direct empirical support for this view (Cowan, Cowan, Pruett, Pruett, & Wong, 2009). This is important for both practical and theoretical reasons. At a practical level, promoting fathers' involvement with their children is a key priority for family policy makers: more than thirty years of research has shown that fathers' engagement is a powerful predictor of positive cognitive, social and emotional outcomes for children (see Cowan, Cowan, Cohen, Pruett, & Pruett, 2008). Theoretically, the strong link between parents' relationship quality and fathers' involvement supports a family systems model of father involvement, and challenges the common assumption that father absence simply reflects a societal decline in "family values".

Beyond its impact on family relationships, caregiver depression can also affect children in other ways. For example, recent findings from the Environmental Risk Study (a nationally representative British cohort study of 1116 twin pairs) indicate that, among low-income families, maternal depression (or other mental-health problems) increases children's risk of having a food intake that is insufficient, unsafe or low in nutritional value (Melchior et al., 2009). This interplay between the effects of caregiver depression and family poverty is important; after all, low-income caregivers are twice as likely as other caregivers to show high levels of depression (e.g., Jackson, Brooks-Gunn, Huang, & Glassman, 2000). That said, distinct risk factors (e.g., maternal depression, family poverty) show contrasting associations with distinct outcomes (e.g., cognitive development, behavioural adjustment). In particular, while caregiver depression is a key predictor of behavioural outcomes, poverty and low maternal education are key predictors of cognitive outcomes (see Kiernan & Mensah, 2009; Perry & Fantuzzo, 2010, for recent epidemiological findings). In other words, with regard to parental influences on children's social understanding, effects of maternal depression may be eclipsed by effects related to variation in socioeconomic status.

However, very few studies of maternal depression have actually examined links with children's social understanding directly; the few exceptional studies have focused heavily on children's understanding of emotion (rather than belief).

In one study that examined maternal depression in relation to both aspects of social understanding, Greig and Howe (2001) also included a story-completion task to assess children's attachment security. Their findings (from 45 40-month-old children) indicated that, compared with securely attached children, insecure children had lower verbal mental ages, poorer emotion understanding and mothers with higher scores for depression, but did not differ in their understanding of false belief. A regression analysis showed that verbal mental age and attachment security (but not maternal depression or socioeconomic status) predicted unique variance in children's emotion understanding. Effects of maternal depression on children's emotion understanding have, however, been reported in a longitudinal study conducted by Raikes and Thompson (2006), involving children from low-income families, followed from age 2 to age 3. From their findings, these authors concluded that maternal depression directly impairs emotion understanding in preschoolers, while secure attachment relationships support children's emotion understanding by promoting mother–child discussion of emotions.

The Toddlers Up study has provided an opportunity to build on the above studies (Hughes & Ensor, 2009). For example, the Toddlers Up sample compares favourably with each of the above studies in terms of both size (n = 235) and social diversity (the sample shows an even split between "white collar" and "blue collar" occupations for heads of households). Consistent with Raikes and Thompson's (2006) findings, emotion understanding (but not false-belief comprehension) at age 4 was significantly inversely related to maternal symptoms of depression. Although this association appeared stronger for boys ($r = -.24$) than girls ($r = -.03$), this gender contrast was not statistically significant. As an aside, it is worth noting that Hughes and Ensor (2009) demonstrated that (alongside child executive function) maternal depression and children's emotion understanding both independently predicted variation in problem-behaviour scores, even when effects of gender, verbal ability and maternal education were all controlled. In other words, maternal depression predicted *both* poor social understanding and problem behaviours. In addition, results from boot-strapping mediation analyses (based on cross-sectional data, and hence to be viewed with caution) again highlighted the importance of multi-pronged interventions. In particular, the results suggested that enhancing children's understanding of emotions and their self-regulatory skills may steer children towards more positive trajectories with respect to behavioural as well as cognitive milestones; we return to this possibility in the third part of this book.

Culture, parenting and children's social understanding

This chapter opened with a brief summary of three historical shifts within research on parenting; the third of these was a move to more nuanced and complex accounts, with increased attention to moderator and mediator variables. Culture is clearly an important moderator: studies of family processes need to be culturally sensitive. Moreover, cross-cultural studies provide a valuable means of testing the strength and generality of theories about both basic developmental processes and the origins of individual differences in social development (Bukowski & Sippola, 1998, p. 742). Given their potential importance, the scarcity of cross-cultural studies is striking and exposes several different issues. Psychology is, in relative terms, a "Western" discipline, such that research interests have, historically at least, been constrained by ethnocentric attitudes. Even when these are overcome, practical challenges (such as the need to match samples in terms of socioeconomic status, and for researchers to have first-hand knowledge of the local culture) make cross-cultural research very difficult. This situation is not helped by a lack of meta-theoretical frameworks. To address this problem, it makes sense to turn to anthropology, which has a well-established distinction between "emic" and "etic" approaches (these terms loosely translate as insider/outsider and subjective/objective, and are derived from the linguistic distinction between the terms "phonemic" and "phonetic").

Within the emic approach, social constructs are culture bound, such that comparisons are simply invalid. Within the etic approach, basic processes are universal, with cultural influences limited to how the details of these processes are manifest.

With regard to children's understanding of mind, early support for the etic view came from the finding that Baka pygmy children in Cameroon pass false-belief tasks at a similar age to children in the USA or the UK (Avis & Harris, 1991). More recently, researchers have reported synchrony in the onset of mental-state reasoning in five cultures: Canada, India, Peru, Samoa and Thailand (Callaghan et al., 2005). However, as noted by Lillard (1997), there may still be important cultural variation in the *nature* of children's understanding of mind, including, for example, differences in what children understand about the content of the mind, the characteristics of the mind and the importance of mind. Moreover, in direct contrast with the findings reported by Callaghan et al. (2005), a recent meta-analysis of theory of mind in Chinese children highlights cultural variation in the onset of mental-state reasoning (Liu et al., 2008). Specifically, alongside parallel developmental trajectories of false-belief understanding for children in China and North America, Liu et al. (2008) found delays of up to 2 years in the onset of mental-state reasoning in Chinese children, as compared with children from the USA or Canada. Adding to this "cultural variation" perspective, similar delays have been reported for Japanese children (e.g., Lewis et al., 2009; Naito & Koyama, 2006). As discussed later in this chapter, my own research group working in collaboration with researchers in Japan has confirmed this delay (Hughes, Devine, Koyasu, Mizokawa, & Ensor, 2010a).

Evidence is also slowly accruing for variations in false-belief performance within the Western world. For example, in another meta-analysis Wellman et al. (2001) found that children in the USA and the UK performed less well on false-belief tasks than children from Australia and Canada, but better than children from Austria (and Japan). Moreover, a recent direct comparison of children in Italy and the UK (matched for socioeconomic background, age, gender and verbal ability) showed similar performances in emotion understanding, but a significant lag in Italian children's understanding of first- and second-order false beliefs (Lecce & Hughes, 2010). At first glance, this group difference is rather surprising;

after all, the traditional Italian way of life includes children in frequent (and emotionally expressive) social interactions; Hsu and Lavelli (2005) have also reported that Italian mothers are more affectionate towards their children than mothers in the USA (and so, by inference, British mothers). In contrast, however, Tardif, Shatz, and Naigles (1997) have reported that, compared with their Italian counterparts, British caregivers talk more often with their toddlers and ask more genuine questions (e.g., "Are you hungry?") and fewer test questions (e.g., "What's that called?"). In addition, beyond contrasts in the relative frequency of parent–child talk (Tardif et al., 2008), British versus Italian families may also differ in the form and function of parent–child talk in English. For example, several studies have noted the frequency with which British parents read books to their children (e.g., Sénéchal, Lefevre, Thomas, & Daley, 1998) while others have shown that parent-reported frequencies of book reading with their children at home are associated with individual differences in preschoolers' false-belief understanding (e.g., Adrián et al., 2005). As Liu et al. (2008) note, findings such as these highlight the importance of both universal trajectories and specific experiential factors in the development of theory of mind and so underscore the importance of bridging the emic/etic divide.

Interestingly, within the field of social development more generally, several cross-cultural studies have succeeded in integrating emic and etic approaches within a "local-knowledge" model in which, when significant cultural variation in the salience of social constructs are taken into account, universal developmental processes can be identified (Bukowski & Sippola, 1998). For example, Keller and colleagues (Keller, Edelstein, Schmid, Fang, & Fang, 1998) reported that differences in how children from China and Iceland resolve moral dilemmas reflect cultural variations in social goals, but argued that similar processes underpinned these differences. In support of this view, across-country differences were most striking for school-aged children: a period in which children (in all cultures) are most likely to base moral judgements on social conventions.

This "local knowledge" model can be used to characterize sociocultural perspectives on theory of mind, as these assume that basic processes (perception, information processing, concept formation) are universal, but vary across culture in how they are organized, integrated and implemented. Although cross-cultural research on theory of mind remains very thin on the ground, this sociocultural perspective on the development of social understanding has a long history: the phrase "folk psychology" (often used as a layman's term for theory of mind) was coined by Wundt (1900/1921), who argued that higher order functions (e.g., remembering, reasoning, learning – *völkerpsychologie*) emerge from group experiences, such that their study via ethnographic analysis should accompany lab-based studies of physiological psychology (Gauvain, 1998). At this point, however, it is also worth noting that sociocultural perspectives on theory of mind appear to lead to quite distinct conclusions from more general "local-knowledge" models of children's cognitive development. Specifically, while children's understanding is generally held to develop from the concrete and specific to the abstract and general, research on children's understanding of mind suggests a progression from commonality to variability, such that cultural differences become more striking in later years of development (Gauvain, 1998; A. Lillard, 1997).

Perhaps, however, it is simply too early to attempt to construct a developmental model of cross-cultural differences, given that the few studies that exist typically involve small samples (rarely matched for socioeconomic status) and tasks that have yet to be tested for measurement invariance. Each of these points is important: socioeconomic contrasts appear to be at least as large as across-culture contrasts (e.g., Shatz et al., 2003); in addition, at the heart of cross-cultural research is a dilemma: how do we know whether similar responses have similar meanings across cultures? Fortunately, recent advances in statistical modelling (e.g., confirmatory factor analysis) have fuelled progress in assessing equivalence across groups. Hui and Triandis (1985), (cited in Krishnakumar, Buehler, and Barber, 2004), distinguished four types of equivalence: (i) conceptual (i.e., items have the same meaning and indicative behaviours across cultures); (ii) operational (i.e., items are operationalized using the same method and response scale across cultures); (iii) scalar (i.e., scores on items assessing a construct are similar in strength across cultures); and (iv) functional (i.e., scores for a construct have similar correlates across cultures).

Recently, my research group has addressed the issue of measurement invariance in a study comparing 5- to 6-year-old British and Japanese children's social understanding (i.e., performance on tests of first- and second-order false belief) and social competence (as rated by teachers; Hughes et al., 2010a). These analyses (based on data from 89 British children and 99 Japanese children) showed tenable measurement invariance for all latent factors (i.e., false-belief understanding and teacher-rated empathy/prosocial behaviour). Confirming findings from previous studies (e.g., Lewis et al., 2009; Naito & Koyama, 2006), comparison of group means showed a robust contrast in social understanding (equivalent to almost two thirds of a standard deviation). Note, however, that this contrast may indicate difference rather than delay in social understanding. In particular, as argued by Naito and Koyama (2006), Japanese children may simply be more likely to focus on social norms than internal states when explaining people's actions. Interestingly, although robust in size, the group difference in social understanding was not mirrored by group differences in social behaviour; in addition, latent factors for social understanding were unrelated (in either group) to latent factors for teacher-rated empathy or prosocial behaviour. Clearly, this area of research is still very much in its infancy. One of my research team, Nao Fujita, is currently embarking on a doctoral study that aims to improve our comprehension of this cross-cultural contrast in social understanding by including ratings (from parents/teachers and from direct observations) of talk and control strategies within adult–child interactions.

In addition, building on the décalage in Italian versus British children's understanding of false belief mentioned earlier (Lecce & Hughes, 2010), our research group has very recently conducted a second study that involved approximately 380 children (170 from Italy, 190 from the UK; screened for monolingualism and matched for age and gender) attending the final year of primary school (i.e., aged 10 to 11 years). This larger sample enabled us to employ latent variable analysis to test for measurement invariance in children's scores on the "Strange Stories" theory-of-mind task (Happé, 1994). Our results confirmed that Italian and British children's scores on this task show conceptual, operational and scalar equivalence, but indicated less functional equivalence, in that the correlates for these scores were not exactly the same. In particular, children's social worries about the transition to secondary school were associated with theory-of-mind performance in Italian children, but not in British children (Lecce & Hughes, 2009). These results provide an encouraging starting point for future research.

In particular, much more work is needed to understand whether the role of parenting in explaining cultural differences in children's understanding of mind declines in importance as children mature and develop wider social horizons. For example, whereas Lecce and Hughes (2010) related the lag in false-belief understanding shown by Italian 5-year-olds to cultural contrasts in parental goals and practices, this study of older children focused on links between theory of mind and children's social experiences with classmates. This shift echoes the suggestion, noted earlier, that links between theory of mind and children's relationships with other children begin to eclipse associations between theory of mind and parent–child relationships (Humfress et al., 2002).

Chapter summary

Building on the relationship perspective introduced at the end of the last chapter, this chapter has reviewed the literature on parental contributions to individual differences in social understanding. The first part of this chapter adopted a historical perspective on parenting research, leading to a summary of three cardinal features within current models of optimal parenting. The first of these is an authoritative parenting style, in which a balance between freedom and control is achieved through a focus on communication, as this enhances children's openness to socialization efforts. The second is reciprocity, which depends upon parents' ability to maintain multiple perspectives, in order to align children's and parents' goals as closely as possible. The third is emotion, or more specifically positive emotions, which promote patient, sensitive and supportive parenting, but in turn depend on being able to see the humour in any situation. As outlined here, each of these three features of good parenting clearly depends on both parents' and children's mindreading skills. Thus, adverse effects on parental mindreading skills (e.g., as a result of maternal depression) are likely to compromise children's social understanding *and* socialization outcomes (e.g., behavioural control), raising the interesting possibility that children's social understanding may actually mediate parental influences on children's socialization. In addition, successful socialization appears to depend on parents' abilities to juggle between multiple perspectives (e.g., between the conflicting agendas of different family members, or between competing short-term and long-term goals), suggesting that executive functions may also contribute to parental influences on children's social understanding. In future, these two fields might be integrated more closely, by examining parental influences on executive function and social understanding in tandem.

The second half of this chapter presented three strands of parenting research that directly focus on how parents can influence children's social understanding. The first of these is attachment research. Here, one simple yet plausible proposal is that exposure to positive and confident parenting fosters not only secure attachment but also the ability and motivation to engage in social interactions that enhance children's social understanding (or indeed the ability to express what they know in a testing situation). An alternative model, proposed by Meins, Fernyhough, Fradley, and Tuckey (2001), is that maternal mind-mindedness underpins both secure attachments and positive child outcomes (note that this echoes the point made in the preceding paragraph). The second strand of parenting research that has considered children's social understanding as an outcome concerns the adverse effects of depression in caregivers. This literature shows that, in general, caregiver depression is more strongly associated with adverse behavioural outcomes than with cognitive delay; this association shows a complex interplay with several distinct processes, including the quality of caregivers' relationships with both their children and their partners. In addition, although relatively few studies have directly included experimental tests of children's social understanding, the evidence to date suggests that caregiver depression is specifically associated with deficits in children's understanding of emotion (rather than belief); moreover, this association is stronger when children from low-income families are included.

The third strand of research on parenting and children's understanding of mind is much more recent, and adopts a cultural perspective; here the debate has been between emic and etic viewpoints, which highlight, respectively, the culturally bound versus universal nature of knowledge. One solution to this problem is to adopt an empirical approach, by using model-fitting methods to assess directly whether measures of social understanding show conceptual, operational, measurement and functional equivalence across different cultural groups. My research group has just begun to adopt this approach, with promising results for comparisons of British, Italian and Japanese school-aged children; more work is needed to address this question with regard to different age groups.

6 Social understanding: Siblings and friends

Sibling relationships are almost universal and among the most enduring of our close relationships. They also stand apart from other relationships in several ways, of which perhaps the most studied is in their potential for rivalry (e.g., Freud, 1918/1963). With regard to the development of mindreading skills, it is perhaps significant that rivalry is often closely linked with deception. For example, as the biblical story of Jacob and Esau tells us, the urge to displace a sibling with regard to a parent's affection is a powerful incentive for deceptive behaviour. At a more everyday level, having a sibling on whom one can pin the blame may well encourage young children to attempt to deceive their parents. Feelings of rivalry may also serve as a powerful catalyst for children to recognize or invent new forms of teasing and provocation. Many parents watching their offspring bicker and argue will have experienced moments of reluctant admiration as their young children devise impressively effective new taunts or forms of revenge. More formal evidence for sibling influences on children's social understanding comes from experimental studies demonstrating that children with siblings succeed on false-belief tasks at substantially younger ages than children without siblings (McAlister & Peterson, 2007; Perner et al., 1994; Ruffman, Perner, Naito, Parkin, & Clements, 1998).

Interestingly, however, the very first study to highlight the potential contribution of sibling relationships to individual differences in young children's social understanding emphasized the importance of cooperative interactions (rather than deceit or rivalry). Specifically, Dunn and colleagues (J. Dunn et al., 1991b) noted that children who enjoyed frequent cooperative interactions with an older sibling at 33 months outperformed their peers on tests of emotion and false-belief understanding administered at 40 months. This finding anticipates, by almost two decades, the results from studies of mother–child interactions (discussed in the last chapter), which highlight the importance of conversational partners being "in tune" with each other (e.g., Ensor & Hughes, 2008). From this perspective, the potential importance of child–child relationships is clear: compared with their interactions with parents, children are much more likely to find themselves on the same wavelength as other children, who are more likely than adults to find the same things exciting or dull, funny or annoying.

Here, as an aside, it is worth noting that with regard to the importance of being "in tune" with another, children's friendships may be an even more important influence on children's social understanding than sibling relationships, for the simple reason that friendships are voluntary and often based on shared interests. In addition, the growth of women returning to work within a few years (or less) of having children means that more and more children regularly play with children from outside the family, such that friendships often begin very early in life. Figure 6.1, for example, shows a triptych of pictures of my younger daughter, Malaika, playing with Charlotte who, thanks to ACE nursery school in Cambridge, has been her very best friend for almost three years now. If siblings provide important opportunities for mindreading, it seems likely that close friendships, especially those characterized by intimacy, cooperation and shared humour, matter just as much. Indeed, Judy Dunn has written a wonderfully accessible book on this topic (J. Dunn, 2004).

To date, however, researchers have typically examined friendships as an outcome rather than a predictor of social understanding (see Chapter 8). And perhaps, for younger children at least, sibling relationships are, on average, more intimate than friendships, both because children can express themselves "warts and all" without jeopardizing the sibling relationship, and because siblings often share all the trials and tribulations of family life and so come to understand each other more completely.

Siblings, friends, pretend play and mindreading skills

Another clear example of the division between children's and adults' worlds (which applies equally to interactions with siblings and friends) is the case of pretend play. While often glad to enter children's imaginary worlds, adults are also quick to tire when the same pretend scenario is enacted time after time, whereas children often relish opportunities for repeat performances. This opportunity to rehearse and practise pretend scenarios may well be an important arena for children's growing mentalizing skills. For example, in an early theoretical study, Leslie (1987) argued that the capacity for pretend play was itself an early manifestation of children's developing skills in mindreading. His argument, backed by findings that children who have imaginary friends typically perform well on theory-of-mind tasks (Taylor & Carlson, 1997), hinged on the "structural isomorphism" of pretend play and false-belief understanding. That is, both share a similar logic in which the pretend scenario/belief floats free of reality, such that to pretend or believe X does not entail that X is true or even that X exists.

However, subsequent observational studies showed that children's performances on theory-of-mind tasks were unrelated or only weakly related to children's ability to recognize pretend play (A. S. Lillard, 1993; C. Rosen, Schwebel, & Singer, 1997) or to the overall frequency of pretend play, but were significantly associated with the frequency with which children engaged in *joint* pretend play (Schwebel, Rosen, & Singer, 1999). These results suggest that it may not be pretend play *per se* that matters, but rather the ability to co-construct a fantasy narrative with another child. Illuminating the processes underlying this association is the finding that children refer to mental states (thoughts, feelings, beliefs,

Figure 6.1 Best friends – Malaika and Charlotte.

intentions) significantly more frequently within pretend play than within other forms of play (Hughes & Dunn, 1997). Similarly, Dr Alex Marks, one of the Toddlers Up research team, has found that at two time-points 36 months apart (i.e., when the target children were aged 3 and 6) both children and siblings referred to desires and cognitive states preferentially within *connected* turns (Marks, 2010).

In other words, joint pretend play may require children to refer explicitly to their own and others' mental states and hence promote children's ability to reflect on the causes and consequences of these mental states. Indeed, developmental changes in children's ability to engage in joint pretend play with other children may well explain why, between the ages of 33 and 47 months, children's talk about mental states shows a developmental shift in preferred conversational partner, such that talk with siblings (and friends) comes to eclipse talk with mothers (Brown, Donelan-McCall, & Dunn, 1996). This shared enjoyment of pretend play is a powerful motivator for children to align their viewpoints in order to initiate or maintain joint pretend play.

A good illustration of how children willingly adopt different roles or viewpoints in pretend play comes from the following excerpt from the Toddlers Up study, in which the 3-year-old target child (whom we'll call Gail) is playing with her 5-year-old sister (whom we'll call Anna). All of this conversation between 3-year-old Gail and her 5-year-old sister Anna was conducted in "pretend voices". Note that Gail opened the play by inviting her older sister to assume the role of the baby, and Anna agreed willingly, referring to Gail as "Mama" and crying "Wah wah wah". This short excerpt was very typical of the entire 15-minute play session, and conforms to a "sugar and spice" view of little girls enacting domestic themes with real harmony.

Gail/Anna:	Annie, do you want to be that baby giraffe?
Anna/Gail:	Yeah.
Anna/Gail:	Mama.
Gail/Anna:	It's time to go to bed.
Anna/Gail:	When do I, when do I grow up?
Gail/Anna:	When you're four.
Anna/Gail:	Hi mum.
Gail/Anna:	Let's have another friend come round?
Anna/Gail:	Yeah, which one?
Gail/Anna:	Polar bear?
Anna/Gail:	Yeah, polar bear. Hello. Hello giraffe, I want to come with you. There I'll put you on my back and I'll take you.
Gail/Anna:	I need another mum.
Anna/Gail:	Mama.
Gail/Anna:	Yeah.
Anna/Gail:	Can I go to giraffe's house? To play with giraffe.
Gail/Anna:	Yeah.
Anna/Gail:	Thanks mum.

Anna/Gail:	Can you come please?
Gail/Anna:	For a little while, then I'll go back.
Anna/Gail:	OK.
Gail/Anna:	Then I'll go back, 'cause my other little baby's crying.
Anna/Gail:	OK. Mama, mama, he came, look.
Gail/Anna:	I'm his mum as well.
Anna/Gail:	Mummy, come on. Come in. Baby, come on. Right.
Gail/Anna:	I get you. Darling, where are our babies?
Anna/Gail:	Wah, wah, wah.

In this exchange, both sisters assume a new role or perspective, with Gail acting as a mummy giraffe and her older sister taking on the role of baby giraffe. Chapters 3 and 4 outlined various different theoretical accounts of why language may matter for theory of mind; note that one of these accounts focused on language as a means of highlighting different points of view (Harris, de Rosnay, & Pons, 2005). In other words, language and pretend play may make similar contributions to children's growing understanding of other people's thoughts and feelings.

Of course, not all siblings show either such companionship and support for each other or such interest in domestic themes for role play; for example, many boys in the Toddlers Up study were fascinated by the toys in our bag that could be used as weapons (a toy chainsaw/hedge-trimmer set, and a Star Wars light sabre). Among sisters, too, themes of pretend play often extended beyond the domestic. This point is illustrated by another excerpt, selected from the Toddlers Up study pool of transcripts simply because it also involved two sisters aged 3 and 5 (although in this family there is also an older brother). The excerpt starts 10 minutes into the filmed play session, because for the first 10 minutes the older sister (here, called Sally) has been dressing up and pretending to be an opera singer, leaving the younger sister (here, called Libby – aka Boba) to amuse herself in solitary exploration of the other toys. At this point, Sally has discovered a pair of handcuffs, and invents a game of pretend in which she imprisons Libby behind a large pot plant.

Sally/Libby:	Boba, pretend you are a baddy and I'll catch you. Come on Boba. You are a baddy and you fight me and I catch you up.
Sally/Libby:	Boba, don't. Do this.
Sally/Libby:	Will you just put that on there? [*putting a handcuff on Libby's wrist*]
Sally/Libby:	Make a fist.
Sally/Libby:	OK you need to [*speech unintelligible*] and I'll take you into prison. Now stay there for the night. Get in Boba. Get into that little space.
Libby/Sally:	Getting in it.
Libby/Sally:	Why do I need this? Why do I need this to fight you?
Sally/Libby:	Now you be on my team or you die. [*thrusting light sabre*]
Libby/Sally:	No.
Sally/Libby:	You said you wanted to be on your team.
Libby/Sally:	Be on my team.

Sally/Libby:	No your team.
Libby/Sally:	My team.
Sally/Libby:	Your team. [*loudly*] Be on your team.
Libby/Sally:	Be on my team.
Sally/Libby:	That means you die. Say, "Be on your team".
Libby/Sally:	Be on my team.
Sally/Libby:	OK, then you die. Boba, say "Your team. Be on your team".
Libby/Sally:	Be on your team.
Sally/Libby:	Good. [*turns round and walks out of view*]

Note that Libby appeared to welcome her older sister's attention and joined in the pretend game willingly, even though it did involve being squashed in a corner of the room, menaced by a light sabre and coerced into repeating a declaration of submission. However, having achieved her objective of sending her little sister to "jail" behind the pot plant, Sally loses interest in the pretend game and the two sisters then spend much of the remainder of the session playing independently.

Overall, the tone and quality of these sisters' shared pretend play is in clear contrast with that shown by Gail and Anna, such that it is easy to see why, as noted earlier, individual differences in social understanding are associated with individual differences in the sophistication rather than the frequency of children's pretend play. Although not assessed directly within the Toddlers Up study, this proposal is supported by findings (from the first time-point, when the target children were aged 2) that individual differences in both the frequency and diversity of children's use of inner-state terms, which we can treat as a proxy index for social understanding (Hughes, Lecce, & Wilson, 2007), showed significant independent relations with the frequency of their reciprocal play with siblings, even when age, verbal ability and overall rates of talk were controlled (Hughes et al., 2006). Similarly, other studies involving preschoolers have reported associations between false-belief performance and socially competent forms of resolving conflict with siblings (e.g., Foote & Holmes-Lonergan, 2003; Randell & Peterson, 2009).

As an interim summary, this chapter has thus far addressed the question of how sibling relationships contribute to children's understanding of mistaken beliefs from three distinct perspectives. In the first two of these perspectives, siblings are viewed either as rivals or as allies. This juxtaposition is perhaps unsurprising; after all, the ability to understand mistaken beliefs is important for a variety of social situations, including sharing jokes, repairing misunderstandings, avoiding blame, teasing and taunting. In the third perspective, siblings (and friends) are viewed as important partners for games of pretend play, which foster children's ability to juggle different representations of reality, as well as the need to align their viewpoints in order to sustain the pretend narrative.

In addition, as illustrated by the excerpts provided above, individual differences in sibling relationships are striking and evident in multiple dimensions. These include: affection, reciprocity, support, rivalry and conflict (J. Dunn, 2000). Thus, the presence of a sibling may stimulate children's awareness of mental states for many different reasons, ranging from facilitating enjoyable and collaborative games of pretend play to providing a means of deflecting parental anger. In fact, individual children may be influenced by a sibling in each of these diverse ways, as many sibling relationships also show a distinctive "love–hate" quality. For example, video-based coding of the sibling play sessions conducted at the first time-point of the Toddlers Up study showed that almost two thirds of the sibling dyads displayed at least some conflict, but the quarter who showed high levels of angry conflict (defined as 4 + angry turns per hour) did not display less frequent or less complex positive social interactions than other sib dyads. This combination of conflict and cooperation within sibling interactions suggests that it may be unwise to place too much emphasis on any one particular aspect of sibling interactions.

Indirect effects of siblings on children's mindreading skills

The striking contrast between the quality of the interactions between the two pairs of sisters illustrated above prompts questions about the origins of individual differences in sibling interactions. Here, research findings are quite clear: sibling interaction quality typically mirrors the quality of other family interactions. Thus sibling conflict is associated with differential parenting (e.g., Boer & Dunn, 1990), marital discord (e.g., Stocker & Youngblade, 1999) and negative parent–child interactions (e.g., Volling & Belsky, 1992).

Do the transcripts from our two example families support this view of close ties between sibling interactions and more general family interactions? Consider first the case of Gail and her older sister Anna, who so willingly adopted the role of baby assigned to her by her little sister. Here, it may come as no surprise to the reader that the girls' father is a teacher and their mother is a playgroup leader. Below is an excerpt from the unstructured family mealtime interaction, filmed during the same home visit as the sibling play session.

	[Anna hugs mum, who kisses her head]
Mum/Anna:	Keep eating.
Gail/Mum:	Another piece.
Mum/Gail:	Another piece.
Anna/Mum:	Me – Gail – Me – Gail – Me – Gail. *[Mum has ended up feeding them both]*
Mum/Gail:	Open up then.
Anna/Mum:	It goes, Me – Gail – Me – Gail – Me – Gail. Yeah?
Mum/Anna:	I don't know why I'm doing this.
Anna/Mum:	Me – Gail – Me – Gail – Me – Gail.
Dad/Anna:	Oh, Anna, you don't need mummy to feed you. You're a big enough girl now.
Gail/Mum:	More food.
Mum/Anna:	Shall I feed daddy as well? I've got three babies. Who's going to feed me?
Anna/Mum:	Me.
Gail/Mum:	Me. I want to feed you.

Mum/Gail: No. I don't want. Mummy doesn't really want anything. No, take a little, take a little bite off.
                [Anna gets mum's attention to be fed and she continues to feeds them both]

During this meal, Anna capitalizes on the fact that her mother is spoon-feeding her younger sister to secure the same indulgent treatment for herself. The closeness and reciprocity between Gail and Anna that was evident in the previously described sibling session is indeed mirrored in the playful harmony of this meal-time interaction. How might all of this contribute to children's mindreading skills? Here, at least three distinct points can be made. First, the presence of a sibling means that children need to become quite adroit at getting parents to attend to their needs. And indeed, in the excerpt above, Anna displays real competence. She begins by giving her mother a hug and then she says "Me – Gail – Me – Gail – Me – Gail", highlighting the parity between her sister and herself, and suggesting a game that might enliven the mealtime.

Second, when there are many actors on the scene (as in this excerpt, in which both parents and both daughters are present) one effective means of sustaining harmonious interactions is to ensure that each actor pays attention to the others' thoughts, feelings and desires. When Gail says, "I want to feed you", her mother replies, "No. I don't want. Mummy doesn't really want anything", and so high-lights the contrast between her daughter's plan and her own feelings. Third, role-reversal games that are initially introduced into family life in the context of sibling play can be extended to other family members. In the excerpt above, for example, the mother uses wry humour to highlight the absurdity of spoon-feeding a five-year-old, saying, "Shall I feed Daddy as well? I've got three babies. Who's going to feed me?" Note also that through this playful suggestion the mother also skil-fully diffuses the father's (mild) disapproval. Thus, in this single utterance the mother achieves three distinct ends: making a joke about family role reversals; sending a gentle message to the older daughter that her request to be spoon-fed is not developmentally appropriate; and deflecting any potential criticism the father may have felt compelled to make. In short, family interactions such as those presented in the above excerpt provide Gail and Anna with clear opportunities to appreciate that speech acts are not always to be taken literally, and can reflect many different motives.

The transcript from the parallel mealtime observation at Libby and Sally's home is much less playful. In particular, at the start of the family observation, Libby was frustrated and unhappy. At the start of the excerpt below Libby is calmer, but still quite fragile and so is having a cuddle with her mother. They have a rather sad conversation about her difficulty in finding a friend to play with at school.

Mum/Libby: What did you do at school?
Libby/Mum: Nobody likes me. *[muffled into mum's shoulder]*
Mum/Libby: Nobody likes you.

Libby/Mum:	No. [*sad voice*]
Mum/Libby:	Did no one play with you?
Libby/Mum:	No. [*sad voice*]
Mum/Libby:	So, what did you do?
Libby/Mum:	[*Speech unintelligible; muffled into mum's shoulder*]
Mum/Libby:	Did you?
Libby/Mum:	[*Pause*] on my own. [*muffled into mum's shoulder*]
Mum/Libby:	And did you cry, or not cry?
Libby/Mum:	Not cry. [*sad muffled voice*]
Mum/Libby:	Did no one play with you?
Libby/Mum:	No. [*sniffs*]
Sally/Mum:	Don't believe her Mum, it's just because she's sad.
Mum/Sally:	I know, I think that's right. I think she is just sad.
Mum/Libby:	Did anyone else play with you apart from [*speech unintelligible*]? Did you play with Darcy? [*looks down at Libby, still cuddling her*]
Libby/Mum:	Erm, yes. [*slightly more cheerful*]

In this excerpt, the mother shows both warmth and support through her desire to listen to her children's problems and to be sensitive to their feelings of sadness. This excerpt also demonstrates how the presence of a sibling can provide opportunities for eavesdropping on parent–child conversations. In this role of bystander Sally shows both agency and concern, intervening to reassure her mother that Libby was not excluded by her classmates at school. In other words, the presence of a distressed sibling causes Sally to reflect both on how her sister's current unhappiness is likely to colour her views of school-life, and on how her mother may be affected emotionally by thoughts of a daughter's social isolation. She says, "Don't believe her mum, it's just because she's sad". Her insights are acknowledged and confirmed by her mother, who says, "I know, I think that's right. I think she is just sad". In this case, then, Libby in her distress indirectly contributes to Sally's growing understanding of the intimate ties that exist between people's thoughts and feelings.

A second point worth making is the sharp contrast between Sally's rather unsupportive attitude towards Libby during the sibling play session, and the insight and sensitivity towards her mother she displays during this family conversation. For many parents, this variability in children's behaviour will be recognizable as part of the rich tapestry of family life. From a research perspective, however, the contrast in Sally's behaviour highlights two points. First, interactional quality is an emergent property of the relationship. This may explain why studies that have attempted to draw links between children's real-life interactions and their performance on sociocognitive tasks have typically yielded only modest results. Second, the quality of any specific relationship is dependent on other relationships within the family. For example, the fact that Sally lost her place as the baby in the family when Libby was born may help explain why, in this home visit at least, she showed sympathetic concern for her mother coupled with a somewhat controlling attitude towards her little sister. Note, however, that sibling relationships are strikingly developmentally dynamic in nature; thus, just as some parent–child attachment relationships take longer to develop than others, so too siblings such as Sally and Libby who do not appear close at one time-point may well develop a very supportive relationship in years to come. We return to this point later in this chapter.

As these excerpts illustrate, the presence of a sibling changes children's relationships with caregivers. In particular, as documented in longitudinal observational studies, the arrival of a new baby in the family is often a time of emotional upheaval that can jeopardize the security of children's attachment to caregivers (Teti, Sakin, Kucera, & Corns, 1996) and adversely affect caregivers' sensitivity towards the older children, such that the birth of a sibling is associated with a marked increase in conflict between firstborns and their caregivers (J. Dunn & Kendrick, 1980). From the child's perspective, the arrival of a sibling can evoke very mixed feelings, ranging from affection and concern, to frustration and jealousy. Caregivers can also find themselves experiencing divided emotions: joy, pride and delight coupled with anxiety, fatigue and concern. Add to this potent mix of emotions a new divide between caregivers' and children's goals and the potential for conflict is obvious. However, conflict is not necessarily negative. Indeed, from a theoretical perspective, conflict is often seen as a fertile context for learning about different points of view (Duveen & Psaltis, 2008). In other words, conflict can provide caregivers with the impetus to adopt parental strategies that enable their older children to achieve new levels of maturity. As discussed in Chapter 5, one successful parental strategy is the use of inductive reasoning (i.e., encouraging children to reflect on how their actions will make others think or feel). In other words, the presence of a sibling is likely to have an important but indirect stimulating effect on children's sociocognitive development. In addition, in families with caregivers who adopt a pre-emptive approach, by discussing the feelings and needs of the baby, friendly child–child interactions are more common (J. Dunn & Kendrick, 1980; Howe & Ross, 1990). Thus, how mothers communicate with their young children at the time of the sibling's birth (and hence children's attributions about the young baby) may contribute to the quality of the relationship that develops between the siblings over time.

The excerpts from mealtime interactions in Gail and Anna's family and in Libby and Sally's family also illustrate a second key contrast in family life associated with the presence of a sibling. This concerns the extent to which children have opportunities for observing caregivers interacting with other family members. From as early as the second year of life, younger siblings show intense interest in what happens between their older siblings and their mothers (J. Dunn, 1988; J. Dunn & Munn, 1985). They respond to disputes between mother and sibling, and their reactions show sensitivity both to the topic of the disputes and to others' expressions of emotion. As younger siblings are less able than their older siblings to monopolize conversations with a caregiver, this opportunity to eavesdrop on conversations that fall within their "zone of proximal development" (Vygotsky, 1962) may contribute to younger siblings' accelerated development in social understanding (Ruffman et al., 1998). Support for this proposal comes from the finding that 4-year-olds with an older sibling produced and heard more talk about cognitive states (e.g., thoughts, beliefs) than did children without an older sibling (Jenkins et al., 2003). Much of this talk about cognitive states occurred in conversations between parents and children, rather than directly between the children themselves, highlighting the variety of ways in which the presence of a sibling can enrich a child's social life.

Developmental change in sibling relationships and links with social understanding

Returning to the same two pairs of sisters three years later (i.e., when the girls are 6 and 8 years old), we can see evidence for both change and continuity across development. For example, Gail and her older sister Anna, who spent most of the previous play session engaged in a pretend game of animal mummies and babies, now show very little use of pretend voices. Nevertheless, their interactions remain characteristically harmonious, as they share the task of setting out a Playmobil zoo.

Anna/Gail:	Look, Gail.
Gail/Anna:	Where does it go, Anna, do you think? [*Anna takes flag from Gail*]
Anna/Gail:	I think it might go in here. [*trying to put flag on roof*]
Anna/Gail:	No, won't go in there will it?
Gail/Anna:	Where's the tiger, where's the tiger, I put it there.
Anna/Gail:	Put it there. I don't know where that goes. [*pause; still holding flag*]
Gail/Anna:	What's that? What's that? [*taking something out of bag*]
Gail/Anna:	Ouch. [*watching toy gorilla fall into cage*]
Anna/Gail:	Yeah, it would hurt wouldn't it?
Gail/Anna:	That might be there.
Anna/Gail:	I don't think it's open yet is it?
Gail/Anna:	No.
Anna/Gail:	No, it's not open yet is it?
Gail/Anna:	Put the people where, but Anna some people go there. [*points*]
Anna/Gail:	Oh, yeah they do, can this one go? [*picking up a figure*]
Gail/Anna:	No this one does. [*picking up another figure*]
Anna/Gail:	Oh, yeah it's got a lion on it, that must be someone else.
Gail/Anna:	That might be for the gorillas. [*pointing to another enclosure*]
Anna/Gail:	I think that goes there, um. [*places shelf in cage; Gail takes it and does similarly*]
Gail/Anna:	Ah, the gorilla might go under it, their little home![*excited*]
Anna/Gail:	Well, we'll have to see about that.
Gail/Anna:	Tiger might. [*putting shelf in cage, and tiger under shelf*]
Anna/Gail:	Oh, yeah! Actually that's a good idea isn't it? Shall we put that in there for now?
Gail/Anna:	Baby could go in there.

Note also that Anna: (i) frequently refers to cognitive states (e.g., know, think); (ii) phrases her thoughts as questions that invite Gail, her younger sister, to share in the decision making; (iii) elaborates on Gail's "Ouch" as the toy gorilla falls by saying, "Yeah, it would hurt wouldn't it?"; and (iv) endorses Gail's idea about where to place the tigers. In short, Anna appears highly proficient at scaffolding Gail's involvement in the game.

The age-6 play session between Libby and her older sister Sally also shows similarities and contrasts with their interactions at age 3 (in which Sally switched pretend roles from opera singer to jailer). In particular, these sisters now show much more talk, and appear to be on much more of an equal footing; at the same time, their interactions remain combative. The excerpt given below is very typical of the full play session, such that in the transcript the conversation about farts covers about 4 to 5 pages.

Libby/Sally:	Tart, fart.
Sally/Libby:	Lady says, I'm going to fart.
Libby/Sally:	And do farts! [*happy, laughing*]
Sally/Libby:	Oh, stop saying the word f, a, r, t.
Libby/Sally:	We need to sweep the rest animals out.
Sally/Libby:	Hey! Oh you wrecked everything. [*annoyed*]
Libby/Sally:	Yes you fart. [*laughing*]
Sally/Libby:	Huh?
Libby/Sally:	OK, dart.
Sally/Libby:	You don't need to say fart.
Libby/Sally:	Do a fart and pick up your dart. I hope you fart and pick up a dart.
Sally/Libby:	I hope you fart and pick up a dart, I hope you fart and pick up a dart. [*imitating in silly voice, both giggling*] [*Sally starts singing; Libby picks up a toy and pretends it's growling at Sally*]
Libby/Sally:	It's stretching, it's stretching, it's stretching. [*holding up tiger for Sally to see*]
Sally/Libby:	Yeah, it's stretching, really really interesting. You know in fact I am amazed, I wonder if I'll ever ever see this again. No, I don't think I will because it's just so, so rare, so amazing. Wow, I think I'm going to faint. [*sarcastic tone; Libby goes back to playing by herself*]

Compared with their interactions when she was aged 3, Libby now shows no sign of submitting to her older sister. Instead, she initiates this play on words with a scatological theme that has them giggling for minutes on end; at the same time, her words and actions frequently provoke her older sister, Sally, who responds with annoyance and then with heavy sarcasm (and, later in the session, with physical force). Thus, the contrast between the two pairs of sisters, so evident when the younger sister was aged 3, remains clear three years later. At the same time, like the other older sister Anna, Sally also shows a greatly increased reference to cognitive states: for example, in the final turn alone Sally uses the terms *interesting, amazed, wonder* and *think*. In addition, all of this is delivered in a voice that is dripping with sarcasm, making it clear that she is actually very unimpressed by Libby's trick of stretching the toy tiger. Thus, although it is clearly not her intention to scaffold Libby's involvement in the game, it seems likely that she is inadvertently boosting Libby's mindreading skills, both by her rich use of language and by her sarcastic tone, which highlights the contrast between literal and intended meanings of speech.

Of course, the above examples from Gail and Anna and from Sally and Libby and their families are simply meant to illustrate the diversity of processes that might underpin associations between the presence of a sibling and children's performances on tests of social understanding. We have yet to test these ideas out formally for the full sample, but one of my research group, Dr Alex Marks, has recently conducted latent variable growth curve modelling of developmental changes in both talk and prosocial behaviour across the full sample of siblings between the age-3 and age-6 time-points (Marks, 2010). Of the many interesting findings to emerge from this analysis, three are particularly relevant to this chapter. First, echoing the findings from mother–child interactions (Ensor & Hughes, 2008), sibling talk about mental states (specifically, desires and cognitions) occurred primarily within connected utterances. This kind of connected discourse about thoughts and desires was: (i) more frequent at the later time-point; (ii) related to the older sibling's age and verbal ability; and (iii) unrelated to child or sibling gender. At the age-3 time-point, the study children showed lower rates of mental-state talk than their older siblings, but this difference between siblings was not evident three years later. In other words, the study children were, in general, successful in their efforts to converse on an equal footing with their older siblings. Second, the overall frequencies of prosocial behaviour did not change across time-points; older siblings' prosocial behaviour did, however, show a decline, presumably because at the later time-point there was less need for them to adopt a caretaking role. Consistent with this care-taking model, at the age-3 time-point, sibling age was positively related to frequencies of prosocial behaviour towards the younger child. Third, there was a significant association between age-related changes in mental-state talk and in prosocial behaviour (with 25–33% of the variance being shared). Given that these measures were based on the same play sessions, this overlap is quite modest, suggesting that mental-state talk and prosocial behaviour are relatively distinct dimensions of individual differences in sibling relationships. In the near future we plan to examine whether and how these distinct trajectories are related to individual differences in social understanding. For now, however, we turn to the question of whether sibling influences on social understanding are universal, or vary according to child, family or cultural characteristics.

Are sibling influences on social understanding universal?

In this chapter we have seen that siblings may contribute to young children's social understanding in many ways: directly or indirectly; and deliberately or inadvertently. The multiplicity of processes through which children can learn from having a sibling around may help to explain the positive findings that have emerged from studies that simply index how many siblings a child has. However, given the striking individual differences that exist both in sibling relationships themselves and in the ways in which the presence of a sibling affects children's relationships with other family members, it seems likely that the magnitude of sibling influences on children's growing understanding of mind is also likely to vary for different children. Indeed, several moderating influences on the impact of sibling relationships on children's growing social understanding have been noted, including child, family and cultural characteristics.

Child characteristics

Three distinct child characteristics may moderate the magnitude of sibling influences on social understanding: age (and age gap); verbal ability; and gender. With regard to child age, Ruffman et al. (1998) analysed pooled data from 444 English and Japanese children and reported that the sibling advantage was restricted to the presence of older siblings and not apparent for children younger than 3 years 2 months (although it is possible that the false-belief tasks used in these studies were not sensitive to individual differences in younger children's fledgling theory-of-mind skills). However, age differences also appear important in two further studies. Cassidy, Fineberg, Brown, and Perkins (2005) found that, in a sample of twins, the presence of additional younger or older siblings predicted higher scores for false-belief understanding. Similarly, Wang and Su (2009) found that Chinese 4-year-olds were more likely to succeed at false-belief tasks if they were being taught in mixed-age classrooms. One further interesting point concerns the contrasts in the ways in which the presence of an older or a younger sibling benefits children's social understanding. For example, young children are so determined to be with and like their older siblings that they tackle not only physical but also cognitive milestones at the earliest opportunity. Conversely, the presence of a younger child provides older siblings with opportunities for adopting the role of caregiver or teacher, which in itself is often an instructive experience (A. Lillard, 2005). At the same time, indirect effects (e.g., impact on family interactions, opportunities for eavesdropping on adult–child conversations) may be quite similar and in each case both minimum and maximum age gaps appear likely (Peterson, 2000).

  With regard to verbal ability, Jenkins and Astington (1996) found that the positive effect of sibs on false-belief performance was restricted to verbally less able children. As they suggest, this may be because verbally more competent children can engage in activities with adults (such as book reading) that provide alternative channels to acquiring an understanding of mistaken beliefs, such that interactions with siblings have less influence. Turning to gender, at least three previous studies have reported gender contrasts in associations between theory of mind and social interactions, including preschoolers' interactions with their caregivers (Hughes, Deater-Deckard, & Cutting, 1999) and friends (Hughes & Dunn, 1998), and older school-aged children's social competencies with peers (Bosacki & Astington, 1999). Findings from the first time-point of the Toddlers Up study (when the study children were aged 2) suggest that gender contrasts are also apparent in the relation between social understanding and quality of sibling interactions. Specifically, among boys, individual differences in theory-of-mind scores were related to overall variation in the frequency and diversity of inner-state talk, whereas for girls these associations were specific to inner-state talk within pretend play. That is, context effects were significantly more important for girls than for boys.

Family characteristics

Associations between false-belief comprehension and numbers of siblings have typically been much weaker (and even non-significant) among studies involving socially diverse samples (e.g., Cole & Mitchell, 1998; Cutting & Dunn, 1999). One plausible interpretation, offered by Cutting and Dunn (1999), is that quality of sibling interactions matters at least as much as quantity. Detailed observations of children in the Toddlers Up study offer direct support for this hypothesis. Specifically, at the first (age-2) wave of the study, individual differences in theory-of-mind task performance were unrelated to the number of siblings each child had, but showed a significant association with mothers' ratings of sibling relationship quality, even controlling for child age, verbal ability and executive function, family social disadvantage and quality of parent–child relations.

This strong and specific association is open to at least two different explanations (Hughes & Ensor, 2005). On the one hand, 2-year-olds who get along well with their siblings are likely to spend more time with them, and therefore have more opportunities to develop their theory-of-mind skills. Equally, 2-year-olds with more advanced theory-of-mind skills are likely to make better playmates for their older sibs (most of the siblings in this study were older sibs), and so enjoy more frequent and more positive interactions with their siblings. Another important finding to emerge from this study was that, unlike the quality of children's relationships with caregivers, which showed overlapping associations with theory-of-mind skills and verbal ability, the association between theory-of-mind skills and the quality of children's sibling relationships was essentially independent from associations between theory-of-mind skills and verbal ability. This contrast lends weight to Jenkins and Astington's (1996) finding that beneficial effects of siblings were clearest for verbally less able children, who presumably are less able to participate in the kinds of parent–child interactions (such as book reading) that support children's growing social understanding.

Cultural characteristics

To date, all the evidence for a beneficial effect of siblings on children's social understanding comes from studies of children growing up in the UK, the USA, Canada and Australia. Indeed, in an early study of children growing up in Crete and Greece (two Mediterranean countries characterized by contrasts in kinship contact) children's performance on false-belief tasks was related to the overall number of family members (both child and adult) with whom children had daily contact, rather than to the number of siblings *per se* (Lewis, Freeman, Kyriakidou, Maridaki-Kassotaki, & Berridge, 1996). More recently, the same research group have reported that among Chinese children frequent contact with other children in the family (typically cousins) was associated with *worse* performance on false-belief tasks (Lewis et al., 2009). Note also that in their meta-analytic review, Liu, Wellman, Tardif, and Sabbagh (2008) found that children from mainland China outperformed children from Hong Kong (who are much more likely to have at least one sibling).

These cultural contrasts can be explained in at least two different ways. First, there may be important cultural differences in the nature of the sibling relationship. For example, children growing up in non-Western countries often play a key role in caregiving, such that sibling relationships are likely to be characterized by responsibility or dependence, and so mirror parent–child relationships more closely. Note that, in the West, many of the social interactions that theorists (e.g., J. Dunn, 1999; Harris & Leevers, 2000; Wellman & Lagattuta, 2000) consider as crucial to children's developing understandings of mind (e.g., conflict, pretence, emotional exchanges) occur most frequently between siblings, rather than in parent–child conversations. Thus, to the extent that sibling relationships in non-Western countries resemble rather than contrast with parent–child relationships, weaker sibling influences on social understanding are predicted.

Second, there may be significant cultural differences in the ways in which the presence of a sibling affects family life more generally. Note here that Lewis et al.'s (2009) study focused, by necessity, on Chinese children's contact with cousins rather than siblings: while cousins may well be valued playmates, they are less likely than siblings to be fierce rivals; equally, the presence of a cousin is less likely to introduce conflict into children's relationships with their parents. Thus, cross-cultural comparisons may provide an interesting perspective from which to tease apart which aspects of family life associated with the presence of a sibling really matter most for children's developing social understanding. For example, in a study in which groups of 5- to 11-year-olds were given distractor toys while their siblings were shown how to construct a novel toy, Guatamalan children from traditional Mayan families with little maternal involvement in Western schooling were found to be much more likely to pay attention and learn than were Westernized Mayan children, who in turn showed greater observational learning than their European-American counterparts (Correa-Chávez & Rogoff, 2009). In other words, there appear to be differences across cultures in the relative salience of opportunities for observational learning, with children from traditional indigenous communities being particularly astute observers of family life. However, much more research is needed to establish whether and why sibling influences on children's developing social understanding vary in importance across distinct cultures.

Chapter summary

Following the work on family talk and parenting reviewed in the two previous chapters, this current chapter examined how children's social understanding may be accelerated by interactions with other children, and especially siblings. The chapter began with the classical Freudian perspective on siblings as rivals whose relationship is significant only as a derivative of more overpowering early experiences with parents. This viewpoint emphasized negative aspects of the sibling relationship that result from their battle for parental resources and love. In fact, the balance of empirical evidence leans towards siblings as a positive resource, that is, as allies who are on the same "wavelength" for humour and interests and so particularly adept at sustaining games of shared pretend play that may be particularly helpful for fostering children's growing awareness of the representational nature of mental states. Some of the mechanisms that might underpin this influence implicate adults (e.g., opportunities to eavesdrop on parent–child conversations; rivalry for parental attention/affection as an incentive for children to engage in deception or impression management), but many involve distinctly child-like interactions (teasing, pretend play, conflict); thus this chapter connects with earlier language chapters through its emphasis on the pragmatic functions of discourse. In particular, conversational excerpts between two pairs of sisters in the Toddlers Up study (and their families) were used to: (i) illustrate the magnitude and complexity of individual differences in sibling relationships; (ii) describe how interactions with siblings may benefit children's social understanding through intended and incidental effects; (iii) discuss how sibling influences may operate through direct and indirect processes; and (iv) illustrate the variety of developmental changes that can be seen in sibling relationships as children grow from preschool to early school age. Finally (linking in with a theme that emerged from the previous chapter on parenting), this chapter addressed the question of whether sibling influences are universal or moderated by child, family and cultural characteristics.

Part III

Social understanding and social outcomes

7   Social understanding and antisocial behaviour

Social understanding and antisocial behaviour are each multi-faceted constructs; unravelling the connections between them could therefore fill an entire book. The aim of this chapter, therefore, is not an exhaustive review, but rather an "*assiette* of ideas" that I hope will whet the reader's appetite for more comprehensive findings from individual lines of research. Specifically, the chapter is organized by five points that are drawn from research in this field. The first of these is that theory-of-mind skills are *socially neutral*: although acquiring an understanding of mind is generally recognized as fundamental to more sophisticated social interactions, it is important to hold in mind that social consequences can be negative as well as positive. The second theme is that *deviance as well as delay* in children's social understanding may affect social outcomes. That is, it may be more useful to ask whether processing of social information is biased (rather than simply delayed) in children with conduct disorder. The third theme concerns the importance of adopting a *developmental perspective* in order to assess whether early and late milestones in social understanding show distinct links with problem behaviours in childhood. The fourth theme is that *links between social understanding and bullying are heterogeneous*, reflecting the different roles assumed by children who engage in (or are exposed to) bullying. The fifth theme is that one promising avenue for expanding the scope of this research field and making contact with research on adults is to bring *deontics* into the picture. That is, children's understanding of social norms is likely to be at least as important an influence on their behaviour as their understanding of mental states; moreover, these two domains of knowledge appear to be closely entwined. Findings from the Toddlers Up study are outlined within several of these specific themes and brought together in the chapter summary.

Theory-of-mind skills are socially neutral

Amid the many different points of debate generated by three decades of research into children's understanding of mind is a general consensus that the ability to attribute mental states to the self and others is an important but socially neutral tool. Why might this be? One reason is that there is an important distinction between the ability to recognize or infer mental states and what one does with this information. Indeed, terms such as "callous" (commonly used to describe psycho-paths) imply that an individual *knowingly* causes harm to others. In other words, the understanding of others' thoughts and feelings does not necessarily ensure concern for others, still less prosocial action. Interestingly, in a recent review, Frick and White (2008) concluded that callous unemotional traits are character-istic of children who show particularly severe, aggressive and persistent patterns of antisocial behaviour. Such children also often appear to be fearless thrill-seekers; perhaps as a result they are typically unresponsive to many disciplinary strategies but do respond to rewards. In consequence, interventions aimed at reducing problem behaviours in these children need to adopt a tailored approach, as disciplinary techniques such as time-out or withdrawal of privileges that work well with other children are likely to be ineffectual with these children. More generally, these findings highlight interactions between temperament, cognition and behaviour. That is, children who are temperamentally emotionally unreactive will experience reduced arousal in response to either punishment (Kochanska, 1993) or others' distress (R. Blair & Mitchell, 2009) and so are more likely than their peers to show impaired conscience development (i.e., guilt, empathy) and to display callous behaviour. Another example of the contrast between knowing and caring is the "happy victimizer" phenomenon (in which typically developing chil-dren judge actions as wrongdoings but nevertheless ascribe positive feelings to the perpetrators (Keller, Lourenço, Malti, & Saalbach, 2003).

Cognitive accounts of moral development (e.g., Kohlberg, 1984; Piaget, 1932) have therefore been criticized for paying too little attention to children's moral reasoning in real-life situations. To address this gap, Toddlers Up data from 222 4-year-olds who completed a moral-sensitivity task (Kochanska, Padavich, & Koenig, 1996) and were filmed at nursery playing with a friend have been analysed by Helen Sharpe as part of her final-year dissertation (Sharpe, 2008). This moral-sensitivity task indexed: (i) whether children judged diverse transgressions against distinct social partners to be OK or Not OK; and (ii) the social sophistication of children's justifications for these judgements (using a simple 3-point scale that ranged from "don't know", through justifications oriented towards punishments or other external factors to interpersonal justifications, such as concern for others' feel-ings). The young friends' dyadic play sessions were coded (from video) for aggres-sive, unfriendly and prosocial behaviours and cluster analysis was used to distinguish six groups: socially "busy" (i.e., high levels of all three sets of behaviours; $n = 46$); both prosocial and unfriendly, but not aggressive ($n = 43$); aggressive and unfriendly, and not prosocial ($n = 57$); aggressive, but neither unfriendly nor prosocial ($n = 22$); socially quiet (i.e., low levels of all three sets of behaviours; $n = 25$); and prosocial with no aggression or unfriendliness ($n = 29$). Across-group comparisons of average scores on the moral-sensitivity task showed no differences for moral judgements, but more advanced moral justifications in both the prosocial group *and* the socially busy group as compared with children in the two antisocial groups; interestingly, children who were socially quiet (i.e., neither antisocial nor prosocial) performed as poorly as the two antisocial groups. Of course, the conclusions that can be drawn from these results are constrained by the fact that the observational coding was based on children's interactions with a friend, making it difficult to generalize to children's interactions with peers in general. However, these findings do suggest that prosocial and antisocial behaviours should be seen as independent dimensions, with only the former showing a clear relationship with moral reasoning.

A second reason for considering theory-of-mind skills as socially neutral concerns the heterogeneity of both positive and negative social acts. In particular, many different kinds of social acts, both positive and negative, require very little in the way of understanding others' minds; conversely, mentalizing skills can be applied to both good and bad ends. Empirical evidence supporting the four categories of behaviour shown in Table 7.1 comes from a birth-cohort study of more than 5000 pairs of twins in which exploratory factor analyses were used to investigate parents' ratings of child behaviour at ages 2, 3 and 4 (Ronald et al., 2005). These analyses yielded the predicted four scales (dubbed "nice", "nasty", "nice theory of mind" and "nasty theory of mind"). Modelling the results from identical *versus* fraternal twins demonstrated that, although both "nice" and "nasty" theory of mind showed moderate heritability, individual differences in these two scales also showed distinct aetiological influences (Ronald et al., 2005). As these authors noted, this finding is open to at least two different interpretations. The first hinges on an interaction between temperament and theory-of-mind skills, akin to the interaction between emotional reactivity and conscience development described above for callous and unemotional children. That is, temperamentally sociable children apply their understanding of mind to foster close harmonious relationships; in contrast, children with negative temperamental dispositions are likely to apply their understanding of mind to manipulate situations in order to achieve social dominance or material gains.

An interaction between temperament and theory-of-mind skills may also shed light on the contrasts Ronald et al. (2005) observed between ratings for girls *versus* boys. Specifically, at ages 2, 3 and 4, female twins were reported as displaying more "Nice" and "Nice theory of mind" behaviours, while male twins were reported as displaying more "Nasty" behaviours (supporting the nursery rhyme view of girls being made of "sugar and spice" and boys of "slugs and snails"). This contrast is unlikely simply to reflect parents' gender stereotypes because direct observational ratings from another study (involving 3½-year-old twins who completed a battery of theory-of-mind tasks and were filmed in triadic play with a caregiver) yielded a very similar contrast. Specifically, Hughes and

Table 7.1 Subsets of both positive and negative behaviours involve mentalizing

Mentalizing needed?	No	Yes
Positive act	Displays of affection, compliance with social norms	Cooperation, empathy, teaching
Negative act	Overt displays of aggression	Lying, stealing, cheating

colleagues (Hughes et al., 1999) found that good theory-of-mind performance in girls was associated with warm and positive mother–child interactions, whereas good theory-of-mind performance in boys was associated with maternal reports of elevated rates of conflict and physical discipline. That is, girls appeared to apply their theory-of-mind skills to affiliative goals, whereas boys appeared to apply their theory-of-mind skills to find new ways of making mischief. Similar findings of contrasting correlates of theory-of-mind skills for boys and girls have also been reported in a study in which ratings were gathered from teachers (Walker, 2005).

A second interpretation of the distinct aetiological influences on "nice theory of mind" versus "nasty theory of mind" offered by Ronald et al. (2005) is that these measures tap into genetically and cognitively distinct aspects of social understanding. This hypothesis parallels Zelazo and colleagues' (Zelazo & Müller, 2002) recent distinction between *hot* and *cool* executive function (i.e., adaptive decision making and inhibition of maladaptive prepotent responses vs. emotionally more neutral abilities, such as working memory span and attentional set-shifting). Perhaps the strongest argument for this distinction of *hot vs. cool* executive function is that at a neuroanatomical level there is a very clear division of labour. Specifically, evidence from neurophysiological studies of primates and both neuroimaging and lesion studies of humans (e.g., Hornak et al., 2004) suggest that the orbitofrontal cortex is involved in representing reward values (i.e., in learning associations between visual stimuli and rewarding or punishing outcomes), whereas lesions to the dorsolateral prefrontal cortex result in impaired control of attentional processes. By analogy, "nice theory of mind" and "nasty theory of mind" may also show distinct neural substrates. At this stage, however, much more work is needed to establish whether "nice theory of mind" and "nasty theory of mind" are genuinely distinct aspects of social understanding. As noted by Ronald et al. (2005), one avenue for future research is investigating theory-of-mind skills in the context of real-life cooperative *versus* competitive situations, in order to test whether these show differential associations with distinct measures of social understanding.

Deviance matters as much as delay

The traditional image of the bully as a "social oaf" reflects a popular belief that children who engage in antisocial behaviour do so because they lack the social skills to win friends and influence people by other means. But at least two sets of findings challenge this lay view. First, children characterized by profound delays in social understanding (e.g., children with autism) do not show elevated rates of antisocial behaviour; thus delayed social understanding is not sufficient to explain increased rates of antisocial behaviour. Second, as discussed in the next section of this chapter, seminal work by Sutton and colleagues (e.g., Sutton, Smith, & Swettenham, 1999a) demonstrates that some bullies (specifically, "ringleader" bullies) show an intact or even superior understanding of others; thus delayed social understanding is not even necessary to explain increased rates of antisocial behaviour.

Perhaps the simplest reason why there is no straightforward necessary and sufficient relationship between social understanding and antisocial behaviour is that the term "antisocial behaviour" covers a multitude of sins, and different forms of antisocial behaviour may well have very different origins. Indeed, even one particular form of antisocial behaviour (e.g., physical aggression) may arise for different reasons in different individuals or contexts. A good illustration of this point is the contrast between proactive and reactive aggression. Proactive aggression is often also described as instrumental or "cold-blooded" aggression. Here it is worth noting that the children described earlier as callous and unemotional have also been viewed as having psychopathic traits; this narrowly defined group of children account for less than 1% of the school population and have been found to show poor impulse control, but are *not* impaired in their performance on theory-of-mind tasks (J. Blair et al., 1996). Conversely, children with autism (who *are* impaired in performance on theory-of-mind tasks) do not show any clear deficits in moral reasoning (Grant, Boucher, Riggs, & Grayson, 2005; Leslie, Mallon, & DiCorcia, 2006) that might relate to both physically and relationally aggressive behaviour (Murray-Close, Crick, & Galotti, 2006). In short, there does not appear to be any strong evidence linking impairments in theory of mind with instrumental or proactive aggression. As we shall see later, however, it is possible that deviant *use* of intact theory-of-mind skills is associated with proactive aggression (cf. Machiavellian behaviour).

Reactive aggression is quite different from proactive aggression, and can be characterized as "hot-headed" aggression. In other words, children characterized by elevated rates of reactive aggression are easily provoked, responding angrily to actions that inadvertently bring negative outcomes. An impressive body of research has demonstrated an association between reactive aggression and "hostile attribution biases" (i.e., the attribution of hostile intentions to neutral or ambiguous acts; see Hubbard, McAuliffe, Morrow, & Romano, 2010, for a recent review). Simply put, children are much more likely to retaliate or respond aggressively to negative events (e.g., being pushed, having a toy damaged) that they think were caused deliberately by others. This suggests that children's understanding of *intentions*, rather than beliefs, may be pivotal for understanding individual differences in antisocial behaviour. (The third section of this chapter provides a brief account of developmental milestones in children's understanding of intentions.)

Dodge and Coie (1987) were the first to argue that hostile attribution biases play a role in reactive aggression. More recently, a meta-analytic review of 41 studies with a total of more than 6000 participants showed that the association between hostile attribution of intent and aggressive behaviour was especially robust in middle childhood, particularly for peer-rejected and/or severely aggressive children (Orobio De Castro, Veerman, Koops, Bosch, & Monshouwer, 2002). In his early work, Dodge proposed that experiences of abuse or neglect at home shape children's expectations of others and lead to hostile interpretations of neutral or ambiguous actions (Dodge, Pettit, Bates, & Valente, 1995). More recently, Dodge has radically revised his model to propose that, in the world of nature, "red in tooth and claw" (Tennyson, 1850) hostile attribution biases are evolutionarily adaptive and therefore likely to be innate (Dodge, 2006). By this account, *positive* experiences of relationships with caregivers and close others are needed to enable children to shed their suspicions and adopt a more benign view of others' intentions.

Interestingly, few researchers have tried to integrate findings from the extensive literature on hostile attribution biases with the even greater body of work on children's theory-of-mind skills. In one exception, a group of "hard-to-manage" preschoolers, known to display elevated rates of peer-directed antisocial behaviour (Hughes et al., 2000b), completed parallel tasks that tapped understanding of emotions related to false-belief in the context of either a nasty or a nice surprise (Hughes et al., 1998). Unlike their typically developing peers (who performed consistently across the two vignettes), the hard-to-manage group performed better on the vignettes that involved a trick rather than a treat, supporting the proposal that such children are predisposed to attend to hostile intentions. Findings from neuroimaging studies provide further indirect evidence for a bridge between theory of mind and hostile attribution biases. Specifically, performance on theory-of-mind tasks has been shown to activate the orbitofrontal prefrontal cortex (e.g., Stone, Baron-Cohen, & Knight, 1998), and lesions to this brain region are associated with poorly modulated responses to displays of anger (e.g., Berlin, Rolls, & Iversen, 2005) and with reactive aggression in both children (e.g., Pennington & Bennetto, 1993) and adults (R. Blair & Cipolotti, 2000).

Further work is needed, however, to elucidate the relationship between theory of mind and attribution biases. One important distinction to be made is that theory of mind is an index of children's *competence*, whereas hostile attribution biases index children's *performance*. As a result, success on theory-of-mind tasks is relatively unaffected by changes in task format (e.g., props, pictures, questions about self vs. other) whereas hostile attribution biases are strongly influenced by contextual factors. In particular, hostile attribution biases appear maximized under conditions of threat to self (Dodge & Somberg, 1987), a finding that may well explain the effectiveness of teaching children to count to ten before responding to provocation.

Developmental perspective

By now it should be apparent that the term "antisocial behaviour" encompasses a wide variety of acts. In addition, it is clear that age of onset will differ for individual antisocial acts (e.g., physical aggression will precede substance abuse). However, one key finding to emerge from the literature is that antisocial behaviour shows *heterotypic continuity*. That is, although its form varies with age, antisocial behaviour shows strong continuity over time, in that it is the same individuals who are likely to display elevated rates of antisocial behaviour at any age. In particular, children characterized by problems of antisocial behaviour very early in life are especially likely to show severe and life-course persistent problems (Moffitt, 1993). By inference, then, although later milestones in social understanding may shed light on age-related shifts in form of antisocial behaviour, it is the early milestones that are especially salient for identifying which children are at risk of entering antisocial trajectories.

As outlined in Chapter 1, two important and early emerging aspects of children's social understanding are the understanding of emotion and the understanding of intention. Many interesting questions surround the connections between these two domains of social understanding. For example, recent adult clinical studies have demonstrated that anxiety plays a key role in the formation and maintenance of paranoid delusions, in which patients believe that others are trying to persecute them (Freeman, 2007); likewise, depression has also been shown to be associated with a hostile attribution bias (e.g., Hoglund & Leadbeater, 2007). Conversely, how we interpret others' intentions can have a powerful impact on our emotions. This emotional impact can be positive: young children frequently display pleasure when offered a low-value "gift" (e.g., a leaf) by a baby sibling, showing that even from an early age children recognize that it is the thought that counts. Equally, the emotional impact can be negative, as illustrated by the case of reactive aggression, defined as an angry response to perceived intention to harm. However, children's understandings of emotion and intention have typically been examined separately in relation to antisocial behaviour and so, for simplicity's sake, are considered separately below.

Understanding intentions

As discussed above, at least one type of aggression (reactive aggression) appears to result from children misreading others' intentions, for example by jumping to the conclusion that an action was deliberately intended to cause harm. This finding begs the question: what can we expect children of different ages to understand about intentions? This question has received remarkably little attention from researchers. In addition, Astington's (2001) careful review of the field highlighted a paradox: intentions are, in general, more obvious and more easily understood than beliefs, but because intention is a complex construct, a complete and precise attribution of intentions is harder than the attribution of belief.

In particular, children's understanding of intentions may differ from adults in three respects: motivational, causal and epistemic (Moses, 2001b). That is, describing an agent's action as intentional implies that: (i) the agent *wanted* to do the action (or at least wanted to achieve the outcome associated with the action); (ii) the agent *caused* the action (i.e., the outcome was not achieved by accident); and (iii) the agent *believed* that s/he could and would perform the action. As one might expect, these three components are mastered at different developmental stages. The motivational component of understanding intentions appears very early in children's development: from 2 years of age, children understand how actions relate to desires (see Wellman & Phillips, 2001, for a review). In contrast, the causal aspect of intention emerges only much later: children do not appear to understand that desired aims can be achieved *unintentionally* before the age of 4 or 5 years; likewise it is not until this age that children have a mature understanding of belief and so can master the epistemic aspect of intention (Astington, 2001). As a result, children aged 3 or younger treat intentions as more or less synonymous with desires; only later do they recognize that desires can be fulfilled by unintentional acts, and that we can desire (but not intend) outcomes that we believe to be impossible.

A key question for this chapter is: are all three components relevant for understanding individual differences in antisocial behaviour? Probably not: the third component (belief in possibility of action) is salient for individual differences in self-efficacy and well-being (Bandura, 2001) and might conceivably be relevant in determining whether acts of extreme violence were premeditated, but is unlikely to be relevant for everyday antisocial acts. The first two (motivational and causal) aspects of intention are typically conflated within studies of how hostile attribution biases lead to reactive aggression. Yet the age difference in children's mastery of motivational versus causal aspects of intention raises the possibility of refining our understanding of the nature of hostile attribution biases. That is, if it is the causal aspect that really matters, then links between individual differences in the accuracy with which children monitor others' intentions should only become associated with individual differences in reactive aggression around the age of 4 to 5 years.

In fact, findings from the Toddlers Up study indicate that from as early as 2 years of age deficits in children's mindreading skills predict antisocial behaviour, even when effects of individual differences in verbal ability, family background and exposure to harsh parenting (a key predictor of conduct problems) are all taken into account; interestingly, there was also an interaction effect, such that the association between harsh parenting at age 2 and antisocial behaviour at age 4 was attenuated for children who, at age 2, already showed good mindreading skills (Hughes & Ensor, 2006, 2007b). However, by age 4, links between mindreading skills and problem behaviours in the Toddlers Up study appeared non-specific, whereas other cognitive domains (such as executive functions) showed independent relations with problem behaviours (Hughes & Ensor, 2008). Although the theory-of-mind measures used in the study did not directly examine distinct aspects of intention understanding, this juxtaposition of findings, viewed alongside the *décalage* in children's mastery of motivational versus causal aspect of intention outlined above, indicates that interventions aimed at reducing hostile attribution biases should focus on the motivational rather than causal aspect of intention.

Understanding emotion

From a very early age infants show preferential attention to faces (e.g., Gliga, Elsabbagh, Andravizou, & Johnson, 2009) and respond differentially to distinct facial expressions (e.g., Repacholi, 2009; Repacholi & Meltzoff, 2007). Cross-cultural studies show that from around 18 months children can identify simple displays of emotions, even when the desires are different from their own (Repacholi & Gopnik, 1997). From 2 years, children begin to interpret emotional displays in others (Zahn-Waxler & Radke-Yarrow, 1990). By 3 years, children can recognize that a situation can evoke different emotions in different people, depending upon personality and situational factors (e.g., Denham & Couchoud, 1990). These early perspective-taking skills predict individual differences in prosocial behaviour (Denham, 1986; Iannotti, 1985) and are typically impaired in "hard-to-manage" preschoolers (Hughes et al., 1998).

By school age, children also appreciate that individuals can experience simultaneous conflicting emotions and may mask their true emotions (Gnepp & Hess, 1986; Harris, 1994; Pons, Harris, & de Rosnay, 2004). For instance, when shown pictures that include conflicting cues (e.g., a child smiling while waiting to be injected with a needle), preschoolers typically rely on facial cues whereas older children focus on the situation and can explain the discrepancy by referring to display rules (e.g., "She's smiling to hide her fear from the doctor"). Children with impaired understanding of mixed emotions and emotion display rules appear more likely to display anger and aggression with their peers at school (e.g., Denham et al., 2002; Dodge et al., 2003). Each of these studies controlled for effects of delayed verbal ability and so, taken together, demonstrate that children with problem behaviours display a specific impairment in both early and late milestones of development in emotion understanding. The Toddlers Up study findings add to this literature by elucidating the role that emotion plays as a mediator of family influences on children's behaviour. For example, analyses of data from 102 children at each of the first three time-points of the Toddlers Up study showed that emotion understanding at age 3 was not only a strong predictor of prosocial behaviour at age 4, but also mediated associations between verbal ability/mother–child mutuality at age 2 and prosocial behaviour at age 4 (Ensor, Spencer, & Hughes, in press). In addition, analyses of age-4 data from the target children and their friends ($n = 235$) showed that poor emotion understanding partially mediated the relationship between low maternal education and problem behaviours (as indexed by multi-measure ratings from mothers, teachers and researchers; Hughes & Ensor, 2009).

Taken together, the above findings demonstrate that individual differences in emotion understanding play a key role in the influence of the quality of early mother–child interactions on children's propensities to be prosocial or antisocial. This conclusion has both theoretical and practical implications. At a theoretical level, emotion understanding appears to play a pivotal role in mediating the influence of adverse family factors (low maternal education, low levels of mother–child mutuality) on young children's problem behaviours. At a practical level, the above results suggest that interventions aimed at reducing problem behaviours in young children should include ways of improving children's emotion understanding. As discussed in Chapter 4, these might include interventions to raise both the quantity and the quality of mother–child talk, with a particular focus on promoting connected parent–child conversations about thoughts and feelings. Interestingly, caregivers' hostile attribution biases have also been reported to predict children's aggressive behaviour (e.g., MacKinnon-Lewis, Starnes, Volling, & Johnson, 1997). However, a recent study has shown no relationship between hostile attribution biases in caregivers and children (Halligan, Cooper, Healy, & Murray, 2007), supporting indirect models in which caregivers' hostile attribution biases predict children's aggressive behaviour by serving as a useful index of more proximal factors such as frequency of harsh parenting (Nix et al., 1999).

Understanding knowledge or belief

Children's knowledge about epistemic mental states continues to increase after the age of four. These late developments include understanding: (i) mistaken beliefs about beliefs (Perner & Wimmer, 1985); (ii) the role of pre-existing biases and expectations in influencing both personal tastes (Carpendale & Chandler, 1996) and how people interpret ambiguous events (Pillow & Henrichon, 1996); and (iii) subtle forms of social deception such as bluffs and white lies (Happé, 1994). On the one hand, these late-developing theory-of-mind skills should lead to increased social harmony, as conflicts arising from misunderstanding become less frequent, and as children develop a new repertoire of skills for avoiding distressing or embarrassing situations. On the other hand, these later developments also enable children to conceal or clarify their motives as needed, in order to manipulate social situations. Thus, while physical aggression peaks in early childhood (Tremblay et al., 1999), relational aggression is most evident in middle childhood (Crick & Grotpeter, 1996; but see also Crick, Casas, & Mosher, 1997), and continues into adulthood (Werner & Crick, 1999). Thus the social implications of age-related developments in children's understanding in mind are very unlikely to be uniformly positive.

Links between social understanding and bullying are heterogeneous

As noted above, school bullies were traditionally viewed as socially inept individuals who resort to force because they lack more subtle means of persuasion. In a refinement of this idea, Crick and Dodge (1996) proposed that aggressive children show distorted or deviant social information processing. In particular, evidence from vignette-based studies suggests that aggressive children attend to fewer social cues and are more inclined both to attribute hostile intentions to others and to choose an aggressive solution to a social problem (e.g., Crick & Dodge, 1994). Aggressive children also commonly experience peer rejection and so have limited opportunities for positive social interactions, such that their deviant social information processing often worsens across the school years (Dodge et al., 2003).

However, it is important to recognize that bullying comes in many shapes and sizes. As a result, a taxonomic approach has proved useful. Specifically, following a seminal study by Salmivalli and colleagues (Salmivalli, Lagerspetz, Björkqvist, Österman, & Kaukiainen, 1996), bullying is now seen as a group process, such that children can assume a variety of roles, from outsider to bully (or their assistants or reinforcers) to victims and their defenders. In addition, as argued by Sutton et al. (1999a), at least some forms of bullying are likely to require intact or even superior mindreading skills. In particular, "ringleader" bullies appear able to manipulate and organize others in inflicting suffering while avoiding detection. Support for this proposal comes from a study of 7- to 10-year-olds, in which ring-leader bullies obtained higher scores on the Strange Stories task than either "follower" bullies (those who helped or supported the bully), victims or defenders of the victim (Sutton et al., 1999b). Similarly, more recent studies have shown that at least some bullies are popular, sociable, assertive and well integrated in their peer group (e.g., Perren & Alsaker, 2006). In contrast, other children who bully are also the victims of bullying themselves. These "bully victims" are typically impulsive and have difficulty regulating both their emotions and their behaviours (Schwartz, 2000), leading to high levels of rejection and victimization from peers (Veenstra et al., 2005). In other words, three distinct groups of children are involved in bullying: victims, bullies and bully victims who are both bullies and victims of bullying.

Recently, the genetic and environmental influences on these social roles have been examined, using mothers' and teachers' reports of victimization and bullying for a representative sample of 1116 pairs of 10-year-old twins living in the UK (Ball et al., 2008). In this large sample, 12% of children were victims of severe bullying, 13% were frequent bullies and just 2.5% were heavily involved as bully victims. Genetic factors explained 73% of the variation in victimization, 61% of the variation in bullying and all the covariation between victim and bully roles. Examining these two social roles in tandem showed that while some genetic factors influenced both victimization and bullying, other genetic factors were specific.

Given these behavioural genetic findings, it is interesting to note that in a recent study comparing 7- to 8-year-old children categorized as bullies, victims, bully victims and prosocial children on tests of moral sensitivity and theory-of-mind skills, both common and contrasting sociocognitive profiles for bullies versus bully victims were found (Gasser & Keller, 2009). Specifically, both groups showed low moral sensitivity – e.g., making permissive judgements about the acceptability of interpersonal transgressions and inferring that the protagonist would feel happy to have achieved his/her (antisocial) goal – but only bully victims performed poorly on theory-of-mind tasks (which involved either second-order false beliefs or emotional display rules). Taken alongside the findings from Ball et al.'s (2008) twin analyses, these results indicate that different groups of children involved in bullying are likely to require different kinds of interventions.

Developmental maturity is another important dimension to consider when assessing the relationship between social understanding and involvement in bullying. Highlighting this point, studies involving different age groups have yielded contrasting findings. For example, in a study of 4- to 6-year-olds, Monks, Smith, and Swettenham (2005) showed children cartoons depicting four aggres-sive situations: physical, verbal, rumour spreading and social exclusion (e.g., a child saying to another, "You can't play with us"). Children were asked to explain what was happening in each cartoon and given extra information if needed; they were then asked to nominate classmates who were involved in these behaviours, either as a perpetrator or a victim. Children identified by their peers as aggressors, victims or defenders were then compared on a comprehensive battery of theory-of-mind tasks (as well as on tests of inhibitory control and planning and a measure of attachment security). In contrast with the previously described findings from older children reported by Sutton et al. (1999a), Monks et al. (2005) found no group differences in social-understanding scores (nor any difference in the proportion of children with insecure attachment profiles); in addition, defenders showed significantly better inhibitory control than aggressors.

A simple explanation for these contrasting results, offered by Monks et al. (2005), is that the nature of bullying changes with age. Specifically, among younger children bullying typically involves simpler overt antisocial acts (e.g., pushing, grabbing, hitting) that do not require social understanding, whereas among older children bullying is more likely to be indirect in form and therefore more likely to be reliant on children's social cognitive and executive skills. For example, in a study of more than 500 Finnish 10- to 14-year-olds, social intelligence was unrelated to physical and verbal forms of aggression but positively correlated with indirect aggression (Kaukiainen et al., 1999). In other words, as children's social understanding improves with development, socially intelligent individuals appear to choose methods of inflicting suffering on others that are likely to escape detection (e.g., spreading malicious rumours).

In another study that adopted an explicitly developmental perspective, Smith, Madsen, and Moody (1999) reported an age-related decline in children's exposure to bullying that was at least partially explained by an age-related increase in children's mastery of the social skills needed to deal effectively with bullying incidents. Echoing this finding, in a recent study of preschoolers' sibling disputes (recorded in mothers' diaries), Randell and Peterson (2009) showed that false-belief understanding was inversely associated with displays of post-conflict distress and positively associated with displays of positive emotion during the disagreement. Together, these findings highlight the importance of considering sociocognitive skills in victims as well as perpetrators of bullying.

In sum, the evidence reviewed in this section highlights the importance of considering: (i) social understanding in victims as well as perpetrators of bullying (as children's sociocognitive skills improve, they are better able to deflect aggressive interactions from bullies); (ii) distinct groups of children (e.g., both bullies and bully victims show poor moral sensitivity, but only bully victims show poor false-belief understanding); (iii) distinct types of bullying (e.g., links with social understanding are stronger for indirect forms of bullying, which only appear in older children); and (iv) children's genetic endowments (which explain almost three-quarters of the variation in victimization, almost two-thirds of the variation in bullying and all the covariation between victim and bully roles). Examining bullying and victimization in tandem showed both general and specific genetic effects.

Bringing deontics into the picture

As discussed in Chapter 1, the construct of a theory of mind has, over the past 30 years, proved to be a very successful framework for explaining how children come to reach "beyond surface, 'behavioural' descriptions of persons and actions to deeper, more psychologically meaningful understandings and attributions" (Wellman & Miller, 2008, p. 106). However, it is only recently that researchers in this field have acknowledged the difficulty of divorcing these mentalistic accounts of human behaviour from explanations that focus on normative social influences. For example, adults often do things they don't really want to do, because they feel obliged or responsible; equally, we resist the temptation to do things that we know are wrong. The term "deontics" derives from the Greek "deon", which roughly translates as "duty or obligation". Interestingly, even in individualistic Western societies, about a quarter of explanations of everyday behaviour refer to deontic factors within the social context (J. G. Miller, 1987). Deontic influences may be less strong for children, but still matter and include both rules (such as sharing toys, washing hands and saying "please" or "thank you") and social norms (e.g., regarding how one should dress for particular situations). That is, as noted by Baird (2008), behaviour is not expressed in a vacuum, but in a social context that motivates, constrains and guides people's actions, such that deontic reasoning enriches belief–desire reasoning.

At the same time, theory of mind impacts on deontics in several ways (Wellman & Miller, 2008). For example, the notion of intentionality is crucial for establishing what kinds of acts can be made either obligatory or permitted (such that someone who goes overboard in laying down the law may elicit the sarcastic retort "excuse me for breathing"). Similarly, intentions influence how certain acts are evaluated (e.g., accidental harm is viewed as much less reprehensible than intentional harm). Desires also impact on deontics: obligation implies that an action is required, even if it conflicts with one's desires, while permission implies that, if desired, an action is allowed. In their review, Wellman and Miller (2008) provided compelling evidence for close, bi-directional ties between the domains of deontic and mentalistic reasoning.

For example, universal developmental patterns in children's mentalistic awareness (e.g., Liu et al., 2008) co-occur with similarly universal developmental patterns in children's deontic reasoning. Findings from two early studies (Harris, Núñez, & Brett, 2001; Núñez & Harris, 1998) show that preschool children from distinct cultures (England and Colombia) can identify breaches of such normative rules and can also distinguish between deliberate and accidental breaches. As suggested by Núñez and Harris (1998), these findings, when viewed alongside the large body of research on preschoolers' understanding of lies and cheating, raise the possibility that deontic contexts can serve to alert children to the possibility of deceptive cheating. That is, as well as understanding that a breach of social norms is only naughty if it is deliberate, children may also realize that a deliberate breach may be produced in such a way as to escape detection. More recently, Rakoczy (2008) has documented how shared pretend play that involves logical structures of the form "in a context C, X counts as Y" (e.g., in our pretend shop, these buttons count as money) may serve to initiate children into the world of normative, deontic rules (e.g., wearing swimming trunks is fine at the pool, but not OK in the classroom).

This is an exciting new research avenue but, as noted by Baird (2008) in her commentary on the Wellman and Miller (2008) paper, it is also important to be aware of the complex and nuanced nature of relations between mentalistic and deontic reasoning. For example, links may actually reflect some third factor, such as working memory demands (McKinnon & Moscovitch, 2007). Moreover, as noted earlier, studies of children with autism and adults with psychopathy demonstrate dissociations as well as ties between these domains. In a further commentary, Conry-Murray and Smetana (2008) proposed that one way of clarifying the nature of links between these domains was to differentiate between moral versus conventional aspects of deontics, arguing that theory-of-mind skills are much more important for issues of morality than of social convention. Although at first glance this proposal appears quite compelling, a closer look suggests that the distinctions between these aspects of deontics may be somewhat blurred. An example of this that is relevant to the current chapter's focus on problem behaviours is the finding that pragmatic deficits in children with conduct disorder may contribute to their being excluded from school as a result of "insolent" behaviour (Gilmour, Hill, Place, & Skuse, 2004). In other words, these children may use disrespectful language to a teacher not because they mean to insult them, but because they are unaware of the norms that govern appropriate modes of speech to authority figures (rules of politeness depend both on social conventions and on the probability of giving offence, or doing harm).

Findings from the Toddlers Up study suggest another way in which deontics may be brought into the picture. Specifically, at age 6, the study children were invited (in same-sex groups of six children) to take part in a lab session that included parallel half-hour observations of two triads and a 10-minute "tea party" for all six children. These tea parties provided an opportunity to observe the children interacting with members of their in-group (i.e., the two other children from the triadic interactions) and with members of an out-group (i.e., the children who took part in the parallel triadic observations). To reinforce this distinction, the two sets of triads were brought into the room separately and given snacks in party boxes decorated with different designs. As might be expected from groups of 6-year-olds, some of these tea parties (especially those involving six boys) were rather boisterous, and resulted in a significant proportion of the children (in total: 40/140) engaging in rule-breaking behaviours (most commonly, throwing food at one of the other children or at the researchers sitting behind a screen).

For her final year dissertation, Rebekah Tennyson coded these lab tea parties, focusing on children's frequency of talk to members of the in-group/out-group, displays of affect, rule-breaks and responses to rule-breaking by others. One striking finding to emerge from analyses of these ratings was how indulgent the children were in their responses to others' misdemeanours: of 111 coded rule-breaks, 99 elicited positive responses (endorse, imitate, join), while only 12 elicited negative responses (disapprove or tell a researcher). Negative responses were therefore excluded from our analyses, which focused on the 56 children (45 boys and 11 girls) who witnessed at least one rule-break from a member of *both* the in-group and the out-group. Our first step was to assess whether the frequencies of positive responses to these two types of rule-break were associated. No such association was found, suggesting that there were no stable individual differences in children's propensity to applaud or join in misbehaviour. Our next step was to compare the mean number of positive responses to these two types of rule-break. We found that children were, on average, equally likely to respond positively to rule-breaks from either the in-group or the out-group. Note, however, that fewer than half these children showed any positive responses, such that these two null results may simply reflect low power.

Interestingly, there was some variability in this difference-score measure, with almost half the children giving more positive responses to rule-breaks from members of one group than the other. Our next step was to examine what might underpin this variability. To address this question, difference scores were examined in relation to individual differences in children's age, verbal ability and social understanding. This analysis showed that individual differences in children's preferential positive responses were unrelated to either age or verbal ability ($r < .10$) but were related to children's performance on the social-understanding tasks. Specifically, children who showed more frequent positive responses to in-group rule-breaks than to out-group rule-breaks scored significantly higher on tests of false-belief understanding ($r = .31$) and marginally higher on the mixed emotions task ($r = .24$). In other words, children who showed good social understanding were more likely than their peers to act as part of a "gang", approving or joining in misdemeanours initiated by their own triad more frequently than similar misdemeanours initiated by children who were not in their triad.

Running the above analyses, I was unaware that others had already produced similar evidence for a link between children's understanding of mind and their awareness of in-group/out-group distinctions. Specifically, in an innovative study that capitalized on children's interest in and exposure to the 2004 European Football Championship, Abrams, Rutland, Pelletier, and Ferrell (2009) have recently reported that 5- to 11-year-old children's performance on a social perspective-taking task (but not performance on a control test involving multiple classification) was significantly associated with their understanding of intergroup inclusion/exclusion norms. That is, children who showed good social perspective taking were more likely to understand that: (i) football fans show an intergroup bias (viewing fellow supporters as more friendly and smart than rival fans); and (ii) deviance from this is likely to lead to peer rejection. In some ways, although the tea-party results from the Toddlers Up study were, inevitably, messier than these experimental results, they are useful in demonstrating the ecological validity of the findings from Abrams et al.'s (2009) study. That is, the tea-party results indicate that children with superior perspective-taking skills not only have, as Abrams et al. put it, greater group "nous", they are also more likely to put this nous into play, reinforcing their social identity by showing relatively greater favourability towards their in-group (cf. Nesdale, Durkin, Maass, & Griffiths, 2004; Verkuyten, 2001).

Chapter summary

This chapter opened the third part of this book, which is devoted to the question of how and why individual differences in social understanding might matter, addressed with regard to three distinct research areas – antisocial behaviour, positive social interactions and school adjustment. The chapter began by noting that mentalizing is best viewed as a socially neutral tool, which can be applied to either prosocial or Machiavellian ends, such that there is an important distinction between competence and performance. In other words, knowing how someone feels is not the same as caring, a point that has important implications for tailoring interventions aimed at reducing antisocial behaviours. The second section developed this theme, by focusing on the distinction between proactive (instrumental or cold-blooded) aggression and reactive (or hot-headed) aggression. Although individual children who show one type of aggression may well show the other, the underlying processes are quite different. In particular, only reactive aggression is associated with a hostile attribution bias (i.e., a tendency to interpret neutral or ambiguous actions as having a hostile intent). Connecting with the first few chapters in this book, the third section of this chapter highlighted the importance of adopting a developmental perspective. For example, some forms of antisocial behaviour (such as stealing or lying) require a certain level of mental-state awareness (as well as a certain level of proficiency in both executive function and language skills). Equally, children's understanding of intention develops in stages, and findings from the Toddlers Up study suggest that reactive aggression is likely to be associated with the early, motivational component (rather than with later causal or epistemic components). The findings presented in this third section also connect with the previous chapters on social influences; for example, emotion understanding appears to mediate associations between family risk factors and child problem behaviours.

The fourth section outlined the taxonomic approach that has been developed within studies of bullying. This categorical approach helps to make sense of the diverse links between social understanding performance and antisocial behaviour. For example, while both "bully victims" (i.e., children who perpetrate acts of bullying and are also bullied themselves) and bullies (who are not also bullied) show poor moral sensitivity, only bully victims also show deficits in their performance on second-order false-belief tasks, or on mixed-emotions tasks. The final section of this chapter summarized the arguments for drawing together research on children's mentalizing skills with research on children's "deontic reasoning" (i.e., their understanding of social norms of duty, obligation and permission). This section also noted that recent analyses of the lab "tea parties" held at the age-6 time-point of the Toddlers Up study suggest that children who are proficient mentalizers are also more likely than their peers to respond more positively to acts of mischief committed by the "in-group" than by the "out-group" – an interesting direction for future research.

8 Social understanding and positive social behaviours

In Chapter 7, children's understanding of mind was presented as a "socially neutral tool". Consistent with this view, evolutionary perspectives have, over the past 30 years, emphasized both the competitive advantages of Machiavellian behaviour (e.g., Whiten, 2000) and the importance of shared intentionality as a foundation for collaborative activity (e.g., Tomasello et al., 2005). Chapter 7 also considered links between social understanding and children's engagement in anti-social behaviour. This chapter turns the spotlight on how social understanding may underpin children's positive social behaviours, and is organized according to three themes: (i) developmental synchrony of cognitive and social milestones; (ii) differential salience of children's psychological understanding for social behaviour in different groups of children (e.g., typically developing vs. at risk); and (iii) discourse as a consistently strong correlate of children's understanding of mind. In addressing each of these themes, my focus will be on children's interactions with friends, as these provide an ideal window into children's social skills. In particular, in their interactions with friends children are more reliant on their own sociocognitive skills, for the simple reason that friendships typically involve age-mates who, compared with caregivers or older siblings, are less likely to scaffold children's social interactions. In addition, unlike family relationships, friendships are voluntary and can be broken. As a result, children are likely to be especially motivated to initiate and maintain harmonious interactions with friends.

Are milestones in children's psychological understanding and social competence developmentally synchronous?

A central premise within research into children's understanding of mind is that psychological understanding both transforms and is transformed by children's social relationships. Earlier in this book (e.g., Chapters 5 & 6), the focus was on the processes through which social interactions might facilitate and promote children's growing understanding of mind. In this chapter, we consider how milestones in children's social understanding may transform children's interactions with their social partners. On this point it is worth noting that in the first few years of life children show a marked shift in their preference for social partners, from adult caregiver to sibling or friend, suggesting that as they become less reliant on adult conversational "scaffolding" children are more able to sustain connected conversations with other children, who also have the appeal of shared interests and humour (Brown et al., 1996; Brown & Dunn, 1992). Thus, developments in social understanding not only influence *how* children interact socially, but also with *whom* they interact. Beyond this point, however, research findings on links between developmental changes in children's social interactions and milestones in social understanding are surprisingly patchy. This section therefore focuses on three example aspects of social interaction that have been well studied: empathy, social information gathering and pretend play.

Empathy

As noted in Chapter 1, even newborn babies orient their attention to faces, and within weeks babies can respond appropriately to emotional facial expressions. Thus, far from experiencing their perceptual world as a "blooming buzzing confusion" (James, 1890, p. 462), infants play an active role in initiating and maintaining eye contact, enabling them to engage in "proto-conversations" that are so important for ensuring affective contact with close others. However, this emotional contact is not yet shaped by the ability to differentiate between self and other. As a result, when faced with displays of distress (e.g., from another infant), newborns and very young infants often become distressed themselves; this behaviour is termed "global empathy". Around 18 months, infants begin to show self-recognition (e.g., as assessed by the rouge-on-the-nose test; Asendorpf, Warkentin, & Baudonnière, 1996), a form of differentiation that has recently been extended to other species, including the Asian elephant (Plotnik, de Waal, & Reiss, 2006).

This milestone in self–other differentiation brings about a dramatic change in how toddlers respond to distress; rather than becoming upset themselves, toddlers often display signs of empathic concern, such as gentle touching or comforting. That said, the differentiation between self and other shown by toddlers does not necessarily extend to internal states; thus toddlers who show such concern are likely to try to reassure the other person by offering their *own* comforting toy or blanket. By preschool, most children have acquired sufficient perspective-taking skills to enable them to extend their empathic concern to individuals who are not physically present (e.g., story characters) and to abstract groups (e.g., people who are sick or elderly).

Developmental milestones in empathy, such as those described above, are accompanied by striking individual differences. In their meta-analysis, Eisenberg and Fabes (1998) reported significant increases in prosocial behaviour across infancy (0 to 3 years) and the preschool period (3 to 6 years), with school-aged children showing highest rates of prosocial acts. However, these conclusions are based on pooling cross-sectional data, gathered in studies that differed in many ways other than the age of the children. What is really needed are longitudinal data: findings from the few available longitudinal studies indicate that individual differences in the frequencies of prosocial acts eclipse developmental changes (e.g., Côté, Tremblay, Nagin, Zoccolillo, & Vitaro, 2002). In contrast, children's *motives* for prosocial acts do appear to change significantly with age. For example, Bar-Tal (1982) found that older children show fewer self-oriented hedonistic reasons (e.g., material gain, avoidance of punishment) and more other-oriented, internalized and altruistic motives (e.g., concern for others' approval, desire to maintain relationships and to be "good"). That is, across the school years, children learn to regard empathy as a goal in its own right rather than as a means of securing approval from others and thus show greater propensity to help others, even when this entails a cost to themselves.

Social information gathering

Faced with novel or ambiguous situations, we often seek guidance from others. This active search for information is crucial in situations that involve potential danger or threat, but also helps harmonious social interactions, for example by enabling us to avoid embarrassing faux pas (Baldwin & Moses, 1996). However, the cognitive underpinnings of this propensity to capitalize on others' knowledge of the world are a matter of considerable controversy. Classically, the social-referencing paradigm (in which infants, presented with a new object or situation such as a "visual cliff", look towards their caregivers and, depending on whether the caregiver displays positive or negative affect, produce either an approach or an avoid response) has been viewed as evidence that 8- to 12-month-olds understand that caregivers are a useful source of information about novel situations (e.g., W. Rosen, Adamson, & Bakeman, 1992). However, as summarized in Chapter 1, research findings indicate that it is only in the second year of life that infants become aware of others' states of knowledge. Given this paradox, other researchers (e.g., Baldwin & Moses, 1996; Moore & Corkum, 1994) have argued for alternative and more parsimonious interpretations of how infants behave in social-referencing tasks. For example, one possibility is that infants are much more familiar with caregivers' positive expressions and so their avoidant response may be a reaction to their caregivers' negative expressions, rather than to the novel object in the environment.

Addressing this problem, Baldwin and Moses (1996) proposed that evidence for four key component skills is required in order to credit infants with deliberately seeking out social information. These component skills are the abilities to: (i) decode social information; (ii) recognize that the information is "about" some object; (iii) recognize that social sources of information can provide helpful guidance in the face of uncertainty; and (iv) elicit this social information from others. Applying these criteria in their review, Baldwin and Moses (1996) concluded that the capacity to actively seek out social information develops gradually across the second year of life, with children's understanding of others as repositories of knowledge and information being the rate-limiting step in this developmental path. That is, viewing others as knowledgeable beings provides children with access to new sources of information and so has the power to transform children's social interactions. In addition, as discussed in Chapter 5, individual differences in attachment security may lead to individual differences in children's trust in adults as sources of knowledge (Corriveau et al., 2009).

Building on this point, it is worth noting that the consequences of this milestone are not universally positive. For example, among children with socially phobic caregivers, acquiring an understanding of others as sources of knowledge may actually facilitate the social transmission of anxiety. Murray and colleagues (Murray et al., 2008) showed that 10-month-old infants' observations of their socially phobic mothers' expressions of anxiety in the presence of an unfamiliar adult predicted increasing avoidance of adults in the infants themselves over the subsequent four months. A subsequent experimental study by this group showed that such infant responses do not rely on some common, perhaps genetically based, propensity to be fearful on the part of mother and child since, when non-phobic mothers of 12- to 14-month-old infants were taught to display either anxious or non-anxious responses to a stranger, infants were significantly more fearful and avoidant with the stranger following a socially anxious mother–stranger interaction; this effect was particularly strong for temperamentally fearful infants (de Rosnay, Cooper, Tsigaras, & Murray, 2006). More recently, Murray and colleagues (Murray, 2009) have shown that this social transmission of anxiety is also evident in preschool: when given a wordless picture book about starting school to discuss with their children, socially anxious mothers typically introduced anxiety-provoking topics, such as getting lost, not knowing people's names, being worried about bigger children. In turn, when presented, on a separate occasion, with small dolls and a model classroom and playground and asked to narrate a typical school experience, preschoolers with socially phobic mothers also showed an elevated incidence of anxious narratives. Nevertheless, for most children, acquiring new skills for gathering social information is a very positive achievement that increases their confidence in new situations and enables them to recognize (and comply with) social norms.

Pretend play

As noted by Leslie (1987), one of the major developments of the second year of human life is the emergence of the ability to pretend. Evidence for this emergence comes from toddlers as young as 15 months of age, who have been reported to be sensitive to violations in pretend scenarios – for example, by looking more often when an actor pretends to pour liquid into one cup and then pretends to drink from another cup (Onishi et al., 2007). A few months later, at 18 months of age, most children can perform simple pretend acts themselves, and around the end of the second year children begin to coordinate their pretend actions with others, engaging in joint pretend play with other children. From about 2½ years of age, many children are also able to give commentaries on joint pretend play, for example, responding to a pretend pouring action by describing one teacup as full and the other as empty (e.g., Harris & Kavanaugh, 1993).

From a cognitive perspective, this rapid progress is remarkable: from a very early age children can remember, coordinate and follow joint fictional worlds with others without getting confused about reality (Rakoczy, 2008). From a social perspective, these milestones are equally important. For example, one important consequence of developing pretend play skills is the facilitation of cooperative interactions between siblings (Brown et al., 1996; J. Dunn et al., 1991b). By fostering cooperative sibling interactions, fledgling pretend play skills may have indirect but widespread positive effects on children's social lives, since it is well known that sibling relationships are a powerful influence upon children's socio-emotional adjustment (J. Dunn, 2000; Garcia, Shaw, Winslow, & Yaggi, 2000; Patterson, 1986). Shared enthusiasm for particular kinds of fantasy play (e.g., kings and queens, mummies and daddies, cops and robbers) often provides a basis for early friendships (J. Dunn, 2004), such that the ability to initiate and sustain games of joint pretend play is likely to directly contribute to children's early social adjustment. Note, however, that the nature of this influence will depend on the identity of children's playmates. For example, affiliation with deviant peers, through a common interest in violent themes for pretend play, may lead to escalating problem behaviours (J. Dunn & Hughes, 2001). Finally, joint pretend play is also a fertile context for conversations about inner states (e.g., Hughes & Dunn, 1997) and the acquisition of internal-state language opens up new horizons in communication. Again, this is a double-edged sword, which enables not only goal-directed collaborative activity between toddlers but also teasing and provocation (J. Dunn, 1988). On balance, however, the evidence suggests that the ability and propensity to engage in pretend play is associated with positive outcomes. For example, compared with their peers, preschoolers with imaginary companions have been found to show greater expressive and receptive language skills (e.g., Taylor & Carlson, 1997) and to produce much richer narratives (Trionfi & Reese, 2009). In discussing this latter finding, Trionfi and Reese (2009) focused on the value of decontextualized conversations about the children's imaginary friends (interestingly, the narrative advantage was restricted to children whose mothers knew about their imaginary friends). The message, then, is not that parents should attempt to encourage their children to create imaginary friends, but rather that talking to children about their pretend play provides a valuable opportunity for children to produce complex narratives.

Is the link between social understanding and social competence stronger for some children than for others?

Within developmental psychology, there is widespread support for the view that understanding other minds is pivotally important for children's social interactions; indeed, this consensus helps to explain the remarkable number of studies in this field. Empirically, however, much of the evidence for the importance of mentalizing for social competence comes from studies of mentalizing deficits in children with autism: a developmental disorder that is defined by a triad of impairments that includes deficits in social contact and communication. However, among typically developing children, although developmental milestones in children's understanding of mind do appear to coincide with important developments in children's social competencies, studies of individual differences have, to date, led to surprisingly few robust findings.

Perhaps the lack of clear associations should not be a surprise. After all, *knowing* how someone feels is not at all the same as *caring* about those feelings. In her now classic nursery-school study, Lois Murphy (1937) reported that although some preschoolers showed prosocial responses to peer distress with initiatives, unsympathetic responses (e.g., laughing, aggression or ignoring) were not uncommon. Confirming this, a more recent study of toddlers in day-care showed that only 11 out of 345 episodes of peer distress evoked prosocial responses (Lamb & Zakhireh, 1997). Whether and how a child responds to peer distress depends on both external contextual factors, such as the duration and unpredictability of the distress display (Caplan & Hay, 1989), and internal child characteristics, such as age or perspective-taking ability (e.g., Kiang, Moreno, & Robinson, 2004).

Arguably, the most important external influence is the nature of the relationship between actor and recipient: as many parents know all too well, children who are very prosocial towards their friends may behave quite differently with their siblings! Another possible moderating influence is gender: good false-belief performance in girls has been found to predict high levels of cooperative interactions with caregivers (Hughes et al., 1999) and with peers (Walker, 2005); in contrast, in each of these studies good false-belief performance in boys was associated with higher levels of negative interactions (harsher parent–child discipline or peer-directed aggression). However, further work is needed to replicate these results (and elucidate causal directions).

Another possible explanation for the lack of clear results hinges on the distinction between what children know and what they do with their knowledge. As a result, the associations between social understanding and social competence may differ in magnitude for different groups of children. In particular, some children may have difficulty making use of their social understanding – perhaps because they are too impulsive, or because they have difficulty in shifting from one topic or activity to another, or because they find it hard to hold complex instructions in mind. For example, among hard-to-manage preschoolers, negative behaviours towards friends appear to show specific associations with deficits in executive function rather than in social understanding (J. Dunn & Hughes, 2001; Hughes et al., 2000b). In addition, studies of peer rejection in 4- to 6-year-olds indicate only modest relations with theory-of-mind performance (Badenes, Estevan, & Bacete, 2000; Slaughter, Dennis, & Pritchard, 2002), but see also Peterson and Siegal (2002). Similarly, in a longitudinal study of British children who were adopted from Romanian orphanages, Colvert and colleagues (Colvert et al., 2008) reported that emotional difficulties at age 11 were related to prior deficits in emotion recognition, but not theory of mind. Together, these findings suggest that independent associations between understanding of mind and social interactions may be weaker among at-risk groups.

Yet another explanation for the lack of clear associations between social understanding and social behaviour hinges on the importance of context effects.

This point is well illustrated by the peer-entry paradigm used in the Toddlers Up study during the age-6 lab visits to observe individual differences in how children find ways of joining unfamiliar peers at play. In this paradigm, one child from each (same-sex) triad was taken aside to complete a brief interview before rejoining the other two at play; after 5 minutes of triadic play the game was changed and the procedure repeated with the second child (and again with a third game for the last child in each triad). Overall, most of the children were pretty successful at joining others at play, but there was interesting variation both in the nature and variety of children's strategies and in how children responded to other children's efforts to join them at play. Figures 8.1, 8.2 and 8.3 show a trio of girls in an example lab visit: Beth has blonde plaits and a spotty top; Evie has curly hair and a white smock; Tilly has a ponytail and is wearing a skirt. In Figure 8.1, Beth comes directly to the trampoline to join Tilly and Beth, who readily make room for her.

In Figure 8.2, Tilly actively welcomes Evie into the game she is playing with Beth by offering her a bat and ball (and at this point Beth volunteers to become the referee). In Figure 8.3 (overleaf), Tilly watches Evie and Beth at work and waits

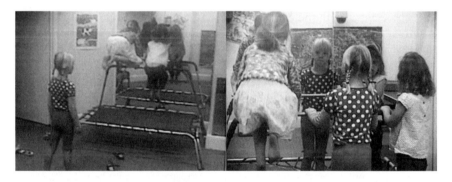

Figure 8.1 Beth joining in trampoline play.

Figure 8.2 Evie joining in the ping-pong game.

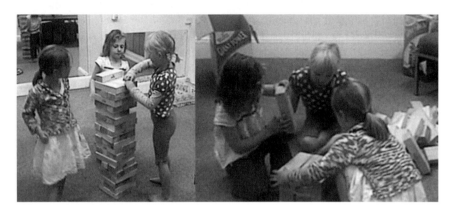

Figure 8.3 Tilly joining in the giant jenga game.

for the tower to topple over so that she can reclaim her place in the trio by helping to rebuild it for a new game.

As these pictures illustrate, the three games used to observe peer entry differed in difficulty: joining in jumping on the trampoline was quite straightforward, whereas joining in games of ping-pong or giant jenga called for more social insight (which might be provided either by the child entering the play or one of the children already in the game). Thus, even simple social challenges such as joining others at play will vary in difficulty depending on contextually specific factors such as the nature of the game, or the behaviour of the child's social partners.

Such moderation effects have an important implication for research, in that they highlight the need to attend to issues of power. This point has particular force for direct observational studies, which are very labour intensive and so often involve quite small sample sizes. Viewed from this perspective, the sample in the Toddlers Up study is relatively large and so provides a promising arena for investigating links between social understanding and social interaction. The findings that have emerged from the study so far are discussed in more detail below.

Discourse and children's understanding of mind

As mentioned earlier, developments in children's understanding of mind influence not only *how* children interact socially, but also with *whom* they engage in social interactions. In particular, increased social understanding means that young children no longer depend on caregivers and older siblings to provide scaffolding, but can rely on their own theory-of-mind skills to engage in cooperative interactions, such as joint pretend play. Support for this proposal comes from the interesting developmental shift reported by Brown and Dunn (1992): at 33 months of age, young children's talk about inner states is predominantly with their mothers (and often in the context of disputes with siblings), whereas at 47 months of age, children show more frequent mental-state talk with their siblings or friends, and this talk is often in the context of cooperative play. Conversations between friends are, on average, more vigorous, mutually oriented and elaborated than those between non-friends (see Newcomb & Bagwell, 1995, for a meta-analytic review). For these two reasons, from preschool onwards, conversations between friends offer a privileged view on how children apply their developing sociocognitive skills to real-life interactions with close others.

One theme to emerge from the findings of previous observational studies is that individual differences in children's social understanding are related to variation in the quality of children's *discourse* with friends. In particular, findings from both cross-sectional and longitudinal studies indicate that individual differences in preschoolers' performance on false-belief tasks are associated with variation in both the content and quality of children's conversations with friends. With regard to conversational content, preschoolers who succeed at false-belief tasks at an early age have been found to talk to their friends about thoughts, feelings and desires more often than other children (Brown et al., 1996; Hughes & Dunn, 1998); more recent work indicates that performance on false-belief tasks is particularly strongly associated with the frequencies of children's talk about *others'* mental states (Hughes et al., 2007). From a social perspective, mental-state reference is clearly an important dimension: conversations that are rich in reference to thoughts, feelings, desires, intentions are likely to play a valuable role in establishing intimacy within a friendship.

However, most communication involves going beyond the literal content of an utterance in order to infer the speaker's meaning, which may depend on a shared understanding of conversational principles (de Rosnay & Hughes, 2006). For example, imagine two young children drawing: the first child shows his (rather mediocre) picture to the second and says, "Do you think this is rubbish?" Should the second child give his honest opinion, or should he respond to this bid for support by saying, "No, it's really good."? Understanding the intention that lies behind a statement may make the difference between a smooth sustained interaction and an awkward or conflictual exchange. Several independent studies have shown that preschoolers who succeed at false-belief tasks at an early age are more likely to engage in more frequent connected conversations and/or coordinated play with their friends (J. Dunn & Cutting, 1999; McElwain & Volling, 2002; Slomkowski & Dunn, 1996).

The extent to which children demonstrate that they are "in tune" with others' thoughts and interests is a salient dimension of children's conversations. This point is best illustrated by an example, taken from the age-6 dyadic play session of the Toddlers Up study, in which each study child was filmed playing with a Playmobil zoo set with a best friend. In the 7-minute excerpt given below, the study child (C) is a girl and her friend (F) is a boy: the two children often talk at once, but rather than interrupting each other, they appear to be co-constructing a seamless narrative. Although this shared narrative is at times confusing to an outsider (both children frequently switch between first and third person voices), the children clearly understand each other perfectly, and are happy to go along with their friend's suggestions, no matter how fanciful. In fact, several conversational turns (shown underlined) show each child actively building on the other's narrative. That is, rather like William Webb Ellis, these children appear to be able to just pick up the ball and run!

F/C: Pretend the duck's swimming then the frog jumped on its head, and the duck was swimming and it couldn't swim anymore

C/F: [*giggling*] then it landed and the frog jumped on

F/C: the frog went there and there and there and [*pause; jumping frog around the pool*]

C/F: pretend it was dinner time so we have to give feed to the animals

F/C: yeah, and pretend this zookeeper said, "Nobody allowed in the zoo, everybody, nobody allowed in the zoo, everybody out, everybody out." She had to feed some of the animals
[*This pretend narrative continues for some minutes. For reasons of space, we will cut to the end*]

F/C: pretend he was and then pretend the door opened as the zookeeper coming in do something with the monkeys and another monkeys jumped out, and it got out and then the door shut, and it was, and he went to join his mate, and it went right [*pause*] there [*pause*] and it hanged like that

C/F: so she [*speech unintelligible*], locked the door, she locked the door, so she lock, tried to make the monkeys jump out

F/C: and then pretend [*pause*]. Some of the, he was coming in and the baby, pretend the baby crept out a little hole [*pause*] and jumped in the pond

C/F: and I heard a big noise so I quickly run to see if, if its and I thought it was the monkey, but the gorilla got out [*speech unintelligible*]

F/C: pretend there was a baby gorilla running all over the place, pretend, pretend he fell into the [*pause*] then pretend he fell into the lions area, argh! Then he got scared to death but luckily, there was a passage way and they jumped right, and he jumped into the giraffe's area and he ended up on here and he fell onto a zookeepers head, and pretend he was hanging on, and he fell off!

C/F: the daddy gorilla was so sad that, he definitely wanted to make a bigger space so they could have much more space to run around

F/C: pretend he squeezed through the hole and went back with his mummy

C/F: and I build it bigger 'cause as it was too small [*speech unintelligible*] running away [*pause*]

F/C: then pretend the elephant just jumped and knocked everyone over

C/F: and then I build it bigger then they had enough space

F/C: and then pretend everyone, and then pretend the monkeys got, got [*speech unintelligible*], and they fell on the giraffe and they [*pause*] they tumbled onto the lion area argh! And then they, and they fell, and were here and the lions all bit, and they, and the little girl was looking over and they took the binoculars off her and he ate them up!

What is also clear from the above excerpt is just how much the friends are enjoying their shared fantasy play. The narrative that they have constructed together is full of action, with lots of different characters and twists in the plot. Note also that although much of the action is fairly physical (e.g., feeding animals, jumping about), it also includes a number of psychological elements. For example:

- I heard a big noise so I quickly run to see if, if its and I thought it was the monkey, but the gorilla got out.
- The daddy gorilla was so sad that, he definitely wanted to make a bigger space so they could have much more space to run around.
- Then he got scared to death but luckily, there was a passage way and they jumped right...

In other words, the children have constructed a storyline that is full of suspense and drama, and that includes comments on how the pretend characters are feeling and why. This narrative shows not only the foundational importance of children's understanding of others' minds, but also indicates how valuable this kind of joint pretend play is for children's emerging literacy skills. Being "in tune" with your friends is thus obviously a hugely important achievement for young children. Although the above excerpt was chosen as being a particularly clear example of how in tune young friends can be with each other, it was not at all unique: many of the other friendship pairs showed similar fluency in their pretend play, which often included shared hilarity at scatological themes, or vivid enactments of nature red in tooth and claw. However, it is worth emphasizing that this fluency was far more characteristic of the children's interactions with their friends than with unfamiliar peers (all the study children were also filmed in the lab in dyadic and triadic play with other same-sex unfamiliar children taking part in the study). For example, in the excerpt above, the study child "C" spoke 18 times in 7 minutes (i.e., at a rate of 154 turns per hour), but when filmed in dyadic/triadic play with unfamiliar peers in the lab she was much less forthcoming, speaking at a rate of just 19 turns per hour. In other words, measures of children's conversations with other children reflect not only the cognitive and linguistic skills of each child, but also the nature and quality of their relationship.

Interestingly, relatively few research groups have investigated associations between children's social understanding and the connectedness of their conversations. Perhaps one key barrier to research has been the difficulty of moving from subjective impressions of connectedness to an operational definition. In analysing children's conversations in the Toddlers Up study we followed the example of Dunn and colleagues in borrowing Gottman's (1983) operational definition of "connectedness" as the frequency with which each speaker's utterances are semantically related to the other speaker's prior utterance. Although very simple, this definition has worked well in previous studies (e.g., J. Dunn & Brophy, 2005; J. Dunn & Cutting, 1999; Slomkowski & Dunn, 1996). The scarcity of research on connectedness and social understanding is therefore rather surprising, not least because links between these measures would provide a simple but generally overlooked "third-factor" explanation of the association between social understanding and mental-state talk. That is, if (as seems plausible) connected conversations are particularly rich in reference to mental states, then it may be the connectedness dimension that actually underpins associations between frequency of mental-state talk and social understanding. As discussed in Chapter 4, this alternative hypothesis provides a compelling account of the links between mother-to-child talk and children's social understanding (see also Ensor & Hughes, 2008). Although it would be interesting to establish whether this "third-factor" account is equally compelling with regard to links between preschool social understanding and later talk with friends, this question is difficult to address, both because so much child–friend talk about inner states occurred within connected turns, and because partner effects were particularly strong within children's conversations with friends.

This brings us neatly to a key methodological point, namely that *both* social partners contribute to individual differences in the quality of their social interaction (e.g., J. Dunn & Cutting, 1999; McElwain & Volling, 2002). In other words, although it is tempting to treat conversational measures (such as the frequency of children's references to mental states) as providing a real-life index of children's social understanding, this view is clearly too simple. Studies that include measures of children's conversations with more than one social partner are very rare, but provide an opportunity to evaluate the magnitude of partner effects. In the Toddlers Up study, we focused on the older siblings to address this issue; this enabled us to compare children's speech with younger siblings (the target sample for the study) and with mothers – i.e., when the children were more competent or less competent than their conversational partners. At each of the first two time-points we found that children talked about inner states (especially others' inner states) more often with younger siblings than with mothers; however, the children's talk about their own inner states was more strongly associated with conflict in their conversations with mothers (mean $r = .46$) than with younger siblings (mean $r = .02$; Hughes et al., in press). One possible reason for this contrast is that children recognize that expressing their own thoughts and feelings is more likely to be an effective means of winning an argument with their mother than with a younger sibling. Alternatively, it may be that mothers provide a scaffolding role, enabling children to articulate their thoughts and feelings.

Together, these findings highlight the influence of partners and the need to take friends' talk into account when examining links between children's social understanding and their conversations with friends. Fortunately, model fitting provides a simple and elegant means of taking partner effects into account. As reported elsewhere (Hughes & Ensor, in press-b), we have recently demonstrated that individual differences in latent variable scores for children's false-belief understanding showed significant stability from ages 3 to 6. Specifically, individual differences in preschool scores explained 43% of the variance in scores at age 6 (with the remaining variance explained by concurrent verbal ability and inhibitory control). Interestingly, individual differences in the frequencies of children's mental-state talk to friends (during a dyadic session in which the friendship pairs were filmed playing with a Playmobil zoo) showed significant independent associations with false-belief performance at both age 3 and age 6, even when effects of children's overall talk and friends' mental-state talk were controlled. Overall, our model explained 48% of the variance in children's mental-state talk to friends; unsurprisingly, the strongest predictor was children's overall rates of talk, which accounted for 25% of the variance; concurrent false-belief understanding accounted for a further 14% of the variance; friends' mental-state talk accounted for an additional 5% and false-belief understanding at age 3 accounted for a modest but significant additional 4%. These findings support the predictive utility of individual differences in false-belief performance at age 3; one possible interpretation is that preschoolers who perform well on false-belief tasks are able to engage in (and hence benefit from) extensive and sophisticated interactions with others: that is, unto those that have, even more shall be given. The next chapter explores these possibilities further, by examining whether early individual differences in children's understanding of mind are useful in predicting variation in children's adjustment to school.

Chapter summary

This chapter was organized according to three themes. The first of these concerned developmental synchrony in cognitive and social milestones. Specifically, this first section considered whether young children's social lives are affected by developmental changes in their abilities to empathize with others, to treat others as sources of knowledge and to engage in pretend play. In general, the social impact of these developmental changes is very positive, enabling children to engage in more extensive and sophisticated interactions with a wider range of social partners. However, developments in children's social understanding may also bring costs, as illustrated by research on how socially phobic mothers transmit social anxiety to their children. The second theme concerned contrasts in the nature or magnitude of influences of children's psychological understanding. Here, moderating factors discussed included characteristics of both the children themselves (e.g., gender, self-regulatory skills, temperament) and their social partner (e.g., sibling *vs.* friend).

The third and longest section of this chapter was devoted to the theme of discourse as a consistently strong correlate of children's understanding of mind. The points raised in this section were illustrated by an excerpt from a conversation between two 6-year-old friends in the Toddlers Up study. While engaged in joint pretend play, these children co-construct a narrative that is full of suspense and drama, and that includes comments on how the pretend characters are feeling and why. In addition, towards the end of the excerpt, one child weaves in the theme of a family needing more space. Quite plausibly, this is a topic of discussion at home, suggesting that the ability to engage in shared fantasy play may also enable children to assimilate and reflect on adults' views of their social worlds.

9 Social understanding and school life

Although the developmental scope of research into children's social understanding has increased significantly over the past decade, most of this expansion has been in a downwards direction, with great strides in our understanding of infant milestones in children's mentalizing skills. Relatively few studies have moved up the age scale to consider the correlates of individual differences in school-aged children's social understanding. These exceptional studies can be divided into two groups, which focus on cognitive and social correlates of children's social understanding. Although the first of these two groups falls some way outside the scope of the Toddlers Up study (and hence of this book) it is worth noting that a number of recent studies have examined the links between social understanding and children's academic competence or understanding of teaching/learning (e.g., Davis-Unger & Carlson, 2008a, 2008b; Lecce, Zocchi, Pagnin, Palladino, & Taumoepeau, 2010b; S. Miller, 2000; Ziv, Solomon, & Frye, 2008). The second group of studies, which focus on social correlates of children's understanding of mind, has typically examined either: (i) the extent to which children are noticed and liked/disliked by their peers (i.e., their "peer status"); or (ii) teachers' ratings of their social competence.

Studies of children's peer status consistently demonstrate that, rather than fitting on a simple uni-dimensional scale (running from popular to unpopular), most children fall into one of five distinct categories (Coie & Dodge, 1983): popular, average, neglected, rejected and controversial (i.e., children who are both liked and disliked by their peers). These categories are characterized by distinct behavioural profiles. For example, popular children are typically highly prosocial, while rejected children are typically more aggressive than their peers. Studies that employ teacher ratings of social competence often focus on these behavioural dimensions, and so often also include measures of peer status. This chapter therefore begins with a review of research linking individual differences in children's social understanding to these two measures of school adjustment. This is followed by a review of research that adopts a child's-eye perspective to examine whether individual differences in theory-of-mind skills show meaningful associations with individual differences in children's own views of themselves and of their experiences at school. This section touches on a variety of topics, including: self-concepts and self-worth; sensitivity to criticism and social anxiety; and children's self-reported relationships with peers and with teachers.

Social understanding and views from peers and teachers

Twenty years ago, Coie, Dodge, and Kupersmidt (1990) showed that cognitive factors could be used to predict individual differences in how much school-aged children were noticed and liked/disliked by their peers (i.e., their "peer status"): popular children generally outperform their peers on tests of IQ, language ability and perspective taking. Examining the links between peer status and perspective-taking abilities in more detail, Dekovic and Gerris (1994) compared rejected *versus* popular school-aged children on tasks that tapped affective perspective taking, interpersonal understanding, prosocial moral reasoning and empathy. Their results confirmed the view that, compared with rejected children, popular children show more advanced sociocognitive functioning and engage in higher levels of prosocial behaviour. Interestingly, this group difference was more striking among older children; one plausible explanation for this age effect is that, as a result of peer rejection, children are excluded from a social context that can foster the very skills necessary to increase their acceptance by peers.

At a practical level, this cumulative model highlights the importance of inter-vening early in children's lives. As a result, subsequent studies have focused on preschoolers. For example, in a study of 3- to 5-year-olds, Cassidy and colleagues (K. Cassidy, Werner, Rourke, Zubernis, & Balaraman, 2003) found that, even with effects of verbal ability controlled, peer popularity (indexed by the number of "most liked" nominations children received from their classmates) was signifi-cantly associated with children's performance on tests of appearance–reality, false-belief and emotion understanding. However, other studies have yielded more complex findings. For instance, Badenes et al. (2000) compared peer-rejected versus average 4- to 6-year-olds on a whole series of theory-of-mind tasks and concluded that rejected children do not show a deficit in mentalizing, but may show a "theory of nasty minds" (i.e., a bias towards attributing hostile inten-tions in neutral or ambivalent situations). Similarly, in two studies of 4- to 6-year-olds, Slaughter et al. (2002) found that theory-of-mind scores (again, based on a whole series of different tasks) independently distinguished between popular and rejected groups, but only for children above the age of 5. For younger children, peer status was better predicted by behavioural measures (i.e., high prosocial behaviour, low aggression). In a further study of preschoolers, Peterson and Siegal (2002) found that the presence of a stable mutual friendship was associated with good theory-of-mind performance for both popular and rejected groups, indi-cating that close relationships matter more for children's social understanding than general peer status.

More recently, researchers have renewed their attention on school-aged children, capitalizing on the development of tests of more advanced understanding of mind. For example, in a series of studies of 8- to 11-year-olds conducted by Banerjee and colleagues (Banerjee, Rieffe, Meerum Terwogt, Gerlein, & Voutsina, 2006; Banerjee & Watling, 2005), rejected children were, as a group, impaired in multiple aspects of social understanding, including understanding faux pas (Banerjee & Watling, 2005) and emotional display rules. In addition, Banerjee et al. (2006) reported that while responses to a victim differed by gender among popular children (with popular girls typically offering comfort and popular boys typically offering advice), rejected boys and girls did not differ in their responses to victims.

Very recently, my own research group has produced results that support and extend the above findings, using data from three studies of British and Italian children. In the first, UK-based study, 300 10- to 11-year-olds completed a series of questions about their social experiences, their views on their classmates and their attitudes to starting secondary school. This questionnaire booklet also included two of Happé's "Strange Stories" (Happé, 1994), in which they were asked to explain the motivation of a story character engaged in either bluff or double bluff. Interestingly, scores on these tasks were unrelated to the number of "most-liked" nominations children received, but were inversely related to frequencies of "least-liked" nominations. In addition, scores on the bluff/double bluff stories were related to children's self-reported excitement about starting secondary school; closer inspection showed that this association was restricted to children of high or average popularity. Taken together, these results suggest that good social understanding may protect children from peer rejection and, in children who already enjoy positive peer relations, may foster a positive attitude to key life events, such as the transition to secondary school. The second parallel study involved 170 Italian 10- to 11-year-olds and led to remarkably similar findings (Lecce & Hughes, 2009). The third study involved 141 British 11- to 12-year-olds and included not only the Strange Stories task, but also a new "Silent Movies" task, developed by one of my PhD students, Rory Devine, using four clips from the classic Harold Lloyd movie "Safety Last" in which a character has either a first- or second-order mistaken belief (Devine & Hughes, 2010). Analyses from this study are still in progress, but have already demonstrated the value of going "live" by adopting a movie format. Specifically, confirmatory factor analyses supported the construction of a single latent factor for the silent movie questions and demonstrated that scores on another latent factor for children's self-reported social inclusion were significantly correlated with latent scores on the Silent Movies task (but not on the Strange Stories task). Of course, each of these studies was cross-sectional in design and so the direction of effects is unclear; follow-up work is in progress to address this question.

Alongside research on links between social understanding and peer success, other studies have examined children's performance on social-understanding tasks in relation to teachers' ratings of their social competence and adjustment. This focus on teacher ratings has several advantages. First, shifting from categorical to continuous data provides an increase in sensitivity. Second, teacher ratings are typically based on their observations of children's behaviour over a period of months, making them more reliable than peer nominations, which may be influenced by day-to-day variability in children's social interactions. Third, given that different sociometric groups show distinct profiles of behaviour, it seems likely that links between social understanding and peer status are underpinned by more direct links between social understanding and specific behavioural propensities (e.g., tendency to display aggressive vs. prosocial behaviour). Fourth, teachers are generally regarded as excellent informants, both because their extended contact with large numbers of children increases the objectivity of their ratings and because they have frequent opportunities to observe children in socially complex and challenging situations.

In the first study to report a significant association between social understanding and teacher-rated social competence, Lalonde and Chandler (1995) adopted a methodology originally applied in autism research (U. Frith et al., 1994) in which 40 items from the Vineland Adaptive Behaviour Questionnaire (Sparrow, Balla, & Cicchetti, 1984) and the Portage checklist (Bluma, Shearer, Frohman, & Hilliard, 1976) were assigned to one of two subscales, depending on whether or not they were judged to involve understanding intentionality rather than mere compliance with social conventions. In Lalonde and Chandler's (1995) study (of 30 3-year-olds), teachers' ratings of social competence were positively related to the intentionality subscale, but were unrelated to the social convention subscale. Unfortunately, these findings are rather difficult to interpret because effects of age or verbal ability were not controlled in this study. However, this oversight was addressed in a subsequent study using the same subscales (with a number of unreliable items removed). Once effects of verbal ability were controlled in this later study, individual differences in 4- and 5-year-olds' performance on theory-of-mind tasks were, as in the previous study, only related to teachers' ratings on the intentionality subscale (Astington, 2003). Similar results have also been reported in a separate investigation in which a standardized instrument (Harter & Pike, 1984) was used to obtain teachers' ratings of children's social competence (Watson, Nixon, Wilson, & Capage, 1999).

However, findings from two subsequent studies involving larger samples suggest that the link between social understanding and teacher-rated social competence may depend on both age and gender. In the first of these studies, Bosacki and Astington (1999) found that, among preadolescents, variation in mentalizing skills was significantly related to peers' (but not teachers') ratings of social competence. One possible explanation for this informant effect is that, as children grow up, peers become more significant than teachers; thus teachers are likely to be less in tune with the social lives of preadolescents than of preschoolers. That said, it is possible that the lack of association between mentalizing and teachers' ratings of social competence in this sample simply reflected a problem of limited sensitivity for the 3-item subscale that was used. Further work is needed to examine age-related changes in the relation between social understanding and teacher-rated social competence in more detail.

In the second study, Walker (2005) examined the theory-of-mind performance of 111 3- to 5-year-olds in relation to teachers' ratings of peer-directed prosocial behaviour, aggressive or disruptive behaviour, and shy or withdrawn behaviour. Her results indicated that, controlling for age, theory-of-mind performance in boys was positively related to aggressive or disruptive behaviour for boys and negatively related to ratings of shy or withdrawn behaviour; in contrast, theory-of-mind performance in girls was positively related to teachers' ratings of prosocial behaviour for girls. This contrast in the correlates of theory-of-mind task performance for boys and girls echoes a finding in an earlier study of 3-year-old twins, in which mothers of girls who performed well on theory-of-mind tasks tended to report close harmonious relationships with their daughters, whereas mothers of boys who performed well on theory-of-mind tasks tended to report greater use of discipline (Hughes et al., 1999). In other words, boys and girls appeared to make very different use of their social understanding.

The Toddlers Up study provides a useful opportunity to assess whether these gender-specific associations can be replicated in a larger and more diverse sample, using teachers' ratings on Goodman's (2001) Strengths and Difficulties Questionnaire (SDQ). Our data, from 234 children seen at age 4 and 288 children seen at age 6, indicate that, at both time-points and for both boys and girls, good theory-of-mind task performance is: (i) positively related to prosocial behaviour; (ii) unrelated to emotional problems; and (iii) inversely related to teachers' ratings of conduct problems, peer problems and hyperactivity. These results remained unchanged when individual differences in verbal ability were taken into account. Although at age 6 the relation between poor theory-of-mind task performance and hyperactivity was stronger for girls ($r = -.48$) than for boys ($r = -.25$; $z = 2.02$, $p < .05$), overall, the pattern of results indicated greater similarities than differences between boys and girls.

In other words, regardless of gender, 6-year-olds who show a good understanding of others' thoughts and feelings are rated by their teachers as high in prosocial behaviour and low in conduct problems, peer problems and hyperactivity. Given these robust and rather global associations, the lack of correlation with teachers' ratings of emotional problems is interesting, and open to at least two alternative explanations. First, compared with the overt displays of social or antisocial behaviour indexed by the other subscales, emotional problems are likely to be difficult for teachers to rate. Second, social understanding may act as a double-edged sword, facilitating children's social behaviours but also increasing their sensitivity to others' hurtful comments or behaviours and thus increasing the risk of children experiencing problems of anxiety or depression. We shall return to this idea later in this chapter.

Alongside the SDQ, teachers in the Toddlers Up study also completed a questionnaire (Pianta, 1992) about their relationship with each study child. Individual differences in theory-of-mind scores were inversely related to teachers' ratings of conflict and dependency, but unrelated to teachers' ratings of closeness; once again, these associations were similar for boys and girls and remained significant when individual differences in verbal ability were taken into account.

All of the findings reported so far involve cross-sectional correlations. However, almost two thirds of the children in the Toddlers Up study had also completed theory-of-mind tasks at age 4, allowing us to assess whether preschoolers' theory-of-mind performances could be used to predict the quality of their relationships with teachers two years later. In brief, with effects of preschool verbal ability partialled, good theory-of-mind performance at age 4 was unrelated to teachers' ratings of conflict or closeness at age 6, but was a significant (albeit modest) predictor of low teacher ratings of dependency at age 6. Interestingly, each of the four items that make up this dependency scale (*This child asks for my help when s/he doesn't need it*; *This child depends on me too much*; *This child has a hard time separating from me*; *This child feels I am unfair to him/her*) can be viewed as reflecting a problem in mindreading – either in children's evaluations of their own knowledge or abilities, or in their ability to recognize that the teacher intends them to work autonomously, or in understanding the motives that underpin a teacher's decisions.

A longitudinal association between preschool theory of mind and teachers' later ratings of social competence has also been reported in a recent study in the USA, conducted by Razza and Blair (2009). Their study (involving a low-income sample of 69 children) showed bi-directional relations between performance on theory-of-mind tasks and teacher-rated social competence. Specifically, preschoolers' false-belief understanding was positively associated with social competence in kindergarten and preschoolers' social competence was positively associated with false-belief understanding in kindergarten. Overall, then, associations between social understanding and teachers' ratings of children's social competence have been reported for several different age groups, in both cross-sectional and longitudinal studies. As expected, this association is clearer for aspects of social interaction that depend on children's understanding of mind.

Social understanding and children's own views of school life

Recent international studies have reported worryingly low levels of well-being among British children (Wilkinson & Pickett, 2009). Amid the controversy about how to measure well-being that has been sparked by these findings is one point of consensus: children's voices need to be heard as emotional problems in childhood often escape adults' notice (Layard & Dunn, 2009). In all of the studies of social understanding and school life discussed thus far in this chapter, children's own views are remarkably absent. Thus, the first section reviewed studies that compared social understanding in children rated by their peers as popular/unpopular, etc., and the second section reviewed studies that examined individual differences in social understanding in relation to teachers' evaluations of their social competence. In this final section, we focus on the relatively small number of studies that have examined individual differences in social under-standing in relation to children's own views of themselves and their adjustment to school.

In a paper entitled *Theory of Mind and the Self*, Happé (2003) concluded that "self-reflection may be, in one sense, an epiphenomenon – an extraordinary side effect of the crucial ability to read other minds" (p. 142). This conclusion was backed up by three lines of evidence: (i) neuroimaging results, which suggested a significant overlap between the network of regions activated by self-reflection tasks or involved in attributing mental states to others; (ii) experimental studies of typically developing children, which suggested a developmental synchrony in children's understanding of their own versus others' minds; and (iii) studies of autism, which suggested that deficits in self-reflection are as striking as the much more intensively studied deficits in attributing mental states to others. Interestingly, however, very few studies have attempted to go beyond charting parallel developments in children's ability to represent their own versus others' thoughts to examine whether individual differences in children's understanding of false beliefs are related to variation in the *content* of either their thoughts about themselves (i.e., children's self-concepts) or their thoughts about others' thoughts (e.g., children's sensitivity to criticism). The findings from the few exceptional studies that have addressed these broader issues are reviewed below, before considering links between children's social understanding and their own views on their relationships with peers and teachers at school.

Bosacki (2000) conducted a study that was exceptional both in its focus on preadolescents (*n* = 128, mean age = 11 years, 9 months) and in its dual exploration (via a storytelling interview) of social understanding versus self-understanding. Specifically, children's scores on a social-stories task (which included a set of comprehension check questions, a set of questions about higher order mental states, i.e., mistaken beliefs about beliefs, and a set of questions that tapped their conceptual role-taking ability) were examined in relation to the justifications children provided for self-statements (i.e., for each of a range of items covering academic, physical and social self-concepts, children were asked "What is the main reason you think that?"). Bosacki found that children with high scores on the social stories also provided more sophisticated justifications for their self-statements; this relationship remained robust even when children's vocabulary scores were partialled.

However, in contrast with the shared-neural-networks model posited by Happé (2003), Bosacki (2000) adopted a sociocultural perspective to explain this robust association between children's understandings of self and others. From this perspective, our sense of self is created from our interactions with others, such that the concepts of self and other are actually one and the same. This position fits nicely with the findings on mother–child interactions and social understanding reviewed in Chapter 5. Further support for this interactional perspective comes from the findings of a recent study in which 125 pairs of 3-year-old (same-sex) twins were filmed in structured and unstructured play with their mothers, and completed a puppet-based self-worth interview, as well as a broad set of social-understanding and verbal-ability tasks (Cahill, Deater-Deckard, Pike, & Hughes, 2007). In this study, the relationship between social understanding and self-worth was moderated by researchers' ratings of maternal warmth and responsivity. Specifically, in the context of high levels of maternal warmth and responsivity, there was good evidence for a positive association between social understanding and self-worth; in contrast, for mother–child dyads characterized by low levels of warmth and responsivity, a weak *negative* association was found between social understanding and self-worth. In other words, for children facing adverse social environments, ignorance may indeed be bliss.

Similarly, Judy Dunn and colleagues have reported findings from two independent studies that suggest that advanced preschool social understanding brings
costs as well as benefits. Specifically, in the first study, based in Pennsylvania,
Dunn (1995) found that the ability to explain false belief at 40 months correlated
with self-reports of negative experiences in kindergarten two years later. In a
second, London-based, study Cutting and Dunn (2002) used a puppet task (developed by Heyman, Dweck, & Cain, 1992) that involved a teacher puppet who gave
different kinds of feedback in response to a child puppet's flawed attempts at a
task (drawing/arithmetic). Five-year-olds ($n = 141$) were asked to imagine that
they were the child puppet and to rate their ability and feelings in each condition.
Low scores on the "teacher criticism" phase of this task were used to index children's sensitivity to criticism and showed specific associations with both concurrent and preschool individual differences in social understanding. Thus, although
"good things go together" is generally a useful maxim, these results suggest that,
in certain situations, accelerated development in children's understanding of the
world has a price: it is only a short step from knowing that others have thoughts to
worrying about what others think of you.

The current Toddlers Up study provided a useful opportunity to assess whether
the association between social understanding and sensitivity to criticism could be
replicated. At age 6, 290 children (164 boys and 126 girls) completed both the
social-understanding task battery and the sensitivity to teacher criticism puppet
task; 182 of these children had also completed a battery of social-understanding
tasks at age 4. Our results were similar, but not identical, to those reported by
Cutting and Dunn (2002). Specifically, we found a significant concurrent association between social understanding and sensitivity to criticism at age 6 that was
independent of verbal ability, $r(289) = .19, p < .01$, but no longitudinal association
between social understanding at age 4 and later sensitivity to criticism, $r(179) =
.10, ns$. In addition, at age 6, the association between social understanding and
sensitivity to criticism was significantly stronger in girls, $r(125) = .32, p < .01$,
than in boys, $r(163) = .09, ns, z = 2.01, p < .05$. This contrast echoes the gender
difference in the correlates of theory-of-mind performance reported earlier, but
should still be viewed with caution, given the similar relations between theory of
mind and *teachers'* ratings of social competence for girls and boys in the Toddlers
Up study (summarized in the previous section of this chapter).

A further related study, involving 60 Italian children at ages 4, 5 and 6, has not
only replicated the association between preschool social understanding and sensitivity to criticism at age 5 reported by Cutting and Dunn (2002) but also shown a
significant predictive relationship between social understanding at age 4 and
teachers' ratings of academic competence at age 6 that was partially mediated by
sensitivity to criticism at age 5 (Lecce, Caputi, & Hughes, 2010a). In other words,
the "cost" of social understanding (in the form of heightened sensitivity to criticism) may itself bring benefits, by driving children's efforts to enhance their
academic performance.

Perhaps a more direct way of assessing the real-life significance of associations
between social understanding and sensitivity to criticism is to examine the nature

and magnitude of associations between social understanding and symptoms of anxiety. At least two research groups have adopted this approach, with convergent findings. First, in a series of studies in the UK, Banerjee and colleagues have shown that social anxiety in a non-clinical sample of school-aged children was unrelated to false-belief performance, but *inversely* related to: (i) performance on a higher order theory-of-mind task, involving social faux pas; (ii) understanding that a character might mask an emotion in order to create a favourable impression with peers; and (iii) teachers' ratings of social skills that required insight into others' mental states (see Banerjee, 2008, for a review). Second, in a recent study of younger Dutch children, Broeren and Muris (2009) have reported modest but significant inverse associations between false-belief understanding and parent-rated anxiety symptoms. Taken together with the positive association between sensitivity to criticism and teacher-rated academic competence reported by Lecce et al. (2010a), these research findings indicate that although advanced social understanding may heighten children's sensitivity to criticism, it is unlikely to have adverse effects on children's well-being.

Social understanding and children's experiences with peers and teachers

As discussed so far in this chapter, several research groups have examined individual differences in social understanding in relation to children's acceptance and liking by peers and teachers' evaluations of children's social competencies. However, two key aspects of children's school lives have been largely overlooked by research in this field. The first of these is the quality of children's relationships with their teachers. The importance of child–teacher relationships is highlighted by recent results from the National Institute for Child Health and Human Development (NICHD) prospective longitudinal study of early care and education (involving 1304 children). Specifically, in this large-scale study, the quality of teacher–child relationships (rated from preschool through third grade) was not only positively associated with achievement, but also buffered children from the adverse effects of insecure maternal attachment on academic achievement (E. O'Connor & McCartney, 2007). Earlier in this chapter, I reported that teachers' ratings of their relationships with the Toddlers Up study children (gathered at age 6) were associated with both concurrent and earlier social understanding. Do these associations remain significant when the *children* are asked about their relationships with their teachers?

Here, one question from the child interviews about school conducted in the Toddlers Up study has proved particularly illuminating. This question asked children how they felt when a teacher was busy with another child and couldn't attend to them immediately. Positive responses to this question (e.g., "I'd just be patient and wait."/"I know a teacher has a lot of children to look after, so I'd feel OK.") were, for boys (but not girls), significantly correlated with both advanced false-belief and understanding of mixed emotions at age 6. In other words, the previously reported inverse association between social understanding and teacher-rated dependency was replicated, but only for boys (the gender difference in the strength of the association between social understanding and self-reported autonomy was statistically significant, $z = 2.39$, $p < .02$, two-tailed). However, the cross-sectional nature of this association makes it difficult to judge whether improvements in social understanding lead to increases in children's self-perceived autonomy, or whether improvements in children's self-regulatory skills foster their reflective awareness of others' mental states (see Chapter 2). Further work (e.g., intervention research) is needed to put these two competing hypotheses to the test.

More generally, children's perceptions of their life at school remain relatively uncharted waters, with very few studies addressing the question of whether individual differences in social understanding predict variation in children's own views of their life at school. This scarcity of studies is striking, given that behavioural genetic research consistently shows important "non-shared" environmental influences that highlight the importance of children's *perceptions* of their environment. For example, children with siblings are acute observers of any signs of parental differential treatment. Equally, the same event (e.g., moving house, family change) is often viewed very differently by different children in the same family. In each case, these contrasting perceptions are a key predictor of children's outcomes (e.g., Conger & Conger, 1994).

Gaining information directly from children is important, not least because children's responses to questions about mental states vary according to the relationship at stake. For example, Dunn and colleagues found that children respond very differently to vignettes involving moral transgressions when the character is presented as a friend or a sibling (J. Dunn, Brown, & Maguire, 1995). Equally, Hughes and Dunn (2002) have reported that children's understanding of maternal anger is more advanced than their understanding of anger in friends, whereas the opposite pattern is found for children's understanding of sadness. Convergent support for this relationship-specific model comes from a study in which teenagers displayed more frequent and less contradictory attributions of mental states when describing the behaviour of their most-liked teacher as opposed to their least-liked teacher (T. O'Connor & Hirsch, 1999).

Turning the findings reported by O'Connor and Hirsch (1999) on their head suggests that mentalistic depth and coherence in children's accounts of their teachers' behaviour can be used as a proxy index of the quality of their relationship – indeed, this is the methodology adopted by attachment researchers to classify attachment security from an individual's interview responses. In other words, as well as making a tally of children's overtly positive or negative comments, we can also extract meaningful information from their ability to engage with the question to provide clear, relevant responses. This is helpful with regard to the Toddlers Up school-interview findings as, although there were no overall associations between children's scores for theory of mind/emotion understanding and the number of positive comments made about schoolwork, classmates or teachers, children's emotion understanding showed a robust inverse association (independent of verbal ability) with the frequency of children's unclear or "don't know" responses to the interviewer's questions, $r(291) = -.35, p < .01$; this inverse association applied equally to girls and boys.

When boys and girls were considered separately, it became clear that the lack of overall associations reflected, at least in part, gender differences. For example, echoing the previously reported association in the Toddlers Up study between social understanding and sensitivity to criticism in girls but not boys, both measures of social understanding (i.e., advanced false-belief tasks, understanding of mixed emotions) were inversely related to girls' (but not boys') positive comments about classmates. This gender difference was highly significant: $z = 3.13, p < .01$. Interestingly, however, children's responses to the more structured Harter interview (Harter & Pike, 1984) indicated that, for both girls and boys, there was a similar inverse association between performance on advanced false-belief tasks and the extent to which children gave positive ratings of their friendship networks: $r(279) = -.15, p = .01$. Given that, as reported earlier, teachers' ratings of social success were robustly and positively associated with social understanding, these inverse associations need to be interpreted with caution. One plausible explanation is that children who do well on social-understanding tasks have a more realistic (i.e., less rose-tinted) view of their relationships with classmates. From this perspective, the fact that gender differences were only found on the open-ended interview indicates that while girls readily apply their social insight to give a realistic picture of their peer relations, boys only do so when supported by structured questioning.

Chapter summary

This chapter began with a review of research on social understanding and children's peer status, with a focus on the perspective-taking skills of popular versus rejected children. Here, group differences are stronger among older children, suggesting that peer status may both cause and reflect contrasts in social understanding, as peer rejection is likely to exclude children from the very social contexts that provide them with a fertile arena for developing their understanding of others. It is also important to recognize that contrasts in the quality of children's friendships may be what really underpin differences in social understanding between popular and rejected children. In addition, findings from a study of 300 children in their final year at primary school suggested that good social understanding may protect children from peer rejection and, in children who already enjoy positive peer relations, may foster a positive attitude to key life events, such as starting secondary school.

The next section of this chapter reported evidence of links between children's social understanding and teachers' ratings of their social competence across a wide age-range. Contrasting with previous reports of gender-specific associations the results from the Toddlers Up study showed that, for both girls and boys, good social understanding was positively related to prosocial behaviour and inversely related to problems of disruptive behaviour. In addition, this study was the first to examine individual differences in social understanding in relation to teachers' reports of their relationships with the children. Here, the key finding was a significant inverse relationship between social understanding and overdependency; again, this finding applied equally to boys and girls.

The third section of this chapter adopted a child's-eye view on school life, as several studies have underlined the importance of children's *perceptions* of their environment. Echoing findings from an earlier study of adolescents, the results from the Toddlers Up study indicated that, even with effects of verbal ability controlled, children who performed poorly on a test of emotion understanding were also more likely to say "don't know" or give unclear responses to questions about life at school; this inverse association applied equally to girls and boys. Likewise, replicating findings from two studies conducted by Dunn and colleagues, children in the Toddlers Up study who performed well on false-belief tasks showed heightened sensitivity to criticism; in this case, however, the association was significantly stronger in girls than in boys. Similarly, both false-belief and emotion-understanding scores showed an inverse relationship with children's positive comments about classmates that was significantly stronger in girls than in boys. However, this gender difference was not found on either a structured task (the Harter Pictorial Scales) or in teachers' ratings. In addition, findings from a study of Italian children highlight the potential benefits of children's sensitivity to criticism (e.g., in motivating children to improve their performance following negative feedback). Together, these findings underline the need for caution in interpreting these results. One plausible account of the link between social understanding and sensitivity to criticism/difficulties with peers is that greater social understanding leads children to have a more realistic (i.e., less rose-tinted) view of their relationships with classmates. From this perspective, the gender differences in this study are best explained in terms of girls' greater willingness to give realistic accounts both of their performance on a task and of their peer relations. Overall, then, these findings converge with the theme (developed in the previous two chapters) of social understanding as a neutral tool. Specifically, for children in the Toddlers Up study, good social understanding was associated with low levels of peer rejection, good relationships with teachers and a positive attitude to key life events (e.g., starting secondary school), but was also linked to heightened sensitivity to criticism and a less rosy (but perhaps more realistic) view of relationships with classmates. In addition, the gender contrasts in associations between social understanding and school adjustment reported in this chapter are consistent with findings from earlier sections of the book that all highlight the importance of moderation effects (e.g., bullies who are also victims show more pervasive socio-cognitive deficits than bullies who are not victimized by their peers; children with socially phobic caregivers are more likely than their peers to experience negative consequences of social understanding). This theme of moderation effects is discussed in the next chapter, which also outlines both developmental and observational perspectives as emerging themes in this book.

Part IV
Conclusion

10 Emerging themes

The previous chapters in this book each included a summary and so, rather than recapitulating these, this chapter outlines three emerging themes (which correspond with the three book parts) as well as two new directions for future research. The first part of the book was concerned with age-related changes in children's social understanding (from infancy to school age), and their links with age-related changes in the related cognitive domains of language and executive function. Development is thus the first theme to emerge from this book. The middle part examined possible social influences on children's social understanding (e.g., family talk, parental characteristics, sibling interactions) and drew heavily on observational research conducted in the Toddlers Up study and in other studies. Thus a second theme to emerge from this book concerns the value of observational methods of working with children. The final part was devoted to exploring behaviour and adjustment outcomes associated with individual differences in social understanding. Here, key emerging themes include the importance of moderation effects (i.e., different processes appear salient for different groups of children) and mediation effects (i.e., indirect associations between two variables that are carried by one or more intervening variables). After discussing these themes of moderation and mediation (i.e., questions of "for whom" and "how"), this chapter turns to two interesting new directions for research, which can be seen as two sides of the same coin, in that each emphasizes adopting a broader and more contextualized approach to children's social understanding. Thus, the first new direction is to expand beyond developmental psychology to include an educational perspective, while the second new direction is to adopt a wider view of social understanding that goes beyond children's mental-state awareness to include their developing understanding of social rules and norms (i.e., "deontics").

Development as an emerging theme

Curiously, developmental psychology has, for many years, relied heavily on (non-developmental) cross-sectional comparisons of different age groups in order to draw conclusions about developmental change. This cross-sectional approach has the obvious merit of being much less time-consuming than longitudinal research (which requires waiting for the children to grow up, in the hope that not too many will be lost along the way). However, there are all sorts of key issues that simply cannot be addressed within a cross-sectional design. This section briefly recaps on the findings described in the previous chapters of this book that relate to four such issues: age-related changes in the nature (as well as content) of children's social understanding; stability of individual differences; distal and proximal links; and individual differences in trajectories over time (a fifth issue, periods of transition, is tackled in the last section of this chapter, which addresses the educational implications of findings from research into children's developing social understanding).

Age-related shifts in the nature of social understanding

In Chapter 1, a key theme was that early intuitive awareness of self and others gives rise to explicit, reflective understanding. Importantly, the later developing explicit theory of mind does not replace the former but both together underpin self-reflection and social understanding from childhood to adulthood. This "dual-track" model helps to explain some of the apparently paradoxical findings that have been reported in the literature on toddlers *versus* preschoolers. In addition, recent work with adults suggests that, in contrast with the significant associations between individual differences in children's social understanding and individual differences in both verbal ability and executive function, impaired executive function has multiple roles in adults' understanding of mind but that severely impaired grammar due to left hemisphere lesions can leave adults' understanding of mind structurally intact (Apperly et al., 2009). To explain these findings, Apperly and colleagues draw an analogy with the domain of number cognition where similarly contrasting results have been observed (Apperly & Butterfill, 2009). That is, while infants (and some non-human animals) possess a cognitively efficient but inflexible capacity for tracking belief-like states that allow them to succeed on measures of implicit false-belief reasoning, improvements in executive control allow preschoolers and older children and adults to develop a more effortful (but also more flexible and explicit) ability to reflect on their own and others' mental states. This shift from intuitive to reflective understanding of mind also enables children to acquire new (and more effective) modes of learning as they grow up. Specifically, Tomasello et al. (1993) have argued for a developmental progression in cultural learning, from imitative learning, to instructed learning, to collaborative learning. Imitative learning involves joint attention, which requires understanding the other as an intentional agent. In contrast with the later two levels, it is not dependent on language and in that sense is "intuitive". Instructed learning is reflective and collaborative learning is recursively reflective – that is, the other is understood *as* a reflective agent. As noted in Chapter 1, this framework provides a fertile foundation for research and may help lay to rest the fruitless, either/or arguments the field has seen between so-called "boosters" and "scoffers" (Chandler et al., 1989) who advocate either rich or lean interpretations of behaviour.

Stability of individual differences

A simple search (in Scopus) for "theory of mind" or "false belief" will yield almost 2000 hits, yet (excluding the handful of studies of test–retest reliability) only about 20 of these (i.e., 1%) relate to studies that include comparable measures at more than one time-point. The scarcity of longitudinal studies in this field is all the more striking given that individual differences in social understanding have attracted considerable research interest (e.g., Hughes et al., 2005; Repacholi & Slaughter, 2003) and yet are only likely to be meaningful if they are also stable over time. On this point, the Toddlers Up study contributes to the literature in two ways: by examining the stability of individual differences in social understanding over a relatively long (three-year) period; and by using latent variable modelling to partition out effects of measurement error and so estimate the stability of individual differences in "true scores" for social understanding. As reported elsewhere (Hughes & Ensor, in press-b), the findings from the Toddlers Up study were encouraging and indicated that, even when stable covarying individual differences in verbal ability were taken into account, latent scores for social understanding showed significant stability over the three-year period from age 3 to age 6, with individual differences at age 3 explaining just under half (43%) of the variance in social understanding 30 months later.

Distal and proximal links

A longitudinal approach is also necessary to distinguish between concurrent (or proximal) and across-time (or distal) associations, in order to elucidate the mechanisms that underpin links between different constructs. For example, Chapter 8 summarized analyses from the Toddlers Up study that examined individual differences in 6-year-old children's talk about thoughts and feelings (in their conversations with a best friend at school) in relation to variation in latent scores for social understanding, both concurrently and three years previously. By applying a modelling approach we were able to control for effects of individual differences in children's verbal ability, in their quantity of talk to their friends and in the frequency with which their friends referred to thoughts and feelings in these conversations. The results showed that, over and above each of these predictive factors, individual differences in children's talk about thoughts and feelings showed independent associations with latent factors for social understanding, both concurrently (i.e., at age 6) and three years previously (see Hughes & Ensor, in press-b, for more details).

The above findings are intriguing, in that they suggest that both distal and proximal components underpin the association between individual differences in age-3 social understanding and in age-6 friendship interactions. That is, age-3 variation in social understanding accounted for significant variance in children's age-6 talk with friends about thoughts and feelings, over and above effects relating to the across-time continuity in individual differences in social understanding (and proximal links between social understanding and talk to friends at age 6). This "distal" effect suggests that individual differences in preschoolers' social understanding may lead to variation in several dimensions that are relevant to the quality of children's talk with friends. Three possible candidate dimensions include: children's adjustment to school (e.g., Razza & Blair, 2009); interpersonal insight (e.g., J. Dunn, Cutting, & Fisher, 2002); and sensitivity to criticism (Cutting & Dunn, 2002). Interestingly, two recent studies have reported distal associations between individual differences in children's understanding of mind and later variation in non-social aspects of development, including (teacher-rated) academic competence at age 6 (Lecce et al., 2010a) and reading meta-knowledge at age 9 (Lecce et al., 2010b). One interesting question for future research concerns whether associations between early individual differences in children's social understanding and these diverse outcomes show overlapping or distinct pathways.

Trajectories

Recent years have seen a dramatic increase in the accessibility of software packages for conducting model-fitting analyses that maximize the advantages of longitudinal data by enabling one to investigate trajectories, either in children's abilities/behaviour or in predictor/outcome measures. This developmentally dynamic approach is important, because static snapshots are likely to be less reliable and less meaningful than developmental measures (e.g., rate of progress over time). For example, one set of latent variable analyses from the Toddlers Up study (summarized in Chapter 2) examined 6-year-old children's self-perceived academic competence in relation to both their concurrent executive function performance and gains in executive function between the ages of 4 and 6. The findings from these analyses demonstrated quite clearly that, when effects of concurrent individual differences in verbal ability were controlled, 6-year-olds' views of their own academic competence were unrelated to their concurrent executive-function scores, but significantly related to variation in improvement in executive function from age 4 to age 6 (Hughes & Ensor, in press-a).

Similarly, as outlined in Chapter 4, predictive relations between variation in mother–child connected talk about thoughts and feelings at age 2 and in children's social understanding at age 6 were especially strong for children who, as they developed, received increasing amounts of mother–child connected talk about thoughts and feelings (Ensor, 2009). That is, the association between mother–child connected talk about thoughts and feelings and children's later social understanding was temporally dynamic; one important direction for future research is to include additional time-points in order to refine our understanding of this relationship by investigating whether the *shape* of these talk trajectories also matters for predicting later individual differences in social understanding.

Observations of children's interactions with others are a valuable research tool

A common criticism of experimental research into children's understanding of mind (and, in particular, the ubiquitous studies of false-belief comprehension) is that this approach is constrained by a reductionist and impersonal theoretical framework (e.g., Chandler, Sokol, & Wainryb, 2000; Nelson et al., 1998). Children are not detached observers of human behaviour, but actively engaged in first- and second-person interactions (Reddy, 2008). In addition, belief–desire reasoning can only provide a partial explanation of behaviour because, in a social world, action also depends on social roles and on moral and social rules. Indeed, just as people may act against their desires when their beliefs are false, so also they may act against their desires in order to obey some moral or social rule. As a result, despite having many advantages (e.g., ease of collection, simplicity of coding), experimental data provide only a pale reflection of children's skills in real-life interactions.

The simplest explanation for the scarcity of direct observational research is the labour-intensive nature of observational studies. In particular, transcribing children's conversations is extremely time consuming; a 20-minute conversation between two children takes about four hours to transcribe. This labour of love is, however, well rewarded in that it yields a rich and detailed picture of children in their everyday lives. In particular, naturally occurring conversations serve as a valuable window into children's interests and preoccupations, as well as a direct demonstration of children's growing skills as communicators. For example, such conversations demonstrate the ease with which children use language as a means of escaping the here and now. This may be in order to engage in enjoyable bouts of pretend play in which they can assume new roles and identities, or to discuss past and future events in their own lives, or to reflect on exciting, scary or puzzling events in story narratives.

After more than a decade of publishing academic papers based on coding and analyses of transcripts, this book was therefore a welcome opportunity to bring some of those findings to life by presenting children in their own words. The excerpts in this book also illustrate the variety that is inherent in conversations, across different children, across different relationships and over time. Indeed, many of the findings from the Toddlers Up study (reported in earlier chapters of this book) depended on the availability of observations of children with different social partners. For example, at the first two time-points of the Toddlers Up study, mental-state talk and conflict were associated in children's conversations with mothers, but not with younger siblings. This suggests that while disagreements with mothers gave children the opportunity to express their own beliefs and desires, disagreements with a younger sibling did not – in fact, such disagreements usually resulted in a breakdown of the interaction (Hughes et al., in press). Conversely, older siblings referred to *others'* mental states more often when talking to their younger siblings (i.e., the study children) than with their mothers, indicating that children are able to tailor their speech to fit the interests and perspective-taking abilities of their conversational partners (Hughes et al., in press).

Indeed, analyses of observational data from the study lab tea parties (see Chapter 7) suggest that the ability to differentiate between social partners may in fact be related to children's growing mental-state awareness. Specifically, although limited by problems of low power and difficulties in interpreting complex interactions, our analyses showed that success on advanced false-belief tasks (and, to a lesser extent, on a mixed-emotions task) was associated with an increased tendency to approve of mischief that was perpetrated by members of the children's own triad (rather than the other triad). This result adds ecological validity to the findings from a recent experimental study of 5- to 11-year-olds, in which social perspective taking (but not performance on a control task) predicted children's understanding of intergroup inclusion/exclusion norms (Abrams et al., 2009). This convergence of findings highlights the value of extending beyond traditional observations of dyadic interactions to include observations of children in groups.

Much of the transcript-based coding discussed in this book focused on children's talk about mental states (thoughts, beliefs, feelings, desires). One conclusion to emerge from this work concerns the significance of *whose* mental states are being discussed. In particular, research findings highlight the different developmental paths and correlates of children's talk about their own *versus* others' mental states and so highlight the importance of interlocutors being able to integrate first- and second-person perspectives (e.g., Hughes et al., 2007). This point is also well illustrated by conversational analyses that go beyond content to assess individual differences in conversational quality. For example, while numerous studies have highlighted mothers' use of mental-state terms as a means of scaffolding children's growing understanding of mind, analyses based on the first time-point of the Toddlers Up study demonstrate that the *connectedness* of mother–child talk (i.e., the extent to which each speaker's turn is semantically related to the previous speaker's turn) predicts children's false-belief performance, even when overall frequencies of mental-state talk are taken into account (Ensor & Hughes, 2008). Moreover, marrying these two coding schemes together revealed that, within both mother–child and sibling conversations, connected talk is particularly rich in reference to mental states (especially cognitive states). Indeed, for mother–child conversations, over and above predictive effects of overall connected and cognitive talk, frequencies of connected cognitive talk predicted additional unique variance in children's false-belief performance. In other words, variation in how often mother–child dyads engage in connected talk about knowledge states or beliefs is a key predictor of children's social understanding. While previous studies have tended to focus on specific aspects of language (e.g., semantics or syntax), these results highlight the value of attending to the pragmatic characteristics of children's conversations. For example, cognitive talk within connected conversation is, by definition, attuned to the child's current focus of attention and this may well be why it is particularly beneficial.

In contrast with the above results for mother–child talk, our sibling observations did not reveal unique predictive effects of connected cognitive talk. This may be because siblings are more likely to focus on their own mental states. Alternatively, even semantically related turns (coded as connected talk) may miss the affective signals from a conversational partner, and young children may, compared with caregivers, be less able or motivated to read these signals. For example, in the age-6 home visit, Libby initially makes her older sister laugh by using the word "fart"; after a while, however, Sally becomes exasperated but Libby continues with this stale joke. This suggests that it may be useful to adopt a more restricted definition of "connected" conversation, to ensure that it applies only to talk that is pragmatically as well as semantically related to the previous speaker's utterance.

That said, the conversational excerpts in Chapter 5 do illustrate how the presence of a sibling provides children with opportunities for "eavesdropping" on conversations between other family members. For example, when Libby talks to her mother about having nobody to play with at school, her older sister Sally is able to offer an insight that demonstrates not only how closely she has been paying attention but also her awareness of the close and reciprocal links between thoughts and feelings ("Don't believe her mum, she's just saying that because she's feeling sad"). Although only an anecdotal example of how children can usefully adopt a third-person perspective on conversations, this proposal is supported by evidence from a study by Jenkins and colleagues (Jenkins et al., 2003) involving lengthy home observations, which showed that 4-year-olds who had older siblings produced and heard more family talk about cognitive states, and that this greater exposure to cognitive talk predicted greater improvements over two years in the children's own cognitive talk, even when initial individual differences in the children's talk and verbal ability were controlled.

One of the simplest merits of conversational analyses is the compelling way in which they demonstrate the sheer magnitude of individual differences. In particular, compared with survey-based studies in which measures often have a very limited range, measures of the frequency and quality of conversations often range from zero to hundreds. At the same time, this variability is also a challenge for statistical analyses, not least because constructing latent variables is very much easier when the indicator measures all have the same range; the latent variable growth models of family interactions achieved by Rosie Ensor and Alex Marks are therefore all the more impressive. Finally, just as conversational measures highlight the magnitude of individual differences, so such measures also demonstrate the magnitude of developmental changes in children's talk; again, this point is well illustrated by the sibling conversations given in Chapter 5. These changes are evident across multiple dimensions, which include increased frequencies of both overall talk and mental-state talk, as well as increased symmetry between the contributions of older and younger siblings (Marks, 2010) and changes in the functional context of mental-state talk (e.g., a clear rise in the proportion of mental-state terms that occur within explanations; Hughes et al., in press). In the next section, the theme of development is discussed more broadly.

Moderators and mediators

The third theme to emerge from this book concerns *moderators and mediators*. Here again, while early research led to growing lists of factors associated with development or individual differences in children's understanding of mind (e.g., executive functions, number of siblings, pretend play, children's own language skills and their linguistic environments), the studies covered in this book go some way to addressing issues of moderation (i.e., do particular factors matter more for some children than for others, or in some contexts more than others?) and mediation (i.e., are there indirect associations that involve other factors?). Putative moderating factors to be considered include age, verbal ability, risk status and cultural background. The discussion of possible mediators highlights the importance of seeing children not as isolated individuals but as growing up within a network of relationships (e.g., siblings may influence each other directly, or via their impact on other family relationships). Almost a quarter of a century ago, Baron and Kenny (1986) published a paper that aimed to elucidate the differences between moderation effects (which concern factors that influence the strength and/or direction of predictive relations between an independent variable X and an outcome Y) and mediation effects (which concern processes that intervene in the predictive relationship between X and Y). This article by Baron and Kenny has been cited almost 1400 times and is viewed by many (e.g., Spencer, Zanna, & Fong, 2005) as responsible for a dramatic increase in the number of studies that examine mediation effects. For example, a Scopus search revealed an exponential increase in the number of hits generated by the terms "children" and "mediation" in each of three consecutive twelve-year periods (1974–1986, 1986–1998 and 1998–2010):148, 250 and 998.

Moderation effects

In sharp contrast with the figures given above, the numbers of hits generated by the terms "children" and "moderation" over the same three twelve-year periods are much more modest: 23, 67 and 19. However, this contrast is deceptive, as the number of hits generated by the terms "children" and "gene–environment interaction" (a special type of moderation effect) shows an equally impressive exponential increase over the same three twelve-year periods: 26, 60 and 1169. Taken together, these figures suggest that moderation (or interaction) effects have been a hot topic within genetic studies over the past twelve years, but appear less prominent in other types of research with children (or, at the very least, have been much less often described explicitly). This is interesting because the identification of moderating influences can be seen as indicative of the maturity and sophistication of a research field (e.g., Judd, McClelland, & Culhane, 1995). Consistent with this view, the research reviewed in the previous chapters of this book demonstrates that, after thirty years or more of research into children's "theory-of-mind" skills, recent work indicates a growing interest in moderation effects.

Specifically, in the first set of chapters that considered a variety of influences on children's social understanding, both individual characteristics (e.g., age, verbal ability) and broader characteristics (e.g., family socioeconomic status, culture) emerged as key moderating influences. For example, as discussed in the previous section on developmental change, Apperly et al. (2009) have recently argued that, unlike individual differences in executive function (which show significant associations with individual differences in understanding of mind in both children and adults), individual differences in language skills are more strongly related to individual differences in social understanding among children than among adults. Similarly, as noted in Chapter 6, sibling influences on children's social understanding may be especially evident within a particular age window (Ruffman et al., 1998) or for less verbally able children (Astington & Jenkins, 1999). In addition, although several studies have reported significant associations between frequencies of mother–child mental-state talk and children's social understanding (see Chapter 5), the evidence from the Toddlers Up study clearly demonstrates that this association is carried by mental-state talk that occurs within the context of connected mother–child conversations (e.g., Ensor & Hughes, 2008). Moreover, cross-cultural studies have begun to challenge the universality of findings based on studies of Western children, whether these concern influences of parental attributes (e.g., Vinden, 2001), contact with siblings or associations with other cognitive domains (e.g., Lewis et al., 2009).

Turning to the third set of chapters that considered a variety of outcomes related to individual differences in children's social understanding, interaction effects are once again evident. A good illustration of this is the taxonomic approach that has become prominent within studies of bullying. For example, reporting on a recent study of 7- to 8-year-olds, Gasser and Keller (2009) found that both "bully victims" (i.e., children who bully and are also bullied by others) and "bullies" (who are not also victims of bullying) showed poor moral sensitivity, but only bully victims performed poorly on theory-of-mind tasks (second-order false-belief and vignettes about emotional display rules). In another recent study, Caravita, Di Blasio, and Salmivalli (2009) have reported an interaction between empathy and peer status as predictors of children's responses to bullying. Specifically, the expected association between empathy and defending behaviour was stronger among boys with a high peer status, highlighting the importance of considering both child characteristics and interpersonal factors when predicting children's social adjustment. Likewise, investigations of the sociocognitive correlates of bullying that involve different age groups have led to divergent findings, perhaps because the nature of bullying changes with age (Monks et al., 2005). Specifically, among younger children bullying typically involves simpler overt antisocial acts (e.g., pushing, grabbing, hitting) that do not require social understanding, whereas among older children bullying is more likely to be indirect in form and therefore more likely to be reliant on children's social cognitive skills.

Moderation effects on the predictive relations between individual differences in social understanding and various measures of adjustment are also evident in the Toddlers Up study. For example, as illustrated by the findings reported in Chapters 8 and 9, individual differences in social understanding within the Toddlers Up sample showed robust (concurrent and predictive) associations with the quality of children's talk to friends (Hughes & Ensor, in press-b), but were unrelated to the quality of children's talk with unfamiliar peers. This differential association may simply reflect the contrasting quantity and quality of talk shown by 6-year-olds interacting with a best friend *versus* unfamiliar peers (e.g., a floor effect in mental-state talk to unfamiliar peers would dampen any potential association with social understanding). Another plausible hypothesis is that temperamental characteristics (e.g., extroversion) are particularly important for how children interact with unfamiliar peers. Clearly more work is needed to tease apart these distinct proposals. More direct evidence for a moderation effect comes from the findings of the study of children making the transition to secondary school. Specifically, excitement about this transition was directly related to children's social understanding (scores on two strange stories), but this association was carried by (and restricted to) children who already enjoyed positive peer relations (i.e., those ranked as average or high in popularity).

Mediation effects

Just as the search for moderating factors has been argued to reflect the maturity of a field of enquiry, researchers have also proposed that the examination of mediated effects is a sign of a maturing discipline (Hoyle & Kenny, 1999). At the same time, however, recent years have seen a growing awareness that mediation analyses often lack both methodological and theoretical rigour. Indeed, Spencer and colleagues have argued that experimental studies are often at least as effective as meditational analyses as a means of examining psychological processes, not least because experimental manipulations do not require direct measurement of mediators; in addition, some mediators, such as unconscious processes, are very difficult to measure (Spencer et al., 2005).

Beyond this conceptual point, Spencer et al. (2005) noted at least three important drawbacks associated with Baron and Kenny's (1986) causal-steps approach to assessing mediation. First, such analyses have lower power than tests of direct effects (or contrasts across experimental conditions). In addition, by stipulating that the predictor and outcome variables should be significantly associated, Baron and Kenny's (1986) model is unlikely to detect mediation effects that run in the opposite direction to the direct effect. Second, this model doesn't directly test the significance of the mediation (as changes in regression coefficients are considered with respect to zero, rather than to each other). Although this gap can be addressed using Sobel's (1982) equation for computing the standard error of an indirect effect, this equation makes numerous assumptions and so can only be applied in studies that have large samples (Preacher & Hayes, 2004). Third, the correlational nature of evidence from mediation analyses means that it is important to ensure both that the predictor, mediator and outcome are all theoretically distinct, and that their interrelationships cannot be explained by another (unmeasured) variable. As a result, mediation analyses are much more interpretable when the predictor, mediator and outcome variables are each assessed at different time-points.

In earlier chapters in this book, the possibility of indirect (i.e., mediated) effects was noted at several points. For example, as described in Chapter 2, predictive relations between children's early executive control and their later social understanding can be explained in terms of both direct effects (e.g., top-down processing may improve children's ability to monitor and reflect on their own mental states) and indirect effects (e.g., better executive control may promote more cooperative social interactions, through which children gain experience of shared and distinct points of view). Data from the Toddlers Up study were used to test these competing views, with executive function at age 3 as the predictor variable, teacher-rated "total difficulty scores" (i.e., emotional symptoms hyperactivity, conduct problems and peer problems) at age 4 as the mediator variable and two distinct aspects of social understanding at age 6 (second-order false-belief comprehension and emotion understanding) as the outcome variables. These analyses showed that behavioural/emotional difficulties at age 4 mediate relations between executive function at age 3 and emotion understanding (but not false-belief comprehension) at age 6.

Mediation effects were also discussed in Chapter 5, which examined parenting and parental characteristics as predictors of child outcomes. In particular, research on the impact of depression in caregivers has highlighted the importance of diverse indirect effects. For example, findings from at least one study (Cummings et al., 2005) suggest that negative marital relations (rather than negative parenting) mediate the association between parental depression and adverse child outcomes. In addition, findings from the Toddlers Up study indicate that maternal depression predicts deficits both in children's understanding of emotions and in their executive functions, each of which are supported as mediators of the relationship between maternal depression and behavioural problems (Hughes & Ensor, 2009). Note, however, that both of these studies involved data from single time-points, such that these results need to be interpreted with caution.

Turning to the chapters that considered individual differences in social understanding as a predictor of later outcome measures, mediation effects again make an appearance, both explicitly and implicitly. One explicit example is from the Toddlers Up study, in which both verbal ability and mother–child mutuality at age 2 were associated with prosocial behaviour at age 4, and these associations were mediated by variation in age-3 emotion understanding (Ensor et al., in press). Another example is from a study of Italian children, in which age-5 sensitivity to teacher criticism mediated the association between age-4 social understanding and age-6 academic competence (Lecce et al., 2010a). Viewed alongside the inverse relationship between performance on tests of social understanding and anxiety symptoms reported in other recent studies (e.g., Banerjee, 2008; Broeren & Muris, 2009), this finding serves as a reassuring counterpoint to the view that children's sensitivity to criticism may represent the "cost" of early success in understanding minds (Cutting & Dunn, 2002).

Implicitly, mediation effects are also suggested by the finding, from the Toddlers Up study, that individual differences in the extent to which 6-year-olds refer to mental states in their conversations with friends show significant relations with variation in performance on social-understanding tasks, both concurrently and three years before (Hughes & Ensor, in press-b). Strikingly, each of these associations was significant even when children's verbal abilities, overall frequencies of talk and friends' frequencies of mental-state talk were controlled.

For reasons of power, the above analyses did not also include a preschool measure of children's mental-state talk to friends; as a result, we cannot rule out the possibility that the distal association between social understanding at age 3 and mental-state talk at age 6 simply reflected stable individual differences in children's mental-state talk. This seems unlikely, however, as many of the friendship pairs filmed at age 6 had only become friends following the transition to school (and other findings from the Toddlers Up study highlight the relationship-specific nature of children's mental-state talk; Hughes et al., in press). Instead, it is more probable that early social understanding motivates and enables children to engage in a variety of social interactions, which in turn foster advances in children's discourse with friends.

New directions for research

Alongside the themes discussed above, the findings presented in this book suggest two interesting new directions for research. The first of these is to examine children's social understanding from an educational perspective. That is, how might schooling help children progress from an intuitive to a reflective understanding of mind? And does this progress in turn help children to meet the social and academic demands of life at school? The other new direction is to examine children's awareness of social norms of duty, obligation or permission (i.e., their understanding of *deontics*); in contrast with the sustained intensity of research into children's mentalizing skills, research into children's awareness of deontic factors is still very much in its infancy, but is likely to enrich our understanding of both developmental change and cultural contrasts.

Bridging psychological and educational perspectives

Schooling has long been considered to play an important role in the development of reflective thinking and so is a promising arena for investigating how children progress from an intuitive to a reflective understanding of mind (see Astington & Hughes, in press). For example, Vygotsky (1962) claimed that, "school instruction plays a decisive role in making the child conscious of his own mental activities" (p. 92). For Vygotskians, language is a key tool for children's cognitive development, such that much of this "decisive role" of school instruction hinges on the provision of supportive opportunities for children to talk about their thought processes. Equally, arguing from a Piagetian perspective, Flavell et al. (1995) suggested that participation in formal school activities may facilitate children's reflective abilities because their thinking about school tasks may be overt, such that children can "literally hear themselves thinking" (p. 91).

Interestingly, recent analyses from the Toddlers Up study (reported in Chapter 2) have highlighted verbal ability as a key predictor of individual differences in the extent to which children improved in their executive function performance across the transition to school (Hughes et al., 2010b). Specifically, between the ages of 4 and 6, verbally less able children showed greater gains in executive function than their verbally more able peers. This finding is open to at least two distinct interpretations. The first is trivial: data tend to show a regression to the mean, and lowest performing children have the most room for improvement. The second, more interesting, account is that verbally less able children are more likely than their peers to come from linguistically impoverished environments, and hence to experience the greatest increase in verbal stimulation when they make the transition to school. One way of pitting these proposals against one another would be to track development in similarly aged groups of children from countries with different age norms for starting school.

Beyond enriching children's linguistic environments, schooling may also stimulate children's social understanding by producing improvements in children's executive functions. Although this idea has yet to be formally tested, some of the findings from the Toddlers Up study (reported in Chapter 9) lend support to this model. For example, in the full sample of 286 children seen at age 6, performance on tests of social understanding was significantly inversely related to teachers' ratings of dependency, even with effects of verbal ability controlled. At least partial convergent support for this association between social understanding and autonomy came from the finding that success on social-understanding tasks was also (in boys, but not girls) directly correlated with children's self-reported ability to wait to get their teacher's attention. Clearly, life at school presents children with multiple small challenges for self-regulation, which may indirectly promote the transition from implicit to reflective understanding of mind. Of course, these results need to be replicated and extended; here again, comparing children who start school at different ages may be a useful approach to teasing apart age-related maturational effects from direct influences of schooling.

Note also that the relationships between social understanding and diverse aspects of self-regulation are likely to be bi-directional; indeed, recent work has shown that preschool false-belief performance predicts teachers' ratings of social competence within the school setting (Razza & Blair, 2009); similarly, the associations between social understanding and social inclusion evident in our own recent work with older children (described in Chapter 9) are likely to reflect reciprocal ties. As yet, however, this work is very much in its infancy as the intersection between social understanding and education has, to date, received remarkably little research attention. This may be partly due to the fact that much of the research on theory of mind is conducted with children under 5 years of age while most education research is with children over 5 years. However, as evident from the material presented in the third part of this book, there is now more interest in exploring developments in social understanding in the school-age years; equally, recent educational initiatives have focused heavily on the early years, creating an overlap that makes this an opportune time to forge stronger links between research in social understanding and education.

For example, is it possible to design curriculum innovations that stimulate reflection on mental states? One promising avenue, suggested by the sophisticated sociodramatic play seen between the young friends in Chapter 8, is to focus on providing children with activities (e.g., storytelling or joint enactments of dramatic themes) that encourage them to coordinate their perspectives to produce shared narratives. Alternatively, interventions might focus on teachers by, for example, demonstrating more open-ended alternatives to the classic "initiation–response–feedback" style of pedagogical discourse that can act as a barrier to children's reflective thinking ability (e.g., Astington, 1997; Kuhn, 2005). Of course, social understanding cannot simply be taught (in the way that literacy is taught); instead it is, like language, a system with biological roots, developing in the preschool years without specific teaching, although certainly environmental factors – such as the nature of family talk and book-reading habits – do influence its development (Astington & Hughes, in press).

Another promising direction would be to investigate the mechanisms that explain why individual differences in social understanding predict individual differences in a variety of outcomes for school children. Here, several findings noted in earlier chapters are relevant. These include the predictive associations between preschool false-belief performance and later academic (Lecce et al., 2010a) and social (Razza & Blair, 2009) competence, as well as the robust and specific concurrent associations (at age 6 in the Toddlers Up study) between social understanding and teachers' ratings of prosocial behaviour and (low levels of) hyperactivity, conduct problems, peer problems and dependency. Clearly, however, there is a need for longitudinal and intervention studies with properly balanced experimental and control groups that together could demonstrate causal relationships. The stage is set for research collaborations between psychologists and teaching professionals aimed at boosting children's success at school.

Putting social understanding in a social context

Social understanding includes not just a mentalistic understanding of belief and desire, but also a deontic understanding of social rules of obligation, permission and prohibitions (Núñez & Harris, 1998). Indeed, as discussed in Chapter 7, these two systems appear fundamentally interconnected (Wellman & Miller, 2008) and together provide a richer research framework by taking account of the social contexts that motivate and constrain people's actions (Baird, 2008). As noted elsewhere (Astington & Hughes, in press), new research directions within this framework include developmental, clinical and cultural perspectives on the relative importance (and interplay) between mentalistic and deontic reasoning. For example, recent research has shown that whereas preschoolers focus on desires as motivating actions and determining emotions, school-aged children incorporate deontic reasoning into their judgements and recognize that people may deny a desire to fulfil an obligation and will feel good about it (Lagattuta, 2005, 2008). This embedding of belief–desire reasoning within a deontic framework provides another example of a developmental shift in the nature of children's social understanding. That said, these are still early days for this field of research and much more work is needed to achieve a full understanding of how deontic reasoning changes as children develop, and how it becomes integrated with belief–desire reasoning.

With regard to clinical studies of atypical groups, it is worth noting (as discussed in Chapter 7) that while children with autism show deficits in belief–desire reasoning coupled with intact moral reasoning (Leslie et al., 2006), psychopathic individuals appear to show the reverse profile (intact belief–desire reasoning coupled with deficits in moral reasoning; e.g., J. Blair et al., 1996). Exploring these dissociations in atypical groups may shed light on how mentalistic and deontic systems of reasoning become, in typical development, two sides of the same folk-psychological coin (Baird, 2008). The third avenue for future research concerns whether contrasts in the relative importance of mentalistic and deontic perspectives help explain the cultural differences in children's developing understanding of mind (Wellman & Miller, 2006). That is, as discussed in Chapter 2, there is consistent evidence that children from China, Japan and Korea pass false-belief tasks about two years later than children from the USA or UK. Very recently, it has been argued that, for Japanese children at least, this delay may be restricted to children's performance on *verbal* false-belief tasks (Moriguchi, Okumura, Kanakogi, & Itakura, 2010). Specifically, this group found that Japanese children performed significantly better on a nonverbal task that, from a previous study by Call and Tomasello (1999), appears to be as difficult as standard false-belief tasks for Western children to successfully complete. To bolster their argument, Moriguchi et al. (2010) noted that Japanese children appear to avoid binary decisions to interview questions (Okanda & Itakura, 2008).

However, before dismissing reports of cross-cultural differences as merely reflecting contrasts in how children respond to verbal testing, three points deserve note. First, these effects should apply equally to control questions (and so be washed out from the overall results); unfortunately, unlike standard false-belief tasks used in previous research, the verbal task employed by Moriguchi et al. (2010) did not include control questions. Second, a similar contrast has been reported between the performance of British and Italian children (Lecce & Hughes, 2010), and there is no evidence that Italian children have difficulty with binary questions. Third, in recent cross-cultural comparison of British, Japanese and Italian children, we have been able to use confirmatory factor analyses to demonstrate measurement invariance across these three samples (Hughes et al., 2010a). As a result, the significant group difference obtained in our study (on average, British children's scores were around one standard deviation higher than scores for either Japanese or Italian children) cannot be explained in terms of demand characteristics, as measurement invariance indicates that the data from each group can be calibrated on a similar metric. Instead, we argue that this group difference is likely to reflect contrast in the relative salience of individualistic *versus* group-oriented norms, such that British children are more likely than their Japanese or Italian peers to adopt a mentalistic stance when interpreting human behaviour. Of course, what is missing from this account is any direct test of this assumed difference in individualistic *versus* group-oriented processing of information; this is a gap that needs to be addressed in future work.

Conclusions

The Cambridge Toddlers Up study, on which this book is based, has at least three notable features: a broad developmental scope (made possible by including several time-points from age 2 to age 6); a clear relationship perspective (provided by observations of children with several distinct social partners); and the assessment of independence and interplay between cognitive predictors (specifically, language and executive function) of individual differences in social understanding. These features have led to progress in elucidating the complex processes that underpin developmental change and individual differences in social understanding (and their consequences). Alongside this complexity, however, three simple conclusions can be made. First, characterizing developmental changes from infancy to school age in children's social understanding by a progression from intuitive to reflective awareness not only integrates theoretical perspectives that emphasize nature or nurture but also makes sense of the strong associations between individual differences in social understanding and in both language skills and executive function (as well as the prevalence of social-understanding deficits in children with disorders chiefly characterized by problems of language or executive function). Second, direct observations of children's social interactions with family and friends highlight associations between relationship quality and social understanding and illuminate the features of close relationships (e.g., familiarity, emotional ties, shared interests) that enable children to construct an understanding of mind from the implicit and fragmentary social cues that typify so many conversations. Third, building on these two points, it is clear that social understanding will show contrasting links with social behaviour or adjustment among children with different cognitive and/or social profiles. Thus, a shift from variable-based to person-centred perspectives may help to develop early interventions to promote successful transitions to school that are tailored to suit the needs of individual children – a challenging but important goal!

Appendices

Appendix 1: Participant characteristics for the Toddlers Up study

As a counterpoint to the narrow focus on children from well-educated and affluent families that is so prevalent in developmental research, the Toddlers Up study adopted an "enriched sampling design" that was aimed at maximizing participation of children from less advantaged families (by recruiting from toddler groups that served mixed or relatively disadvantaged communities). Table A1.1 presents both the distributions of a variety of family background measures (as percentages of all families, averaged across time-points) as well as the percentages of families who reported each of seven markers of social disadvantage (as adopted in other studies; Moffitt & the E-Risk Study Team, 2002). Averaged across time-points, 34% of the sample reported no indicators of disadvantage, 48% reported 1 to 3 markers and 18% of the sample reported 4 or more markers of disadvantage.

Table A1.1 Family background measures (% families, averaged across time-points)

	Specific marker
Marital status	With partner: 75; Single: 25
No. adults in home	One: 26; Two: 67; Three: 7
No. children in home	One: 10; Two: 46; Three: 29; Four or more: 15
Social disadvantage	Head of household: No educational qualifications (quals): 28
	Head of household: Unemployed: 17
	Family income < £10,000: 21
	Family living in council accommodation: 44
	Family receiving non-contributory benefits: 33
	Family has no access to a car: 25
	Family living in a very poor neighbourhood: 9

(*Continued overleaf*)

Table A1.1 continued

	Specific marker	
Occupational status	Head of household:	
Professional/managerial:	41	
Clerical/services:	22	
Unskilled/unemployed:	37	
Parental education	Mothers:	Fathers (N = 107):
College degrees:	20	23
Age 18 quals:	27	19
Age 16 quals:	36	37
No quals:	17	21

$N = 140$.

Retention

Over the four study time-points (ages 2, 3, 4 and 6) the Toddlers Up study lost just 10% of the original sample. To a large extent this impressive retention rate reflects the trust and rapport that was built up with families at the recruitment stage (and maintained during later time-points by ensuring that the same researcher remained the primary contact for all families). Other strategies that also helped to retain the families' good will included: giving families £20 and a DVD of each visit, as a "thank you" for their time; arranging taxi-escorts to and from the university play-room; and presenting the age-6 lab visit as a party with a magician, in order to kindle the children's enthusiasm.

Appendix 2: Observations

Table A2.1 Summary of filmed observations with children (C)

Where?	With?	Age	Setting
Home	Mother (M)	2, 3	Triadic play (M, C, S), Tidy-up task
		6	Etch-a-sketch task, Sharing stories
	Sib (S)	2, 3, 6	Unstructured
		6	Cooperative task, Competitive game
	Family	2, 3	Unstructured
Lab	Mother	2, 3	Unstructured, Structured, Tidy
	Peer	2, 3	Unstructured, Sharing, Trampoline
		6	Ping-pong, Giant Jenga, Trampoline
	Group	6	Magic show, Tea party
Nursery/school	Friend	4, 6	Unstructured
		6	Cooperative task, Competitive game

Video-based coding

Mother–child interactions

Each minute interval of our mother–child interactions was coded using Deater-Deckard and colleague's *Parent–Child Interaction System* (Deater-Deckard, Pylas, & Petrill, 1997), with a particular focus on four 7-point Likert scale ratings:

1   Mother responsiveness to child's comments, questions, and behaviours (0 = ignored child's comments, questions and behaviours; 3 = responded to about half of child's comments, questions or behaviours, although some responses may be delayed; 6 = always responds immediately to child; expands on some comments made by child).
2   Child responsiveness to mother's comments, questions and behaviours.
3   Dyadic reciprocity: shared positive affect, eye contact and "turn taking" (conversation like) quality of interaction.
4   Dyadic cooperation: explicit agreement and discussion about how to proceed with and complete task.

To simplify analyses and maximize reliability, average scores for each of these four scales, for each session, were calculated. In addition, mother/child responsiveness and dyadic reciprocity/cooperation scores were averaged to construct a global index of mother–child mutuality (Cronbach's $\alpha \geq .73$) that could be compared with mutuality indices used in other studies (Deater-Deckard & O'Connor, 2000; Deater-Deckard & Petrill, 2004). Note also that more detailed, temporally dynamic coding of mother–child interactions is currently being conducted by one of my research team, Gabriela Petrut, as part of her PhD thesis.

Dyadic child–child interactions

Three video-based coding systems were applied to children's interactions with siblings and friends. The first two allowed us to assess the frequency of children's antisocial and prosocial acts; the third was developed for structured interactions and provided global ratings of negative interactions. With regard to antisocial behaviour, the findings from our earlier London study of hard-to-manage preschoolers (Hughes et al., 2000b) highlighted the importance of adopting a child's-eye view of antisocial behaviour, in order to focus on acts that regularly evoked distress or anger from peers (e.g., refusals to share, snatching, harming and bullying) rather than attending to acts that might appear antisocial from an adult perspective, but do not evoke negative reactions from peers (e.g., name calling or rule-breaking). In the Toddlers Up study, the same coding system was applied to observations of children interacting with both siblings and friends. Specifically, we noted the frequencies of each of the following four categories of antisocial behaviour:

1   Refusal to share/interact: child declines to relinquish an object in their posses-
    sion (e.g., by shouting, "No, that's mine."), declares ownership of an object
    not in their possession (e.g., bodily blocks peer's access to toy) or rejects
    another child's bid for interaction or help (e.g., "I know how to do that but
    I'm not going to show you.").
2   Snatching: child takes toy from peer, either from their hands or from another
    part of their body (e.g., child pulls headphones from peer's head).
3   Bullying: child threatens or intimidates peer (e.g., "I'm going to tell on you,
    you'll get in trouble.").
4   Hurting: child pushes/pulls, hits, kicks or throws toy at peer.

In addition, adapting the procedures developed by Hay, Castle, Davies, Demetriou, and Stimson (1999), we also coded three distinct categories of prosocial
behaviour that occurred between children:

1   Share: child offers object previously in their possession or gives object into
    other's hands or lap or adds object to array within which other is situated.
2   Help: child provides physical or verbal assistance.
3   Comfort: child expresses concern or offers physical or verbal reassurance.

The structured interactions between children included a rigged competitive game
of SNAP that had been adapted for use with the hard-to-manage preschoolers in
our London study (Hughes et al., 2001, 2002). In the Toddlers Up study we used
a simplified coding system that comprised four 5-point global scales:

1   Disruptive behaviour – both minor acts (e.g., challenging researcher, doing
    something despite being asked not to, initiating or escalating an argument)
    and more overt acts (e.g., throwing game materials about, refusing to relin-
    quish task materials). A score of 1 indicated full cooperation throughout the
    game; a score of 3 indicated several instances of non-cooperation or disrup-
    tive behaviour; a score of 5 indicated disruptive behaviour for almost all
    the task.
2   Social negativity – conflict between the children (e.g., gloating, critical or
    negative remarks about what other child is doing, refusal to sit near other
    child). Here, a score of 1 indicated no display of negativity; a score of 3
    indicated negative interactions for about half the session; and a score of 5
    indicated negative interactions throughout the task.
3   Arousal. Here, a score of 1 indicated no display of tension; a score of 3 indi-
    cated displays of tension (e.g., verbal or physical displays of frustration) for
    about half the session; and a score of 5 indicated displays of tension throughout
    the task, or one extreme sign (e.g., hitting self or other things).
4   Aggression – both verbal aggression (e.g., swearing or insults such as, "Your
    mother's dead.") and physical aggression (e.g., snatching, hitting other child,
    researcher or object, threatening behaviour). Here, a score of 1 indicated no

aggression; a score of 3 indicated at least three displays of aggression; and a score of 5 indicated multiple displays of clear aggression.

Group interactions between children

At age 6, the children were all filmed in the lab in both small groups (same-sex triads) and large groups (two triads brought together for a tea party). Coding for triadic interactions is still being developed, and will focus on children's strategies for joining others (in a peer-entry paradigm) and their welcoming/excluding behaviour towards another child attempting to join in the play. Coding for the tea party is now complete – given the complexity of interactions between six children, our coding focused on just three simple aspects of interaction: talk, affect and rule-breaking/response to rule-break.

1   Talk: For each child, verbal utterances were coded for frequency and addressee – self/other individual child or pair of children (identified)/general, i.e., whole group or 3+ children. Coding addressees for all verbal utterances allowed us to calculate the frequency with which each child interacted with his or her "in-group"(i.e., members of the same triad) or with the "out-group" (i.e., members of the other triad).

2   Affect: For each 30-second interval, we used a 7-point Likert scale to code the valence and intensity of affect displays (Strong/Moderate/Mild displays of positive/negative affect, plus neutral affect). Strong negative affect was rare, but indexed by crying, screaming, clear verbal displays of anger or sadness). Moderate negative affect was indexed by whimpering, whining, frowning or negative vocalization. Mild negative affect was indexed by mild distress, protests, frowning, verbal messages of annoyance or disapproval. Mild positive affect was indexed by brief smiles and by positive but calm vocalization. Moderate positive affect was indexed by singing, bright smiles, giggling, excited laughter, expressed happiness or pleasure in a very excited tone. Strong positive affect was indexed by laughter or very excited expressions of happiness or pleasure. When intervals included more than one affect display within the period, the more intense display was coded.

3   Rule-breaking: At the start of each tea party, the researchers made it clear that they wanted the children to stay seated. The most frequently observed rule-breaks included children leaving their seat with the intention of being disruptive, peeking around the dividing screen and throwing food. For each event, we also coded whether and how each of the other five children responded. Negative responses were rare, but included telling adult/warning (e.g., "That's naughty, I'm going to tell!") and verbal expressions of disapproval (e.g., "You're not supposed to do that."). Positive responses were relatively frequent and included laughter and verbal endorsements (e.g., "Throw it again!"), imitations and joining behaviour (e.g., "Here, throw this!").

Transcript-based coding

Many of the Toddlers Up observations were also transcribed, which allowed us to use detailed speech-based coding. In addition, the investment of time required for transcription was rewarded by increased ease of establishing inter-rater reliability – while even short intervals of video footage can be interpreted in a number of different ways, conversational transcripts make the task of identifying particular events (e.g., use of mental-state terms) much easier and operational rules for coding (e.g., trumping systems) are also easier to apply.

Talk about mental states

At each time-point, transcripts were coded, using Brown et al.'s (1996) scheme, for references to three categories of mental states: cognitions, desires and feelings. References to cognitive states included terms used to denote thoughts, memories or knowledge of the mother, child or a third party. The most common cognitive terms recorded were: *think, know, forgot, mean* and variations. Other cognitive terms that occurred were: *assure, believe, concentrate, distract, expect, figure, guess, idea, ignore, imagine, interest, learn, pretend, recognize, trust, understand, wonder* and variations. The desire terms observed were: *fancy, keen, hope, want, wish, would like, would love* and variations commonly used to capture both desires and goals. For example, "*want*" was coded when the term referred to a goal-directed behaviour. References to feelings included those that referred to an emotional state. The feeling terms noted were: *cross, disgust, enjoy, excited, fed up, frightened, fun, grumpy, happy, like, love, pleased, proud, scared, surprise, upset, worried* and variations. For example, "*like*" was only coded when the term referred to a state of enjoyment and not when it indicated "to want to have". References to mental states that were conversational, repetitive (within an utterance) and imitative were excluded.

Quality of verbal interactions

The transcripts were divided into conversational turns; a turn was defined as the utterances of one speaker bounded by another speaker's utterances (Shatz & Gelman, 1973) or a significant silence (usually 5 seconds or more). Adopting procedures from previous studies (J. Dunn & Cutting, 1999), each conversational turn that mothers directed to the target child was assigned to one of the following five quality codes:

1   Connected: speaker's utterance is semantically related to the other interlocutor's previous turn.
2   Initiation: speaker initiates a new topic that is both unrelated to the other interlocutor's previous turn and successful in eliciting a semantically related response from the other interlocutor.
3   Failed: speaker's turn is directed (either explicitly or implicitly) to the other interlocutor but fails to elicit a semantically related response.

4   Conflict: speaker's utterance includes a prohibition, threat or insult. Note that a trumping system was used such that turns that could be categorized as either conflict or connected were always coded as connected.
5   Unclear: inaudible or unintelligible.

Reliability of observational coding

All of the coding conducted for the Toddlers Up study included independent double coding of at least 20% of the DVDs/transcripts, with additional spot checks conducted to avoid problems of researchers "drifting" from established coding procedures. A minimum value of Cohen's modified kappa of .80 was set as the criterion for coding reliability. In addition, to maximize consistency, the same researcher was, as far as possible, responsible for carrying out a particular coding system at all time-points.

Appendix 3: Summary of tasks used in the Toddlers Up study

At each time-point, assessments (see Table A3.1) were spread across two visits, to minimize loss of data through fatigue, task refusal, etc. Full scripts and details of test–retest reliability for many of the social understanding tasks are available elsewhere (Hughes et al., 2000a).

Table A3.1 Social-understanding tasks administered at each time-point

Construct	Age	Task	Measure
Emotion	2	Denham's puppets	Receptive/Expressive identification; Unambiguous stories
Understanding	3, 4	Denham's puppets	Receptive/Expressive identification; Unambiguous and ambiguous stories
	6	Gordis stories	Explaining/Inferring/Generating mixed emotions
Standard ToM	2	Elicited pretence	Single/Double substitutions (e.g., pretending to feed junk hay to junk horse)
	2, 3, 4	Penny hiding	No. correct elements (both hands behind back; both hands forward; hide coin)
	2, 3, 4	Picture book FB*	Recall of own FB*; Predict other's FB
	3	Object transfer FB	Predict other's FB; Explain other's FB
	3, 4	Deceptive contents FB	Recall of own FB; Explain other's FB
Advanced ToM	6	2 × Second-order FB	Predict and explain FB about another's belief
	6	2 × Belief-based emotion	Use FB to infer and explain emotion

ToM = Theory of Mind. *Success on FB (false-belief) questions depends on also passing reality/memory control questions.

References

Abrams, D., Rutland, A., Pelletier, J., & Ferrell, J. (2009). Children's group nous: Understanding and applying peer exclusion within and between groups. *Child Development, 80*, 224–243.

Adrián, J., Clemente, R., & Villanueva, L. (2007). Mothers' use of cognitive state verbs in picture-book reading and the development of children's understanding of mind: A longitudinal study. *Child Development, 78*, 1052–1067.

Adrián, J., Clemente, R., Villanueva, L., & Rieffe, C. (2005). Parent–child picture-book reading, mothers' mental state language and children's theory of mind. *Journal of Child Language, 32*, 673–686.

Alexander, M. P., Benson, D. F., & Stuss, D. T. (1989). Frontal lobes and language. *Brain and Language, 37*, 659–691.

Amsterdam, B. (1972). Mirror self-image reactions before age two. *Developmental Psychobiology, 5*, 297–305.

Apperly, I., & Butterfill, S. (2009). Do humans have two systems to track beliefs and belief-like states? *Psychological Review, 116*, 953–970.

Apperly, I., Samson, D., & Humphreys, G. (2009). Studies of adults can inform accounts of theory of mind development. *Developmental Psychology, 45*, 190–201.

Appleton, M., & Reddy, V. (1996). Teaching 3-year-olds to pass false-belief tests: A conversational approach. *Social Development, 5*, 275–291.

Ardila, A., Rosselli, M., Matute, E., & Guajardo, S. (2005). The influence of the parents' educational level on the development of executive functions. *Developmental Neuropsychology, 28*, 539–560.

Arnold, M., & Gasson, J. (1954). Feelings and emotions as dynamic factors in personality integration. In M. Arnold & J. Gasson (Eds.), *The human person* (pp. 294–313). New York, NY: Ronald.

Asendorpf, J., Warkentin, V., & Baudonnière, P.-M. (1996). Self-awareness and other-awareness. II: Mirror self-recognition, social contingency awareness, and synchronic imitation. *Developmental Psychology, 32*, 313–321.

Astington, J. W. (1997). Reflective teaching and learning: Children's and teachers' theories of mind. *Teaching Education, 9*, 95–103.

Astington, J. W. (1998). Theory of mind, Humpty Dumpty and the icebox. *Human Development, 41*, 30–39.

Astington, J. W. (2001). The paradox of intention: Assessing children's metarepresentational understanding. In B. Malle, L. Moses, & D. Baldwin (Eds.), *Intentions and intentionality: Foundations of social cognition* (pp. 85–104). Boston, MA: MIT Press.

Astington, J. W. (2003). Sometimes necessary, never sufficient: False belief understanding and social competence. In B. Repacholi & V. Slaughter (Eds.), *Individual differences in theory of mind: Implications for typical and atypical development* (pp. 13–38). New York, NY: Psychology Press.

Astington, J. W., & Baird, J. (Eds.). (2005). *Why language matters for theory of mind.* New York, NY: Oxford University Press.

Astington, J. W., & Hughes, C. (in press). Theory of mind: Self-reflection and social understanding. In P. Zelazo (Ed.), *Oxford handbook of developmental psychology.* Oxford, UK: Oxford University Press.

Astington, J. W., & Jenkins, J. (1999). A longitudinal study of the relation between language and theory-of-mind development. *Developmental Psychology, 35*, 1311–1320.

Astington, J. W., Pelletier, J., & Homer, B. (2002). Theory of mind and epistemological development: The relation between children's second-order false-belief understanding and their ability to reason about evidence. *New Ideas in Psychology, 20*, 131–144.

Astington, J. W., & Baird, J. (2005). Representational development and false-belief understanding. In J. W. Astington & J. Baird (Eds.), *Why language matters for theory of mind* (pp. 163–185). Oxford, UK: Oxford University Press.

Austin, J. (1962). *How to do things with words.* Cambridge, MA: Harvard University Press.

Avis, J., & Harris, P. (1991). Belief–desire reasoning among Baka children: Evidence for a universal conception of mind. *Child Development, 62*, 460–467.

Badenes, L., Estevan, R., & Bacete, F. (2000). Theory of mind and peer rejection at school. *Social Development, 9*, 273–283.

Baillargeon, R., Spelke, E., & Wasserman, S. (1985). Object permanence in five-month-old infants. *Cognition, 20*, 191–208.

Baird, J. (2008). Thinking outside the Smarties box: A broader perspective on theory of mind. *Human Development, 51*, 143–147.

Baldwin, D., & Moses, L. (1996). The ontogeny of social information gathering. *Child Development, 67*, 1915–1939.

Ball, H., Arseneault, L., Taylor, A., Maughan, B., Caspi, A., & Moffitt, T. (2008). Genetic and environmental influences on victims, bullies and bully victims in childhood. *Journal of Child Psychology and Psychiatry and Allied Disciplines, 49*, 104–112.

Bandura, A. (2001). Social cognitive theory: An agentic perspective. *Annual Review of Psychology, 52*, 1–26.

Bandura, A., Ross, D., & Ross, S. A. (1963). Imitation of film-mediated aggressive models. *Journal of Abnormal and Social Psychology, 66*, 3–11.

Banerjee, R. (2008). Social cognition and anxiety in children. In C. Sharp, P. Fonagy, & I. M. Goodyer (Eds.), *Social cognition and developmental psychopathology* (pp. 239–269). Oxford, UK: Oxford University Press.

Banerjee, R., Rieffe, C., Meerum Terwogt, M., Gerlein, A., & Voutsina, M. (2006). Popular and rejected children's reasoning about negative emotions in social situations: The role of gender. *Social Development, 15*, 418–433.

Banerjee, R., & Watling, D. (2005). Children's understanding of *faux pas*: Associations with peer relations. *Hellenic Journal of Psychology, 2*, 27–45.

Barkley, R. A. (1997). Behavioral inhibition, sustained attention and executive functions: Constructing a unified theory of ADHD. *Psychological Bulletin, 121*, 65–94.

Baron, R., & Kenny, D. (1986). The moderator mediator variable distinction in social psychological research: Conceptual, strategic and statistical considerations. *Journal of Personality and Social Psychology, 52*, 1173–1182.

Baron-Cohen, S. (1988). Social and pragmatic deficits in autism: Cognitive or affective? *Journal of Autism and Developmental Disorders, 18*, 379–401.

Baron-Cohen, S. (1995). *Mindblindness: An essay on autism and theory of mind.* Cambridge: MA: MIT Press.

Baron-Cohen, S., Leslie, A., & Frith, U. (1985). Does the autistic child have a "theory of mind"? *Cognition, 21*, 37–46.

Baron-Cohen, S., O'Riordan, M., Stone, V., Jones, R., & Plaisted, K. (1999). Recognition of faux pas by normally developing children with Asperger syndrome or high-functioning autism. *Journal of Autism and Developmental Disorders, 29*, 407–418.

Bar-Tal, D. (1982). Sequential development of helping behavior: A cognitive-learning approach. *Developmental Review, 2*, 101–124.

Bartsch, K., & London, K. (2000). Children's use of mental state information in selecting persuasive arguments. *Developmental Psychology, 36*, 352–365.

Bartsch, K., London, K., & Campbell, M. (2007). Children's attention to beliefs in interactive persuasion tasks. *Developmental Psychology, 43*, 111–120.

Bartsch, K., & Wellman, H. (1995). *Children talk about the mind.* Oxford, UK: Oxford University Press.

Bateman, L., & Bharj, K. (2009). The impact of the birth of the first child on a couple's relationship. *Evidence Based Midwifery, 7*, 16–23.

Baumrind, D. (1971). Current patterns of parental authority. *Developmental Psychology, 4*, 1–103.

Berlin, H., Rolls, E., & Iversen, S. (2005). Borderline personality disorder, impulsivity, and the orbitofrontal cortex. *American Journal of Psychiatry, 162*, 2360–2373.

Bettelheim, B. (1987). *A good enough parent: A book on child-rearing.* New York, NY: Alfred A. Knopf.

Bialystok, E. (1999). Cognitive complexity and attentional control in the bilingual mind. *Child Development, 70*, 636–644.

Bird, G., Leighton, J., Press, C., & Heyes, C. (2007). Intact automatic imitation of human and robot actions in autism spectrum disorders. *Proceedings of the Royal Society B: Biological Sciences, 274*(1628), 3027–3031.

Bishop, D. (2002). The role of genes in the etiology of specific language impairment. *Journal of Communication Disorders, 35*, 311–328.

Bishop, D. (2006). What causes specific language impairment in children? *Current Directions in Psychological Science, 15*, 217–221.

Bishop, D. V. M., & Norbury, C. F. (2002). Exploring the borderlands of autistic disorder and specific language impairment: A study using standardised diagnostic instruments. *Journal of Child Psychology and Psychiatry and Allied Disciplines, 43*, 917–929.

Blair, C., & Diamond, A. (2008). Biological processes in prevention and intervention: The promotion of self-regulation as a means of preventing school failure. *Development and Psychopathology, 20*, 899–911.

Blair, C., & Peters, R. (2003). Physiological and neurocognitive correlates of adaptive behavior in preschool among children in Head Start. *Developmental Neuropsychology, 24*, 479–497.

Blair, C., & Razza, R. (2007). Relating effortful control, executive function, and false belief understanding to emerging math and literacy ability in kindergarten. *Child Development, 78*, 647–663.

Blair, R. J. R., Sellars, C., Strickland, I., Clark, F., Williams, A., Smith, M., et al. (1996). Theory of mind in the psychopath. *Journal of Forensic Psychiatry, 7*, 15–25.

Blair, R. J. R., & Cipolotti, L. (2000). Impaired social response reversal. A case of "acquired sociopathy". *Brain, 123,* 1122–1141.

Blair, R. J. R., & Mitchell, D. (2009). Psychopathy, attention and emotion. *Psychological Medicine, 39,* 543–555.

Bluma, S., Shearer, M., Frohman, A., & Hilliard, J. (1976). *The Portage guide to early education checklist.* Portage, WI: Portage Project Cooperative Educational Agency 12.

Boer, F., & Dunn, J. (1990). *Children's sibling relationships: Developmental and clinical issues.* Hillsdale, NJ: Lawrence Erlbaum Associates, Inc.

Boivin, M., & Bégin, G. (1989). Peer status and self-perception among early elementary school children: The case of the rejected children. *Child Development, 60,* 591–596.

Bosacki, S. (2000). Theory of mind and self-concept in preadolescents: Links with gender and language. *Journal of Educational Psychology, 92,* 709–717.

Bosacki, S., & Astington, J. (1999). Theory of mind in preadolescence: Relations between social understanding and social competence. *Social Development, 8,* 237–255.

Bowlby, J. (1969). *Attachment and loss: Vol. 1. Attachment.* New York, NY: Basic Books.

Bowlby, J. (1982). Attachment and loss: Retrospect and prospect. *American Journal of Orthopsychiatry, 52*(4), 664–678.

Bowler, D. (1992). "Theory of mind" in Asperger's syndrome. *Journal of Child Psychology and Psychiatry, 33,* 877–893.

Bradley, R., & Corwyn, R. (2002). Socioeconomic status and child development. *Annual Review of Psychology, 53,* 371–399.

Brinton, B., & Fujiki, M. (1998). Social interactional behaviors of children with specific language impairment. *Topics in Language Disorders, 19,* 49–69.

Broeren, S., & Muris, P. (2009). The relation between cognitive development and anxiety phenomena in children. *Journal of Child and Family Studies, 18,* 702–709.

Brophy, M., & Dunn, J. (2002). What did mummy say? Dyadic interactions between young "hard to manage" children and their mothers. *Journal of Abnormal Child Psychology, 30,* 103–112.

Brown, J., Donelan-McCall, N., & Dunn, J. (1996). Why talk about mental states? The significance of children's conversations with friends, siblings, and mothers. *Child Development, 67,* 836–849.

Brown, J., & Dunn, J. (1992). Talk with your mother or your sibling? Developmental changes in early family conversations about feelings. *Child Development, 63,* 336–349.

Bruner, J. (1985). *Actual minds, possible worlds.* Cambridge, MA: Harvard University Press.

Budwig, N. (2002). A developmental-functionalist approach to mental state talk. In J. B. E. Amsel (Ed.), *Language, literacy, and cognitive development: The development and consequences of symbolic communication* (pp. 59–86). Mahwah, NJ: Lawrence Erlbaum Associates, Inc.

Bukowski, W., & Sippola, L. (1998). Diversity and the social mind: Goals, constructs, culture, and development. *Developmental Psychology, 34,* 742–746.

Burke, J., Pardini, D., & Loeber, R. (2008). Reciprocal relationships between parenting behavior and disruptive psychopathology from childhood through adolescence. *Journal of Abnormal Child Psychology, 36,* 679–692.

Bus, A., & van IJzendoorn, M. (1988). Attachment and early reading: A longitudinal study. *Journal of Genetic Psychology, 149,* 199–210.

Cahill, K., Deater-Deckard, K., Pike, A., & Hughes, C. (2007). Theory of mind, self-worth and the mother–child relationship. *Social Development, 16,* 45–56.

Cairns, R. B. (1979). *Social development: The origins and plasticity of social interchanges.* San Francisco, CA: Freeman.

Call, J., & Tomasello, M. (1999). A nonverbal false belief task: The performance of children and great apes. *Child Development, 70,* 381–395.

Callaghan, T., Rochat, P., Lillard, A., Claux, M., Odden, H., Itakura, S., et al. (2005). Synchrony in the onset of mental-state reasoning: Evidence from five cultures. *Psychological Science, 16,* 378–384.

Caplan, M., & Hay, D. (1989). Preschoolers' responses to peers' distress and beliefs about bystander intervention. *Journal of Child Psychology and Psychiatry, 30,* 231–242.

Caravita, S. C. S., Di Blasio, P., & Salmivalli, C. (2009). Unique and interactive effects of empathy and social status on involvement in bullying. *Social Development, 18,* 140–163.

Carlson, S. (2005). Developmentally sensitive measures of executive function in preschool children. *Developmental Neuropsychology, 28,* 595–616.

Carlson, S., Mandell, D., & Williams, L. (2004). Executive function and theory of mind: Stability and prediction from ages 2 to 3. *Developmental Psychology, 40,* 1105–1122.

Carlson, S., & Moses, L. (2001). Individual differences in inhibitory control and children's theory of mind. *Child Development, 72,* 1032–1053.

Carlson, S., Moses, L., & Breton, C. (2002). How specific is the relation between executive function and theory of mind? Contributions of inhibitory control and working memory. *Infant and Child Development, Special Issue on Executive Functions and Development, 11,* 73–92.

Carlson, S., Moses, L., & Claxton, L. (2004). Individual differences in executive functioning and theory of mind: An investigation of inhibitory control and planning ability. *Journal of Experimental Child Psychology, 87,* 299–319.

Carlson, S., Moses, L., & Hix, H. (1998). The role of inhibitory processes in young children's difficulties with deception and false belief. *Child Development, 69,* 672–691.

Carpendale, J., & Chandler, M. (1996). On the distinction between false belief understanding and subscribing to an interpretive theory of mind. *Child Development, 67,* 1686–1706.

Carpendale, J., & Lewis, C. (2004). Constructing an understanding of mind: The development of children's social understanding within social interaction. *Behavioral and Brain Sciences, 27,* 79–151.

Carpendale, J., & Lewis, C. (2006). *How children develop social understanding.* Oxford, UK: Blackwell.

Carpenter, M., Call, J., & Tomasello, M. (2002). A new false belief test for 36 month-olds *British Journal of Developmental Psychology, 20,* 393–420.

Carroll, L. (1872). *Through the looking glass and what Alice found there.* London, UK: Macmillan.

Carruthers, P. (1996). Autism as mindblindness: An elaboration and partial defence. In P. Carruthers & P. K. Smith (Eds.), *Theories of theories of mind* (pp. 257–273). Cambridge UK: Cambridge University Press.

Caspers, K., Paradiso, S., Yucuis, R., Troutman, B., Arndt, S., & Philibert, R. (2009). Association between the serotonin transporter promoter polymorphism (5-HTTLPR) and adult unresolved attachment. *Developmental Psychology, 45,* 64–76.

Caspi, A., Sugden, K., Moffitt, T., Taylor, A., Craig, I., Harrington, H., et al. (2003). Influence of life stress on depression: Moderation by a polymorphism in the 5-*HTT* gene. *Science, 301,* 386–389.

Cassidy, J., Parke, R., Butkovsky, L., & Braungart, J. (1992). Family peer connections: The roles of emotional expressiveness within the family and children's understanding of emotions. *Child Development, 63,* 603–618.

Cassidy, K. W., Werner, R. S., Rourke, M., Zubernis, L., & Balaraman, G. (2003). The relationship between psychological understanding and positive social behaviors. *Social Development, 12,* 198–221.

Cassidy, K. W., Fineberg, D. S., Brown, K., & Perkins, A. (2005). Theory of mind may be contagious, but you don't catch it from your twin. *Child Development, 76,* 97–106.

Chandler, M., Fritz, A., & Hala, S. (1989). Small-scale deceit: Deception as a marker of two-, three-, and four-year-olds' early theories of mind. *Child Development, 60,* 1263–1277.

Chandler, M., Sokol, B., & Wainryb, C. (2000). Beliefs about truth and beliefs about rightness. *Child Development, 71,* 91–97.

Charman, A., & Campbell, A. (1997). Reliability of theory of mind task performance by individuals with a learning disability: A research note. *Journal of Child Psychology and Psychiatry, 38,* 725–730.

Charman, A., Carroll, F., & Sturge, C. (2001). Theory of mind, executive function and social competence in boys with ADHD. *Emotional and Behavioural Difficulties, 6,* 31–49.

Charman, A., Ruffman, T., & Clements, W. (2002). Is there a gender difference in false belief development? *Social Development, 11,* 1–10.

Chasiotis, A., Kiessling, F., Campos, D., & Hofer, J. (2006). Theory of mind and inhibitory control in three cultures: Conflict inhibition predicts false belief understanding in Germany, Costa Rica and Cameroon. *International Journal of Behavioral Development, 30,* 249–260.

Cheung, H., Hsuan-Chih, C., Creed, N., Ng, L., Wang, S., & Mo, L. (2004). Relative roles of general and complementation language in theory-of-mind development: Evidence from Cantonese and English. *Child Development, 75,* 1155–1170.

Chouinard, M. (2007). Children's questions: A mechanism for cognitive development. *Monographs of the Society for Research in Child Development, 72,* 1–121.

Cicchetti, D. (1993). Developmental psychopathology: Reactions, reflections, projections. *Developmental Review, 13,* 471–502.

Clark, J., Whitall, J., & Phillips, S. (1988). Human interlimb coordination: The first 6 months of independent walking. *Developmental Psychobiology, 21,* 445–456.

Clements, W., & Perner, J. (1994). Implicit understanding of belief. *Cognitive Development, 9,* 377–397.

Cohen, L. (2004). Uses and misuses of habituation and related preference paradigms. *Infant and Child Development, 13,* 349–352.

Coie, J., & Dodge, K. (1983). Continuities and changes in children's social status: A five-year longitudinal study. *Merrill-Palmer Quarterly, 29,* 261–282.

Coie, J., Dodge, K., & Kupersmidt, H. (1990). Peer group behaviour and social status. In S. R. Asher & J. D. Coie (Eds.), *Peer rejection in childhood* (pp. 17–59). New York, NY: Cambridge University Press.

Cole, K., & Mitchell, P. (1998). Family background in relation to deceptive ability and understanding of the mind. *Social Development, 7,* 181–197.

Cole, K., & Mitchell, P. (2000). Siblings in the development of executive control and a theory of mind. *British Journal of Developmental Psychology, 18,* 279–295.

Colvert, E., Rutter, M., Beckett, C., Castle, J., Groothues, C., Hawkins, A., et al. (2008). Emotional difficulties in early adolescence following severe early deprivation: Findings from the English and Romanian adoptees study. *Development and Psychopathology, 20,* 547–567.

Comay, J. (2009). *Individual differences in narrative perspective-taking and theory of mind.* PhD thesis, University of Ontario, Toronto, Canada.

Conger, K., & Conger, R. (1994). Differential parenting and change in sibling differences in delinquency. *Journal of Family Psychology, 8,* 287–302.

Conry-Murray, C., & Smetana, J. (2008). Going out of your mind: Broadening the social in social reasoning. *Human Development, 51,* 136–142.

Conti-Ramsden, G., Simkin, Z., & Botting, N. (2006). The prevalence of autistic spectrum disorders in adolescents with a history of specific language impairment (SLI). *Journal of Child Psychology and Psychiatry and Allied Disciplines, 47,* 621–628.

Coplan, R., Findlay, L., & Nelson, L. (2004). Characteristics of preschoolers with lower perceived competence *Journal of Abnormal Child Psychology, 32,* 399–408.

Corcoran, R. (2003). Inductive reasoning and the understanding of intention in schizophrenia. *Cognitive Neuropsychiatry, 8,* 223–235.

Corina, D., & Singleton, J. (2009). Developmental social cognitive neuroscience: Insights from deafness. *Child Development, 80,* 952–967.

Correa-Chávez, M., & Rogoff, B. (2009). Children's attention to interactions directed to others: Guatemalan Mayan and European American patterns. *Developmental Psychology, 45,* 630–641.

Corriveau, K., Harris, P., Meins, E., Fernyhough, C., Arnott, B., Elliott, L., et al. (2009). Young children's trust in their mother's claims: Longitudinal links with attachment security in infancy. *Child Development, 80,* 750–761.

Costello, E., Compton, S., Keeler, G., & Angold, A. (2003). Relationships between poverty and psychopathology: A natural experiment. *Journal of the American Medical Association, 290,* 2023–2029.

Côté, S., Tremblay, R., Nagin, D., Zoccolillo, M., & Vitaro, F. (2002). The development of impulsivity, fearfulness, and helpfulness during childhood: Patterns of consistency and change in the trajectories of boys and girls. *Journal of Child Psychology and Psychiatry, 43,* 609–618.

Cowan, P., Cowan, C., Cohen, N., Pruett, M., & Pruett, K. (2008). Supporting fathers' engagement with their kids. In D. Berrick & N. Gilbert (Eds.), *Raising children: Emerging needs, modern risks and social responses* (pp. 44–80). New York, NY: Oxford University Press.

Cowan, P., Cowan, C., Pruett, M., Pruett, K., & Wong, J. (2009). Promoting fathers' engagement with children: Preventive interventions for low-income families. *Journal of Marriage and Family, 71,* 663–679.

Crick, N., Casas, J., & Mosher, M. (1997). Relational and overt aggression in preschool. *Developmental Psychology, 33,* 570–588.

Crick, N., & Dodge, K. (1994). A review and reformulation of social information processing mechanisms in children's social adjustment. *Psychological Bulletin, 115,* 74–101.

Crick, N., & Dodge, K. (1996). Social information-processing mechanisms in reactive and proactive aggression. *Child Development, 67,* 993–1002.

Crick, N., & Grotpeter, J. (1996). Children's treatment by peers: Victims of relational and overt aggression. *Development and Psychopathology, 8,* 367–380.

Csibra, G., & Southgate, V. (2006). Evidence for infants' understanding of false beliefs should not be dismissed. *Trends in Cognitive Sciences, 10,* 4–5.

Cummings, E., Keller, P., & Davies, P. (2005). Towards a family process model of maternal and paternal depressive symptoms: Exploring multiple relations with child and family functioning. *Journal of Child Psychology and Psychiatry and Allied Disciplines, 46,* 479–489.

Cutting, A., & Dunn, J. (1999). Theory of mind, emotion understanding, language, and family background: Individual differences and interrelations. *Child Development, 70,* 853–865.

Cutting, A., & Dunn, J. (2002). The cost of understanding other people: Social cognition predicts young children's sensitivity to criticism. *Journal of Child Psychology and Psychiatry, 43,* 849–860.

Darling, N., & Steinberg, L. (1993). Parenting style as context: An integrative model. *Psychological Bulletin, 113,* 487–496.

Davis-Unger, A., & Carlson, S. (2008a). Children's teaching skills: The role of theory of mind and executive function. *Mind, Brain, and Education, 2,* 128–135.

Davis-Unger, A., & Carlson, S. (2008b). Development of teaching skills and relations to theory of mind in preschoolers. *Journal of Cognition and Development, 9,* 26–45.

de Rosnay, M., Cooper, P., Tsigaras, N., & Murray, L. (2006). Transmission of social anxiety from mother to infant: An experimental study using a social referencing paradigm. *Behaviour Research and Therapy, 44,* 1165–1175.

de Rosnay, M., & Harris, P. L. (2005, April). *Maternal comments on strange-situation videos: Natural clusters, and links with child attachment status and emotion understanding.* Poster presented at the biennial meeting of the Society for Research in Child Development, Atlanta, GA.

de Rosnay, M., & Hughes, C. (2006). Conversation and theory of mind: Do children talk their way to socio-cognitive understanding? *British Journal of Developmental Psychology, 24,* 7–37.

de Rosnay, M., Pons, F., Harris, P., & Morrell, J. (2004). A lag between understanding false belief and emotion attribution in young children: Relationships with linguistic ability and mothers' mental-state language. *British Journal of Developmental Psychology, 22,* 197–218.

de Vignemont, F. (2009). Drawing the boundary between low-level and high-level mindreading. *Philosophical Studies, 144,* 457–466.

de Villiers, J., & de Villiers, P. (2000). Linguistic determination and the understanding of false beliefs. In P. Mitchell & K. Riggs (Eds.), *Children's reasoning and the mind* (pp. 191–228). Hove, UK: Psychology Press.

de Villiers, P. (2005). Language as a causal factor in developing a representational theory of mind: What deaf children tell us. In J. Astington & J. Baird (Eds.), *Why language matters for theory of mind* (pp. 186–219). Oxford, UK: Oxford University Press.

Deater-Deckard, K., & O'Connor, T. (2000). Parent–child mutuality in early childhood: Two behavioral genetic studies. *Developmental Psychology, 36,* 561–570.

Deater-Deckard, K., & Petrill, S. (2004). Parent–child dyadic mutuality and child behavior problems: An investigation of gene–environment processes. *Journal of Child Psychology and Psychiatry, 45,* 1171–1179.

Deater-Deckard, K., Pylas, M., & Petrill, S. (1997). *Parent–Child Interactive System (PARCHISY).* London, UK: Unpublished.

Dekovic, M., & Gerris, J. (1994). Developmental analysis of social cognitive and behavioral differences between popular and rejected children. *Journal of Applied Developmental Psychology, 15,* 367–386.

Denham, S. (1986). Social cognition, prosocial behavior, and emotion in preschoolers: Contextual validation. *Child Development, 57,* 194–201.

Denham, S., Caverly, S., Schmidt, M., Blair, K., DeMulder, E., Caal, S., et al. (2002). Preschool understanding of emotions: Contributions to classroom anger and aggression. *Journal of Child Psychology and Psychiatry and Allied Disciplines, 43*, 901–916.

Denham, S., & Couchoud, E. (1990). Young preschoolers' ability to identify emotions in equivocal situations. *Child Study Journal, 20*, 153–169.

Denham, S., & Kochanoff, A. (2002). Parental contributions to preschoolers' understanding of emotion. *Marriage and Family Review, 34*, 311–343.

Denham, S., Zoller, D., & Couchoud, E. (1994). Socialisation of preschoolers' emotion understanding. *Developmental Psychology, 30*, 928–936.

Dennett, D. (1978). Beliefs about beliefs. *Behavioural and Brain Sciences, 1*, 568–570.

Dennis, M., Agostino, A., Roncadin, C., & Levin, H. (2009). Theory of mind depends on domain-general executive functions of working memory and cognitive inhibition in children with traumatic brain injury. *Journal of Clinical and Experimental Neuropsychology, 31*, 835–847.

Dennis, M., Barnes, M., Wilkinson, M., & Humphreys, R. (1998). How children with head injury represent real and deceptive emotion in short narratives. *Brain and Language, 61*, 450–483.

Dennis, M., Purvis, K., Barnes, M., Wilkinson, M., & Winner, E. (2001). Understanding of literal truth, ironic criticism, and deceptive praise following childhood head injury. *Brain and Language, 78*, 1–16.

Devine, R. T., & Hughes, C. (2010). Theory of Mind at the Movies. The Development of a New Measure of Theory of Mind for Older Children and Adolescents. Poster presented at the Developmental Section Meeting of the British Psychological Society, London (September).

Diamond, A. (1988). Abilities and neural mechanisms underlying A not B performance. *Child Development, 59*, 523–527.

Diamond, A., & Goldman-Rakic, P. (1989). Comparison of human infants and rhesus monkeys on Piaget's A-not-B task: Evidence for dependence on dorsolateral prefrontal cortex. *Experimental Brain Research, 74*, 24–40.

Dienes, Z., & Perner, J. (1999). A theory of implicit and explicit knowledge. *Behavioral and Brain Sciences, 22*, 735–808.

Dix, T. (1991). The affective organization of parenting: Adaptive and maladaptative processes. *Psychological Bulletin, 110*, 3–25.

Dix, T., & Meunier, L. (2009). Depressive symptoms and parenting competence: An analysis of 13 regulatory processes. *Developmental Review, 29*, 45–68.

Dodge, K. (2006). Translational science in action: Hostile attributional style and the development of aggressive behavior problems. *Development and Psychopathology, 18*, 791–814.

Dodge, K., & Coie, J. (1987). Social-information-processing factors in reactive and proactive aggression in children's peer groups. *Journal of Personality and Social Psychology, 53*, 1146–1158.

Dodge, K., Lansford, J., Burks, V., Bates, J., Pettit, G., Fontaine, R., et al. (2003). Peer rejection and social information-processing factors in the development of aggressive behavior problems in children. *Child Development, 74*, 374–393.

Dodge, K., Pettit, G., Bates, J., & Valente, E. (1995). Social information-processing patterns partially mediate the effect of early physical abuse on later conduct problems. *Journal of Abnormal Psychology, 104*, 632–643.

Dodge, K., & Somberg, D. (1987). Hostile attributional biases among aggressive boys are exacerbated under conditions of threat to the self. *Child Development, 58*, 213–224.

Dunbar, R. (2003). The social brain: Mind, language, and society in evolutionary perspective. *Annual Review of Anthropology, 32*, 163–181.

Duncan, J. (2005). Frontal lobe function and general intelligence: Why it matters. *Cortex, 41*, 215–217.

Dunn, J. (1988). *The beginnings of social understanding* (1st ed.). Cambridge, MA: Harvard University Press.

Dunn, J. (1994). Changing minds and changing relationships. In C. Lewis & P. Mitchell (Eds.), *Origins of an understanding of mind* (pp. 297–310). Hillsdale, NJ: Lawrence Erlbaum Associates, Inc.

Dunn, J. (1995). Children as psychologists: The later correlates of individual differences in understanding of emotions and other minds. *Cognition and Emotion, 9*, 187–201.

Dunn, J. (1999). Siblings, friends, and the development of social understanding. In W. Collins & B. Laursen (Eds.), *Relationships as developmental contexts: The Minnesota symposia on child psychology* (Vol. 30, pp. 263–279). Mahwah, NJ: Lawrence Erlbaum Associates, Inc.

Dunn, J. (2000). State of the art: Siblings. *The Psychologist, 13*, 244–248.

Dunn, J. (2004). *Children's friendships: The beginnings of intimacy.* London, UK: Blackwell.

Dunn, J., Bretherton, I., & Munn, P. (1987). Conversations about feeling states between mothers and their young children. *Developmental Psychology, 23*, 132–139.

Dunn, J., & Brophy, M. (2005). Communication, relationships, and individual differences in children's understanding of mind. In J. Astington & J. Baird (Eds.), *Why language matters for theory of mind* (pp. 50–69). Oxford, UK: Oxford University Press.

Dunn, J., Brown, J., & Beardsall, L. (1991a). Family talk about feeling states and children's later understanding of others' emotions. *Developmental Psychology, 27*, 448–455.

Dunn, J., Brown, J., & Maguire, M. (1995). The development of children's moral sensibility: Individual differences and emotion understanding. *Developmental Psychology, 31*, 649–659.

Dunn, J., Brown, J., Slomkowski, C., Tesla, C., & Youngblade, L. (1991b). Young children's understanding of other people's feelings and beliefs: Individual differences and their antecedents. *Child Development, 62*, 1352–1366.

Dunn, J., & Cutting, A. (1999). Understanding others, and individual differences in friendship interactions in young children. *Social Development, 8*, 201–219.

Dunn, J., Cutting, A., & Fisher, N. (2002). Old friends, new friends: Predictors of children's perspective on their friends at school. *Child Development, 73*, 621–635.

Dunn, J., & Hughes, C. (2001). "I got some swords and you're dead!": Fantasy and friendship in young "hard to manage" children. *Child Development, 72*, 491–505.

Dunn, J., & Kendrick, C. (1980). The arrival of a sibling: Changes in patterns of interaction between mother and first-born child. *Journal of Child Psychology and Psychiatry and Allied Disciplines, 21*, 119–132.

Dunn, J., & Munn, P. (1985). Becoming a family member: Family conflict and the development of social understanding in the second year. *Child Development, 56*, 764–774.

Dunn, L. (1997). *British Picture Vocabulary Scale – Revised.* Windsor, UK: NFER-Nelson.

Duranti, A. (2006). The social ontology of intentions. *Discourse Studies, 8*, 31–40.

Duveen, G., & Psaltis, C. (2008). The constructive role of asymmetries in social interaction. In U. Mueller, J. Carpendale, N. Budwig, & B. Sokol (Eds.), *Social life and social knowledge: Toward a process account of development* (pp. 183–204). Mahwah, NJ: Lawrence Erlbaum Associates, Inc.

Dyer, J., Shatz, M., & Wellman, H. (2000). Children's books as a source of mental state information. *Cognitive Development, 15*, 17–37.

Eisenberg, N., & Fabes, R. (1998). Prosocial development. In W. Damon (Ed.), *Handbook of child psychology* (Vol. 3, pp. 701–778). New York, NY: Wiley.

Eisenmajer, R., & Prior, M. (1991). Cognitive linguistic correlates of "theory of mind" ability in autistic children. *British Journal of Developmental Psychology, 9*, 351–364.

Elliott, C., Murray, D., & Pearson, L. (1983). *British abilities scales.* Windsor, UK: NFER-Nelson.

Ensor, R. (2009, April). *Dynamics of mother–child talk from ages 2 to 6: Implications for children's social understanding.* Paper presented at the Society for Research in Child Development, Denver, USA.

Ensor, R., & Hughes, C. (2008). Content or connectedness? Early family talk and theory of mind in the toddler and preschool years. *Child Development, 79*, 201–216.

Ensor, R., Spencer, D., & Hughes, C. (in press). "You feel sad?" Emotion understanding mediates predictors of prosocial behaviour: Findings from 2 to 4 years. *Social Development.* (Available online at: doi: 10.1111/j.1467-9507.2009.00572.x)

Fahie, C., & Symons, D. (2003). Executive functioning and theory of mind in children clinically referred for attention and behavior problems. *Journal of Applied Developmental Psychology, 24*, 51–73.

Farmer, M. (2000). Language and social cognition in children with specific language impairment. *Journal of Child Psychology and Psychiatry and Allied Disciplines, 41*, 627–636.

Farrant, B., Fletcher, J., & Maybery, M. (2006). Specific language impairment, theory of mind, and visual perspective taking: Evidence for simulation theory and the developmental role of language. *Child Development, 77*, 1842–1853.

Fernald, A. (1993). Approval and disapproval: Infant responsiveness to vocal affect in familiar and unfamiliar languages. *Child Development, 64*, 657–674.

Filippova, E., & Astington, J. (2008). Further development in social reasoning revealed in discourse irony understanding. *Child Development, 79*, 126–138.

Flavell, J., Green, F., & Flavell, E. (1995). Young children's knowledge about thinking. *Monographs of the Society for Research in Child Development, 60*, 1–96.

Flavell, J., Green, F., & Flavell, E. R. (1986). Development of knowledge about the appearance–reality distinction. *Monographs of the Society for Research in Child Development, 51*, 1–87.

Flynn, E. (2007). The role of inhibitory control in false belief understanding. *Infant and Child Development, 16*, 53–69.

Flynn, E., O'Malley, C., & Wood, D. (2004). A longitudinal, microgenetic study of the emergence of false belief understanding and inhibition skills. *Developmental Science, 7*, 103–115.

Fonagy, P., Redfern, S., & Charman, T. (1997). The relationship between belief–desire reasoning and a projective measure of attachment security (SAT). *British Journal of Developmental Psychology, 15*, 51–61.

Fonagy, P., & Target, M. (1997). Attachment and reflective function: Their role in self-organization. *Development and Psychopathology, 9*, 679–700.

Foote, R., & Holmes-Lonergan, H. (2003). Sibling conflict and theory of mind. *British Journal of Developmental Psychology, 21*, 45–58.

Forman, D., O'Hara, M., Stuart, S., Gorman, L., Larsen, K., & Coy, K. (2007). Effective treatment for postpartum depression is not sufficient to improve the developing mother–child relationship. *Development and Psychopathology, 19*, 585–602.

Freeman, D. (2007). Suspicious minds: The psychology of persecutory delusions. *Clinical Psychology Review, 27*, 425–457.

Freud, S. (1963). *The history of an infantile neurosis: The standard edition of the complete psychological works of Sigmund Freud* (Trans. J. Strachey, A. Strachey, A. Freud & A. Tyson, Vol. XVII). London, UK: Hogarth Press and Institute of Psychoanalysis. (Original work published 1918.)

Frick, P., & White, S. (2008). Research review: The importance of callous-unemotional traits for developmental models of aggressive and antisocial behavior. *Journal of Child Psychology and Psychiatry and Allied Disciplines, 49*, 359–375.

Friedman, O., & Petrashek, A. (2009). Children do not follow the rule "ignorance means getting it wrong". *Journal of Experimental Child Psychology, 102*, 114–121.

Frith, C., & Frith, U. (1999). Interacting minds – A biological basis. *Science, 286*, 1692–1695.

Frith, C., & Frith, U. (2000). The physiological basis of theory of mind: Functional neuroimaging studies. In S. Baron-Cohen, H. Tager-Flusberg, & D. Cohen (Eds.), *Understanding other minds: Perspectives from developmental cognitive neuroscience* (pp. 334–356). Oxford, UK: Oxford University Press.

Frith, U. (2004). Emanuel Miller lecture: Confusions and controversies about Asperger syndrome. *Journal of Child Psychology and Psychiatry and Allied Disciplines, 45*, 672–686.

Frith, U., & Frith, C. (2001). The biological basis of social interaction. *Current Directions in Psychological Science, 10*, 151–155.

Frith, U., Happé, F., & Siddons, F. (1994). Autism and theory of mind in everyday life. *Social Development, 3*, 108–124.

Frye, D., Zelazo, P. D., & Palfai, T. (1995). Theory of mind and rule-based reasoning. *Cognitive Development, 10*, 483–527.

Gallagher, H. L., Happé, F., Brunswick, N., Fletcher, P. C., Frith, U., & Frith, C. D. (2000). Reading the mind in cartoons and stories: An fMRI study of "theory of mind" in verbal and nonverbal tasks. *Neuropsychologia, 38*, 11–21.

Garcia, M. M., Shaw, D. S., Winslow, E. B., & Yaggi, K. E. (2000). Destructive sibling conflict and the development of conduct problems in young boys. *Developmental Psychology, 36*, 44–53.

Garner, P., Jones, D., Gaddy, G., & Rennie, K. (1997). Low-income mothers' conversations about emotions and their children's emotional competence. *Social Development, 6*, 37–52.

Gasser, L., & Keller, M. (2009). Are the competent the morally good? Perspective taking and moral motivation of children involved in bullying. *Social Development, 18*, 798–816.

Gauvain, M. (1998). Cognitive development in social and cultural context. *Current Directions in Psychological Science, 7*, 188–192.

Genesee, F., Nicoladis, E., & Paradis, J. (1995). Language differentiation in early bilingual development. *Journal of Child Language, 22*, 611–631.

Gerstadt, C., Hong, Y., & Diamond, A. (1994). The relationship between cognition and action: Performance of children 3½–7 years old on a Stroop-like day–night test. *Cognition, 53*, 129–153.

Gilmour, J., Hill, B., Place, M., & Skuse, D. (2004). Social communication deficits in conduct disorder: A clinical and community survey. *Journal of Child Psychology and Psychiatry, 45*, 967–978.

Gliga, T., Elsabbagh, M., Andravizou, A., & Johnson, M. (2009). Faces attract infants' attention in complex displays. *Infancy, 14,* 550–562.

Gnepp, J., & Hess, D. (1986). Children's understanding of verbal and facial display rules. *Developmental Psychology, 22,* 103–108.

Goodman, R. (2001). Psychometric properties of the Strengths and Difficulties Questionnaire. *Journal of the American Academy of Child and Adolescent Psychiatry, 40,* 1337–1345.

Gopnik, A., & Astington, J. (1988). Children's understanding of representational change and its relation to the understanding of false belief and the appearance reality distinction. *Child Development, 59,* 26–37.

Gopnik, A., & Wellman, H. (1994). The theory-theory. In L. Hirschfeld & S. Gelman (Eds.), *Mapping the mind: Domain specificity in cognition and culture* (pp. 257–293). New York, NY: Cambridge University Press.

Gorsuch, R. (1997). Exploratory factor analysis: Its role in item analysis. *Journal of Personality Assessment, 68,* 532–560.

Gottman, J. (1983). How children become friends. *Monographs of the Society for Research in Child Development, 48,* Serial no. 201.

Grant, C., Boucher, J., Riggs, K., & Grayson, A. (2005). Moral understanding in children with autism. *Autism, 9,* 317–331.

Greig, A., & Howe, D. (2001). Social understanding, attachment security of preschool children and maternal mental health. *British Journal of Developmental Psychology, 19,* 381–393.

Gross, H., Shaw, D., & Moilanen, K. (2008). Reciprocal associations between boys' externalising problems and mothers' depressive symptoms. *Journal of Abnormal Child Psychology, 36,* 693–709.

Guajardo, N. R., & Watson, A. C. (2002). Narrative discourse and theory of mind development. *Journal of Genetic Psychology, 163,* 305–325.

Hala, S., Hug, S., & Henderson, A. (2003). Executive function and false-belief understanding in preschool children: Two tasks are harder than one. *Journal of Cognition and Development, 4,* 275–298.

Hala, S., & Russell, J. (2001). Executive control within strategic deception: A window on early cognitive development? *Journal of Experimental Child Psychology, 80,* 112–141.

Hale, C. M., & Tager-Flusberg, H. (2003). The influence of language on theory of mind: A training study. *Developmental Science, 6,* 346–359.

Halligan, S., Cooper, P., Healy, S., & Murray, L. (2007). The attribution of hostile intent in mothers, fathers and their children. *Journal of Abnormal Child Psychology, 35,* 594–604.

Happé, F. (1994). An advanced test of theory of mind: Understanding of story characters' thoughts and feelings by able autistic, mentally handicapped, and normal children and adults. *Journal of Autism and Development Disorders, 24,* 129–154.

Happé, F. (1995). The role of age and verbal ability in the theory of mind task performance of subjects with autism. *Child Development, 66,* 843–855.

Happé, F. (2003). Theory of mind and the self. *Annals of the New York Academy of Sciences, 1001,* 134–144.

Happé, F., & Loth, E. (2002). "Theory of mind" and tracking speakers' intentions. *Mind and Language, 17,* 24–36.

Harman, G. (1978). Studying the chimpanzee's theory of mind. *Brain and Behavioral Sciences, 1,* 591.

Harris, P. (1975). Development of search and object permanence during infancy. *Psychological Bulletin, 82*, 332–344.

Harris, P. (1992). From simulation to folk psychology: The case for development. *Mind and Language, 7*, 120–144.

Harris, P. (1994). The child's understanding of emotion: Developmental change and the family environment. *Journal of Child Psychology and Psychiatry, 35*, 3–28.

Harris, P. (2007). Commentary: Time for questions. *Monographs of the Society for Research in Child Development, 72*, 113–120.

Harris, P., de Rosnay, M., & Pons, F. (2005). Language and children's understanding of mental states. *Current Directions in Psychological Science, 14*, 69–73.

Harris, P., & Gross, D. (1988). Children's understanding of real and apparent emotion. In J. Astington, P. Harris, & D. Olson (Eds.), *Developing theories of mind* (pp. 295–314). New York, NY: Cambridge University Press.

Harris, P., Johnson, C., Hutton, D., Andrews, G., & Cooke, T. (1989). Young children's theory of mind and emotion. *Cognition and Emotion, 3*, 379–400.

Harris, P., & Kavanaugh, R. D. (1993). Young children's understanding of pretense. *Monographs of the Society for Research in Child Development, 58*, Serial no. 231.

Harris, P., & Koenig, M. (2006). Trust in testimony: How children learn about science and religion. *Child Development, 77*, 505–524.

Harris, P., & Leevers, H. (2000). Pretending, imagery and self-awareness in autism. In S. Baron-Cohen, H. Tager-Flusberg, & D. Cohen (Eds.), *Understanding other minds: Perspectives from developmental cognitive neuroscience* (pp. 182–202). Oxford, UK: Oxford University Press.

Harris, P., Núñez, M., & Brett, C. (2001). Let's swap: Early understanding of social exchange by British and Nepali children. *Memory and Cognition, 29*, 757–764.

Hart, B., & Risley, T. (1992). American parenting of language-learning children: Persisting differences in family child interactions observed in natural home environments. *Developmental Psychology, 28*, 1096–1105.

Hart, B., & Risley, T. (1995). *Meaningful differences in the everyday experience of young American children.* Baltimore, MD: Brookes.

Harter, S., & Jackson, B. (1993). Young adolescents' perceptions of the link between low self-worth and depressed affect. *Journal of Early Adolescence, 33*, 383–407.

Harter, S., & Pike, R. (1984). The pictorial scale of perceived competence and social acceptance for young children. *Child Development, 55*, 1969–1982.

Hay, D., Castle, J., Davies, L., Demetriou, H., & Stimson, C. (1999). Prosocial action in very early childhood. *Journal of Child Psychology and Psychiatry, 40*, 905–916.

Heyman, G., Dweck, C., & Cain, K. (1992). Young children's vulnerability to self-blame and helplessness: Relationship to beliefs about goodness. *Child Development, 63*, 401–415.

Hobson, P. R., Chidambi, G., Lee, A., & Meyer, J. (2006). Foundations for self-awareness: An exploration through autism. *Monographs of the Society for Research in Child Development, 71*(2), vii–166.

Hobson, R. (1991). Against the theory of "theory of mind". *British Journal of Developmental Psychology, 9*, 33–51.

Hoff, E. (2003). The specificity of environmental influence: Socioeconomic status affects early vocabulary development via maternal speech. *Child Development, 74*, 1368–1378.

Hoglund, W., & Leadbeater, B. (2007). Managing threat: Do social-cognitive processes mediate the link between peer victimization and adjustment problems in early adolescence? *Journal of Research on Adolescence, 17*, 525–540.

Holmes, H. A., Black, C., & Miller, S. A. (1996). A cross-task comparison of false belief understanding in a Head-Start population. *Journal of Experimental Child Psychology*, *63*, 263–285.

Hornak, J., O'Doherty, J., Bramham, J., Rolls, E., Morris, R., Bullock, P., et al. (2004). Reward-related reversal learning after surgical excisions in orbito-frontal or dorsolateral prefrontal cortex in humans. *Journal of Cognitive Neuroscience*, *16*, 463–478.

Howe, N., & Ross, H. (1990). Socialization, perspective-taking, and the sibling relationship. *Developmental Psychology*, *26*, 160–165.

Howlin, P., Mawhood, L., & Rutter, M. (2000). Autism and developmental receptive language disorder–A follow-up comparison in early adult life. II: Social, behavioural, and psychiatric outcomes. *Journal of Child Psychology and Psychiatry and Allied Disciplines*, *41*, 561–578.

Hoyle, R., & Kenny, D. (1999). Sample size, reliability, and tests of statistical mediation. In R. Hoyle (Ed.), *Statistical strategies for small sample research* (pp. 195–222). Thousand Oaks, CA: Sage.

Hsu, H., & Lavelli, M. (2005). Perceived and observed parenting behavior in American and Italian first-time mothers across the first 3 months. *Infant Behavior and Development*, *28*, 503–518.

Hubbard, J., McAuliffe, M., Morrow, M., & Romano, L. (2010). Reactive and proactive aggression in childhood and adolescence: Precursors, outcomes, processes, experiences, and measurement. *Journal of Personality*, *78*, 95–118.

Huey, E., Krueger, F., & Grafman, J. (2006). Representations in the human prefrontal cortex. *Current Directions in Psychological Science*, *15*, 167–171.

Hughes, C. (1998a). Executive function in preschoolers: Links with theory of mind and verbal ability. *British Journal of Developmental Psychology*, *16*, 233–253.

Hughes, C. (1998b). Finding your marbles: Does preschoolers' strategic behaviour predict later understanding of mind? *Developmental Psychology*, *34*, 1326–1339.

Hughes, C. (2001). Executive dysfunction in autism: Its nature and implications for the everyday problems experienced by individuals with autism. In J. Burack, T. Charman, N. Yirmiya, & P. Zelazo (Eds.), *The development of autism* (pp. 255–274). Mahwah, NJ: Lawrence Erlbaum Associates, Inc.

Hughes, C. (2005). Genetic and environmental influences on individual differences in language and theory of mind: Common or distinct? In J. Astington & J. Baird (Eds.), *Why language matters for theory of mind* (pp. 319–339). Oxford, UK: Oxford University Press.

Hughes, C., Adlam, A., Happé, F., Jackson, J., Taylor, A., & Caspi, A. (2000a). Good test–retest reliability for standard and advanced false-belief tasks across a wide range of abilities. *Journal of Child Psychology and Psychiatry*, *41*, 483–490.

Hughes, C., & Cutting, A. (1999). Nature, nurture and individual differences in early understanding of mind. *Psychological Science*, *10*, 429–432.

Hughes, C., Cutting, A., & Dunn, J. (2001). Acting nasty in the face of failure? Longitudinal observations of "hard to manage" children playing a rigged competitive game with a friend. *Journal of Abnormal Child Psychology*, *29*, 403–416.

Hughes, C., Deater-Deckard, K., & Cutting, A. (1999). "Speak roughly to your little boy?" Sex differences in the relations between parenting and preschoolers' understanding of mind. *Social Development*, *8*, 143–160.

Hughes, C., Devine, R., Koyasu, M., Mizokawa, A., & Ensor, R. (2010a, April). *Contrasts between British and Japanese children's understanding of mistaken beliefs: Do comparisons show measurement invariance?*. Paper presented at the Indian Social Sciences Research Council International Workshop on Child Wellbeing and Education, Bangalore, India.

Hughes, C., & Dunn, J. (1997). "Pretend you didn't know": Preschoolers' talk about mental states in pretend play. *Cognitive Development, 12*, 477–499.

Hughes, C., & Dunn, J. (1998). Understanding mind and emotion: Longitudinal associations with mental-state talk between young friends. *Developmental Psychology, 34*, 1026–1037.

Hughes, C., & Dunn, J. (2000). Hedonism or empathy? Hard-to-manage children's moral awareness, and links with cognitive and maternal characteristics. *British Journal of Developmental Psychology, 18*, 227–245.

Hughes, C., & Dunn, J. (2002). "When I say a naughty word." Children's accounts of anger and sadness in self, mother and friend: Longitudinal findings from ages four to seven. *British Journal of Developmental Psychology, 20*, 515–535.

Hughes, C., Dunn, J., & White, A. (1998). Trick or treat?: Uneven understanding of mind and emotion and executive function among "hard to manage" preschoolers. *Journal of Child Psychology and Psychiatry and Allied Disciplines, 39*, 981–994.

Hughes, C., & Ensor, R. (2005). Theory of mind and executive function in 2-year-olds: A family affair? *Developmental Neuropsychology, 28*, 645–668.

Hughes, C., & Ensor, R. (2006). Behavioural problems in two-year-olds: Links with individual differences in theory of mind, executive function and negative parenting. *Journal of Child Psychology and Psychiatry and Allied Disciplines, 47*, 488–497.

Hughes, C., & Ensor, R. (2007a). Executive function and theory of mind: Predictive relations from ages 2 to 4 years. *Developmental Psychology, 43*, 1447–1459.

Hughes, C., & Ensor, R. (2007b). Positive and protective: Effects of early theory of mind on preschool problem behaviours. *Journal of Child Psychology and Psychiatry and Allied Disciplines, 48*, 1025–1032.

Hughes, C., & Ensor, R. (2008). Does executive function matter for preschoolers' problem behaviors? *Journal of Abnormal Child Psychology, 36*, 1–14.

Hughes, C., & Ensor, R. (2009). Independence and interplay between maternal and child risk factors for preschool problem behaviors. *International Journal of Behavioral Development, 33*, 1–11.

Hughes, C., & Ensor, R. (in press-a). Executive function trajectories across the transition to school predict externalizing and internalizing behaviors and children's self-perceived academic success at age 6. *Journal of Experimental Child Psychology, Special Issue on Executive Functions.* (Available online at: doi:10.1016/j.physletb.2003.10.071)

Hughes, C., & Ensor, R. (in press-b). Individual differences in false-belief understanding are stable from ages 3 to 6 and predict children's mental state talk with friends. *Journal of Experimental Child Psychology.* (Available online at: http://dx.doi.org/10.1016/j.jecp.2010.07.012)

Hughes, C., Ensor, R., Wilson, A., & Graham, A. (2010b). Tracking executive function across the transition to school: A latent variable approach. *Developmental Neuropsychology, 35*, 20–36.

Hughes, C., Fujisawa, K., Ensor, R., Lecce, S., & Marfleet, R. (2006). Cooperation and conversations about the mind: A study of individual differences in two-year-olds and their siblings. *British Journal of Developmental Psychology, 24*, 53–72.

Hughes, C., Jaffee, S., Happé, F., Taylor, A., Caspi, A., & Moffitt, T. (2005). Origins of individual differences in theory of mind: From nature to nurture? *Child Development, 76*, 356–370.

Hughes, C., Lecce, S., & Wilson, C. (2007). "Do you know what I want?" Preschoolers' talk about desires, thoughts and feelings in their conversations with sibs and friends. *Cognition and Emotion, 21*, 330–350.

Hughes, C., Marks, A., Ensor, R., & Lecce, S. (in press). Who's she talking to? Children's talk about inner states with younger siblings and mothers. *Social Development*. (Available online at: doi: 10.1111/j.1467-9507.2009.00561.x)

Hughes, C., Oksanen, H., Taylor, A., Jackson, J., Murray, L., Caspi, A., et al. (2002). "I'm gonna beat you!" SNAP!: an observational paradigm for assessing young children's disruptive behaviour in competitive play. *Journal of Child Psychology and Psychiatry*, *43*, 507–516.

Hughes, C., & Russell, J. (1993). Autistic children's difficulty with mental disengagement from an object: Its implications for theories of autism. *Developmental Psychology*, *29*, 498–510.

Hughes, C., Russell, J., & Robbins, T. (1994). Evidence for central executive dysfunction in autism. *Neuropsychologia*, *32*, 477–492.

Hughes, C., White, A., Sharpen, J., & Dunn, J. (2000b). Antisocial, angry and unsympathetic: "Hard to manage" preschoolers' peer problems, and possible social and cognitive influences. *Journal of Child Psychology and Psychiatry*, *41*, 169–179.

Hui, C. H., & Triandis, H. (1985). Measurement in cross-cultural psychology: A review and comparison of strategies. *Journal of Cross-Cultural Psychology*, *16*, 131–152.

Humfress, H., O'Connor, T., Slaughter, J., Target, M., & Fonagy, P. (2002). General and relationship-specific models of social cognition: Explaining the overlap and discrepancies. *Journal of Child Psychology and Psychiatry and Allied Disciplines*, *43*, 873–883.

Iannotti, R. (1985). Naturalistic and structured assessments of prosocial behavior in preschool children: The influence of empathy and perspective taking. *Developmental Psychology*, *21*, 46–55.

Jackson, A., Brooks-Gunn, J., Huang, C.-C., & Glassman, M. (2000). Single mothers in low-wage jobs: Financial strain, parenting, and preschoolers' outcomes. *Child Development*, *71*, 1409–1423.

James, W. (1890). *The principles of psychology*. New York, NY: Holt.

Jeffrey, W., & Cohen, L. (1971). Habituation in the human infant. *Advances in Child Development and Behavior*, *6*, 63–97.

Jenkins, J., & Astington, J. (1996). Cognitive factors and family structure associated with theory of mind development in young children. *Developmental Psychology*, *32*, 70–78.

Jenkins, J., Turrell, S., Kogushi, Y., Lollis, S., & Ross, H. (2003). A longitudinal investigation of the dynamics of mental state talk in families. *Child Development*, *74*, 905–920.

Joseph, R., & Tager-Flusberg, H. (2004). The relationship of theory of mind and executive functions to symptom type and severity in children with autism. *Development and Psychopathology*, *16*, 137–155.

Judd, C., McClelland, G., & Culhane, S. (1995). Data analysis: Continuing issues in the everyday analysis of psychological data. *Annual Review of Psychology*, *46*, 433–465.

Karmiloff-Smith, A. (1992). *Beyond modularity: A developmental perspective on cognitive science*. Cambridge, MA: MIT Press.

Kaukiainen, A., Björkqvist, K., Lagerspetz, K., Österman, K., Salmivalli, C., Rothberg, S., et al. (1999). The relationships between social intelligence, empathy, and three types of aggression. *Aggressive Behavior*, *25*, 81–89.

Keenan, T., Olson, D. R., & Marini, Z. (1998). Working memory and children's developing understanding of mind. *Australian Journal of Psychology*, *50*, 76–82.

Keller, M., Edelstein, W., Schmid, C., Fang, F., & Fang, G. (1998). Reasoning about responsibilities and obligations in close relationships: A comparison across two cultures. *Developmental Psychology*, *34*, 731–741.

Keller, M., Lourenço, O., Malti, T., & Saalbach, H. (2003). The multifaceted phenomenon of "happy victimizers": A cross-cultural comparison of moral emotions. *British Journal of Developmental Psychology, 21*, 1–18.

Kiang, L., Moreno, A., & Robinson, J. (2004). Maternal preconceptions about parenting predict child temperament, maternal sensitivity, and children's empathy. *Developmental Psychology, 40*, 1081–1092.

Kiernan, K., & Mensah, F. (2009). Poverty, maternal depression, family status and children's cognitive and behavioural development in early childhood: A longitudinal study. *Journal of Social Policy, 38*, 569–588.

Kloo, D., & Perner, J. (2003). Training transfer between card sorting and false belief understanding: Helping children apply conflicting descriptions. *Child Development, 74*, 1823–1839.

Kobayashi, C., Glover, G., & Temple, E. (2006). Cultural and linguistic influence on neural bases of "theory of mind": An fMRI study with Japanese bilinguals. *Brain and Language, 98*, 210–220.

Kobayashi, C., Glover, G., & Temple, E. (2007). Cultural and linguistic effects on neural bases of "theory of mind" in American and Japanese children. *Brain Research, 1164*, 95–107.

Kobayashi, C., Glover, G., & Temple, E. (2008). Switching language switches mind: Linguistic effects on developmental neural bases of "theory of mind". *Social Cognitive and Affective Neuroscience, 3*, 62–70.

Kochanska, G. (1993). Toward a synthesis of parental socialization and child temperament in early development of conscience. *Child Development, 64*, 325–347.

Kochanska, G., Murray, K., & Harlan, E. (2000). Effortful control in early childhood: Continuity and change, antecedents, and implications for social development. *Developmental Psychology, 36*, 220–232.

Kochanska, G., Padavich, D., & Koenig, A. L. (1996). Children's narratives about hypothetical moral dilemmas and objective measures of their conscience: Mutual relations and socialization antecedents. *Child Development, 67*, 1420–1436.

Kochanska, G., Philibert, R., & Barry, R. (2009). Interplay of genes and early mother–child relationship in the development of self-regulation from toddler to preschool age. *Journal of Child Psychology and Psychiatry and Allied Disciplines, 50*, 1331–1338.

Kohlberg, L. (1984). *The psychology of moral development: The nature and validity of moral stages* (Vol. 2). San Francisco, CA: Harper Row.

Konrad, K., Gauggel, S., Manz, A., & Scholl, M. (2000). Inhibitory control in children with traumatic brain injury (TBI) and children with attention deficit/hyperactivity disorder (ADHD). *Brain Injury, 14*, 859–875.

Koster, C., Been, P., Krikhaar, E., Zwatts, F., Diepstra, H., & Van Leeuwen, T. (2005). Differences at 17 months: Productive language patterns in infants at familial risk for dyslexia and typically developing infants. *Journal of Speech, Language, and Hearing Research, 48*, 426–438.

Kovács, Á. (2009). Early bilingualism enhances mechanisms of false-belief reasoning. *Developmental Science, 12*, 48–54.

Krishnakumar, A., Buehler, C., & Barber, B. (2004). Cross-ethnic equivalence of socialization measures in European American and African American youth. *Journal of Marriage and Family, 66*, 809–820.

Kuhn, D. (2005). *Education for thinking*. Cambridge, MA: Harvard University Press.

Lagattuta, K. (2005). When you shouldn't do what you want to do: Young children's understanding of desires, rules, and emotions. *Child Development, 76*, 713–733.

Lagattuta, K. (2008). Young children's knowledge about the influence of thoughts on emotions in rule situations. *Developmental Science, 11*, 809–818.

Laible, D. (2004). Mother–child discourse in two contexts: Links with child temperament, attachment security, and socioemotional competence. *Developmental Psychology, 40*, 979–992.

Laible, D., & Thompson, R. (1998). Attachment and emotional understanding in preschool children. *Developmental Psychology, 34*, 1038–1045.

Lalonde, C. E., & Chandler, M. J. (1995). False belief understanding goes to school: On the social-emotional consequences of coming early or late to a first theory of mind. *Cognition and Emotion, 9*, 167–185.

Lamb, S., & Zakhireh, B. (1997). Toddlers' attention to the distress of peers in a day care setting. *Early Education and Development, 8*, 105–118.

Larsson, H., Viding, E., & Rijsdijk, F. (2008). Relationships between parental negativity and childhood antisocial behaviour over time: A bidirectional effects model in a longitudinal genetically informative design. *Journal of Abnormal Child Psychology, 36*, 633–645.

Lay, K., Waters, E., & Park, K. (1989). Maternal responsiveness and child compliance: The role of mood as a mediator. *Child Development, 60*, 1405–1411.

Layard, R., & Dunn, J. (2009). *A good childhood: Searching for values in a competitive age*. London, UK: Penguin.

Lecce, S., Caputi, M., & Hughes, C. (2010a). *Does sensitivity to criticism mediate the relationship between theory of mind and academic competence?* Ms submitted for publication.

Lecce, S., & Hughes, C. (2009, September). *Links between peer relationships, theory of mind and children's hopes and fears about starting secondary school: Findings from the UK and from Italy*. Paper presented at Developmental Section Meeting of the British Psychological Society, Nottingham, UK.

Lecce, S., & Hughes, C. (2010). "The Italian job?": Comparing theory of mind performance in British and Italian children. *British Journal of Developmental Psychology, 28*, 747–766.

Lecce, S., Zocchi, S., Pagnin, A., Palladino, P., & Taumoepeau, M. (2010b). Reading minds: The relation between children's mental state knowledge and their metaknowledge about reading. *Child Development, 81*, 1632–1636.

Leckman-Westin, E., Cohen, P., & Stueve, A. (2009). Maternal depression and mother–child interaction patterns: Association with toddler problems and continuity of effects to late childhood. *Journal of Child Psychology and Psychiatry and Allied Disciplines, 50*, 1176–1184.

Leekam, S. (1991). Jokes and lies: Children's understanding of intentional falsehood. In A. Whiten (Ed.), *Natural theories of mind: Evolution, development and simulation of everyday mindreading* (pp. 159–174). Oxford, UK: Blackwell.

Legerstee, M., & Varghese, J. (2001). The role of maternal affect mirroring on social expectancies in three-month-old infants. *Child Development, 72*, 1301–1313.

Leslie, A. (1987). Pretense and representation: The origins of "theory of mind". *Psychological Review, 94*, 412–426.

Leslie, A. (1994). ToMM, ToBY and agency: Core architecture and domain specificity. In L. Hirschfeld & S. Gelman (Eds.), *Mapping the mind: Domain specificity in cognition and culture* (pp. 119–148). Cambridge, UK: Cambridge University Press.

Leslie, A. (2005). Developmental parallels in understanding minds and bodies. *Trends in Cognitive Sciences, 9*, 459–462.

Leslie, A., Friedman, O., & German, T. (2004). Core mechanisms in "theory of mind". *Trends in Cognitive Sciences, 8*, 528–533.

Leslie, A., & Frith, U. (1988). Autistic children's understanding of seeing, knowing and believing. *British Journal of Developmental Psychology, 6*, 315–324.

Leslie, A., German, T., & Polizzi, P. (2005). Belief–desire reasoning as a process of selection. *Cognitive Psychology, 50*, 45–85.

Leslie, A., Mallon, R., & DiCorcia, J. (2006). Transgressors, victims, and cry babies: Is basic moral judgment spared in autism? *Social Neuroscience, 3–4*, 270–283.

Leslie, A., & Polizzi, P. (1998). Inhibitory processing in the false-belief task: Two conjectures. *Developmental Science, 1*, 247–254.

Lewis, C., Freeman, N., Kyriakidou, C., Maridaki-Kassotaki, K., & Berridge, D. (1996). Social influences on false belief access: Specific sibling influences or general apprenticeship? *Child Development, 67*, 2930–2947.

Lewis, C., Huang, Z., & Rooksby, M. (2006). Chinese preschoolers' false belief understanding: Is social knowledge underpinned by parental styles, social interactions or executive functions? *Psychologia, 49*, 252–266.

Lewis, C., Koyasu, M., Oh, S., Ogawa, A., Short, B., & Huang, Z. (2009). Culture, executive function and social understanding. *New Directions in Child and Adolescent Psychiatry, Special Issue on Social Interaction and the Development of Executive Function, 123*, 69–85.

Lewis, C., & Osborne, A. (1990). Three-year-olds' problems with false belief: Conceptual deficit or linguistic artifact? *Child Development, 61*, 1514–1519.

Lillard, A. (1993). Pretend play skills and the child's theory of mind. *Child Development, 64*, 348–371.

Lillard, A. (1997). Ethnopsychologies: Cultural variations in theories of mind. *Psychological Bulletin, 123*, 3–32.

Lillard, A. (2005). *Montessori: The science behind the genius*. New York, NY: Oxford University Press.

Lillard, A., & Witherington, D. (2004). Mothers' behavior modifications during pretense and their possible signal value for toddlers. *Developmental Psychology, 40*, 95–113.

Lind, S., & Bowler, D. (2009). Language and theory of mind in autism spectrum disorder: The relationship between complement syntax and false belief task performance. *Journal of Autism and Developmental Disorders, 39*, 929–937.

Lindsey, E., Mize, J., & Pettit, G. (1997). Mutuality in parent–child play: Consequences for children's peer competence. *Journal of Social and Personal Relationships, 14*, 523–538.

Liu, D., Wellman, H. M., Tardif, T., & Sabbagh, M. A. (2008). Theory of mind development in Chinese children: A meta-analysis of false-belief understanding across cultures and languages. *Developmental Psychology, 44*, 523–531.

Lock, A. (1980). *The guided reinvention of language*. London, UK: Academic Press.

Lockl, K., & Schneider, W. (2007). Knowledge about the mind: Links between theory of mind and later metamemory. *Child Development, 78*, 148–167.

Lohmann, H., & Tomasello, M. (2003). The role of language in the development of false belief understanding: A training study. *Child Development, 74*, 1130–1144.

Maccoby, E. (1992). The role of parents in the socialization of children: An historical overview. *Developmental Psychology, 28*, 1006–1017.

Maccoby, E., & Martin, J. (1983). Socialization in the context of the family: Parent–child interaction. In E. Hetherington & P. Mussen (Eds.), *Handbook of child psychology. Vol. 4. Socialization, personality, and social development* (4th ed., pp. 1–102). New York, NY: Wiley.

MacKinnon-Lewis, C., Starnes, R., Volling, B., & Johnson, S. (1997). Perceptions of parenting as predictors of boys' sibling and peer relations. *Developmental Psychology*, *33*, 1024–1031.

Marks, A. (2010). *Children's interactions with siblings from ages 3 to 6: Developmental trajectories and links with children's peer experiences.* PhD thesis, University of Cambridge, Cambridge, UK.

Marsh, H., Ellis, L., & Craven, R. (2002). How do preschool children feel about themselves? Unraveling measurement and multidimensional self-concept structure. *Developmental Psychology*, *38*, 376–393.

Maughan, A., Cicchetti, D., Toth, S., & Rogosch, F. (2007). Early occurring maternal depression and maternal negativity in predicting young children's emotion regulation and socioemotional difficulties. *Journal of Abnormal Child Psychology*, *35*, 685–703.

Mawhood, L., Howlin, P., & Rutter, M. (2000). Autism and developmental receptive language disorder–A comparative follow-up in early adult life. I: Cognitive and language outcomes. *Journal of Child Psychology and Psychiatry and Allied Disciplines*, *41*, 547–559.

Mayes, L., Klin, A., Tercyak, K. P., Cicchetti, D. V., & Cohen, D. J. (1996). Test–retest reliability for false-belief tasks. *Journal of Child Psychology and Psychiatry*, *37*, 313–319.

McAlister, A., & Peterson, C. (2007). A longitudinal study of child siblings and theory of mind development. *Cognitive Development*, *22*, 258–270.

McCarthy, D. A. (1930). *The language development of the preschool child.* Minneapolis, MN: University of Minnesota Press.

McElwain, N., & Volling, B. (2002). Relating individual control, social understanding, and gender to child–friend interaction: A relationships perspective. *Social Development*, *11*, 362–385.

McElwain, N., & Volling, B. (2004). Attachment security and parental sensitivity during infancy: Associations with friendship quality and false-belief understanding at age 4. *Journal of Social and Personal Relationships*, *21*, 639–667.

McGlamery, M., Ball, S., Henley, T., & Besozzi, M. (2007). Theory of mind, attention, and executive function in kindergarten boys. *Emotional and Behavioural Difficulties*, *12*, 29–47.

McKinnon, M., & Moscovitch, M. (2007). Domain-general contributions to social reasoning: Theory of mind and deontic reasoning re-explored. *Cognition*, *102*, 179–218.

Mclennan, J. D., Kotelchuck, M., & Cho, H. (2001). Prevalence, persistence, and correlates of depressive symptoms in a national sample of mothers of toddlers. *Journal of the American Academy of Child and Adolescent Psychiatry*, *40*, 1316–1323.

Mehler, J., Jusczyk, P., Lambertz, G., Halsted, N., Bertoncini, J., & Amiel-Tison, C. (1988). A precursor of language acquisition in young infants. *Cognition*, *29*, 143–178.

Meins, E., Fernyhough, C., Fradley, E., & Tuckey, M. (2001). Rethinking maternal sensitivity: Mothers' comments on infants' mental processes predict security of attachment at 12 months. *Journal of Child Psychology and Psychiatry*, *42*, 637–648.

Meins, E., Fernyhough, C., Russell, J., & Clarke-Carter, D. (1998). Security of attachment as a predictor of symbolic and mentalising abilities: A longitudinal study. *Social Development*, *7*, 1–24.

Meins, E., Fernyhough, C., Wainwright, R., Gupta, M., Fradley, E., & Tuckey, M. (2002). Maternal mind-mindedness and attachment security as predictors of theory of mind understanding. *Child Development*, *73*, 1715–1726.

Melchior, M., Caspi, A., Howard, L., Ambler, A., Bolton, H., Mountain, N., et al. (2009). Mental health context of food insecurity: A representative cohort of families with young children. *Pediatrics, 124*, e564–e572.

Meltzoff, A. (1995). Understanding the intentions of others: Re-enactment of intended acts by 18-month-old children. *Developmental Psychology, 31*, 838–850.

Meristo, M., Falkman, K., Hjelmquist, E., Tedoldi, M., Surian, L., & Siegal, M. (2007). Language access and theory of mind reasoning: Evidence from deaf children in bilingual and oralist environments. *Developmental Psychology, 43*, 1156–1169.

Mezzacappa, E. (2004). Alerting, orienting, and executive attention: Developmental properties and sociodemographic correlates in an epidemiological sample of young, urban children. *Child Development, 75*, 1373–1386.

Miller, C. (2001). False belief understanding in children with specific language impairment. *Journal of Communication Disorders, 34*, 73–86.

Miller, J. G. (1987). Cultural influences on the development of conceptual differentiation in person description. *British Journal of Developmental Psychology, 5*, 309–319.

Miller, S. (2000). Children's understanding of preexisting differences in knowledge and belief. *Developmental Review, 20*, 227–282.

Miller, S. (2009). Children's understanding of second-order mental states. *Psychological Bulletin, 135*, 749–773.

Milligan, K., Astington, J., & Dack, L. (2007). Language and theory of mind: Meta-analysis of the relation between language ability and false-belief understanding. *Child Development, 78*, 622–646.

Milton, J. (1671). *Paradise regained: A poem in IV books*. London, UK: John Starkey at the Mitre in Fleet Street.

Mitchell, R., & Karchmer, M. (2004). When parents are deaf versus hard of hearing: Patterns of sign use and school placement of deaf and hard-of-hearing children. *Journal of Deaf Studies and Deaf Education, 9*, 133–152.

Miyake, A., Friedman, N., Emerson, M., Witzki, A., Howerter, A., & Wager, T. (2000). The unity and diversity of executive functions and their contributions to complex "frontal lobe" tasks: A latent variable analysis. *Cognitive Psychology, 41*, 49–100.

Moffitt, T. (1993). The neuropsychology of conduct disorder. *Development and Psychopathology, 5*, 135–152.

Moffitt, T., & the E-Risk Study Team. (2002). Contemporary teenaged mothers in Britain. *Journal of Child Psychology and Psychiatry, 43*, 727–742.

Monks, C., Smith, P., & Swettenham, J. (2005). Psychological correlates of peer victimisation in preschool: Social cognitive skills, executive function and attachment profiles. *Aggressive Behavior, 31*, 571–588.

Montgomery, D. (2005). The developmental origins of meaning for mental terms. In J. Astington & J. Baird (Eds.), *Why language matters for theory of mind* (pp. 106–122). Oxford, UK: Oxford University Press.

Moore, C., & Corkum, V. (1994). Social understanding at the end of the first year of life. *Developmental Review, 14*, 349–372.

Moriguchi, Y., Okumura, Y., Kanakogi, Y., & Itakura, S. (2010). Japanese children's difficulty with false belief understanding: Is it real or apparent? *Psychologia, 53*, 36–43.

Moses, L. (2001a). Executive accounts of theory of mind development. *Child Development, 3*, 688–690.

Moses, L. (2001b). Some thoughts on ascribing complex intentional concepts to young children. In B. Malle, L. Moses, & D. Baldwin (Eds.), *Intentions and intentionality: Foundations of social cognition* (pp. 69–84). Boston, MA: MIT Press.

Müller, U., Zelazo, P., & Imrisek, S. (2005). Executive function and children's under-standing of false belief: How specific is the relation? *Cognitive Development, 20,* 173–189.

Munakata, Y., McClelland, J., Johnson, M., & Siegler, R. (1997). Rethinking infant knowledge: Toward an adaptive process account of successes and failures in object permanence tasks. *Psychological Review, 104,* 686–713.

Mundy, P., Sigman, M., & Kasari, C. (1990). A longitudinal study of joint attention and language development in autistic children. *Journal of Autism and Developmental Disorders, 20,* 115–128.

Murphy, L. B. (1937). *Social behavior and child personality: An exploratory study of some roots of sympathy.* New York, NY: Columbia University Press.

Murray, L. (1992). The impact of postnatal depression on infant development. *Journal of Child Psychology and Psychiatry and Allied Disciplines, 33,* 543–561.

Murray, L. (2009, October). *Maternal "meaning-making" in social phobia: From expres-sion and gesture to narrative.* Paper presented at the ESRC Workshop on Language, Social Understanding and Developmental Psychopathology, Manchester, UK.

Murray, L., de Rosnay, M., Pearson, J., Bergeron, C., Schofield, E., Royal-Lawson, M., et al. (2008). Intergenerational transmission of social anxiety: The role of social refer-encing processes in infancy. *Child Development, 79,* 1049–1064.

Murray-Close, D., Crick, N., & Galotti, K. (2006). Children's moral reasoning regarding physical and relational aggression. *Social Development, 15,* 345–372.

Naito, M., & Koyama, K. (2006). The development of false-belief understanding in Japanese children: Delay and difference? *International Journal of Behavioral Development, 30,* 290–304.

Nelson, K. (2005). Language pathways into the community of minds. In J. Astington & J. Baird (Eds.), *Why language matters for theory of mind* (pp. 26–49). Oxford, UK: Oxford University Press.

Nelson, K., & Fivush, R. (2004). The emergence of autobiographical memory: A social cultural developmental theory. *Psychological Review, 111,* 486–511.

Nelson, K., Plesa, D., & Henseler, S. (1998). Children's theory of mind: An experiential interpretation. *Human Development, 41,* 7–29.

Nelson, K., Skwerer, D., Goldman, S., Henseler, S., Presler, N., & Walkenfeld, F. (2003). Entering a community of minds: An experiential approach to "theory of mind". *Human Development, 46,* 24–46.

Nesdale, D., Durkin, K., Maass, A., & Griffiths, J. (2004). Group status, outgroup ethnicity and children's ethnic attitudes. *Journal of Applied Developmental Psychology, 25,* 237–251.

Newcomb, A., & Bagwell, C. (1995). Children's friendship relations: A meta-analytic review. *Psychological Bulletin, 117,* 306–347.

Nix, R., Pinderhughes, E., Dodge, K., Bates, J., Pettit, G., & McFadyen-Ketchum, S. (1999). The relation between mothers' hostile attribution tendencies and children's externalizing behavior problems: The mediating role of mothers' harsh discipline prac-tices. *Child Development, 70,* 896–909.

Noble, K., McCandliss, B., & Farah, M. (2007). Socioeconomic gradients predict individual differences in neurocognitive abilities. *Developmental Science, 10,* 464–480.

Núñez, M., & Harris, P. (1998). Psychological and deontic concepts: Separate domains or intimate connection? *Mind and Language, 13,* 153–170.

O'Connor, E., & McCartney, K. (2007). Examining teacher–child relationships and achievement as part of an ecological model of development. *American Educational Research Journal, 44,* 340–369.

O'Connor, T., & Hirsch, N. (1999). Intra-individual differences and relationship-specificity of mentalising in early adolescence. *Social Development, 8*, 256–274.

Okanda, M., & Itakura, S. (2008). Children in Asian cultures say yes to yes–no questions: Common and cultural differences between Vietnamese and Japanese children. *International Journal of Behavioral Development, 32*, 131–136.

Onishi, K., & Baillargeon, R. (2005, May). *Do 15-month-old infants understand false beliefs?* Paper presented at International Conference on Infant Studies, Chicago, IL.

Onishi, K., Baillargeon, R., & Leslie, A. (2007). 15-month-old infants detect violations in pretend scenarios. *Acta Psychologica, 124*, 106–128.

Ontai, L., & Thompson, R. (2002). Patterns of attachment and maternal discourse effects on children's emotion understanding from 3 to 5 years of age. *Social Development, 11*, 433–450.

Ontai, L. L., & Thompson, R. A. (2008). Attachment, parent–child discourse and theory-of-mind development. *Social Development, 17*, 47–60.

Orobio De Castro, B., Veerman, J., Koops, W., Bosch, J., & Monshouwer, H. (2002). Hostile attribution of intent and aggressive behavior: A meta-analysis. *Child Development, 73*, 916–934.

Ozonoff, S., Pennington, B. F., & Rogers, S. J. (1991). Executive function deficits in high functioning autistic children: Relationship to theory of mind. *Journal of Child Psychology and Psychiatry, 32*, 1081–1105.

Pardini, D., Fite, P., & Burke, J. (2008). Bidirectional associations between parenting practices and conduct problems in boys from childhood to adolescence: The moderating effects of age and African-American ethnicity. *Journal of Abnormal Child Psychology, 36*, 647–662.

Patterson, G. (1986). The contribution of siblings to training for fighting: A microsocial analysis. In D. Olweus, J. Block, & M. Radke-Yarrow (Eds.), *Development of antisocial and prosocial behavior* (pp. 235–261). New York, NY: Academic Press.

Pellicano, E. (2007). Links between theory of mind and executive function in young children with autism: Clues to developmental primacy. *Developmental Psychology, 43*, 974–990.

Pennington, B., & Bennetto, L. (1993). Main effects or transactions in the neuropsychology of conduct disorder. A commentary on the neuropsychology of conduct disorder. *Development and Psychopathology, 5*, 153–164.

Perner, J. (1998). The meta-intentional nature of executive functions and theory of mind. In P. Carruthers & J. Boucher (Eds.), *Language and thought* (pp. 270–316). Oxford, UK: Cambridge University Press.

Perner, J. (2009). Who took the cog out of cognitive science? Mentalism in an era of anti-cognitivism. In P. A. Frensch (Ed.), *XXIX International Congress of Psychology, 2008 Proceedings*. London, UK: Psychology Press.

Perner, J., & Aichhorn, M. (2008). Theory of mind, language and the temporoparietal junction mystery. *Trends in Cognitive Sciences, 12*, 123–126.

Perner, J., Aichhorn, M., Kronbichler, M., Staffen, W., & Ladurner, G. (2006). Thinking of mental and other representations: The roles of left and right temporo-parietal junction. *Social Neuroscience, 1*, 245–258.

Perner, J., Frith, U., Leslie, A., & Leekam, S. (1989). Exploration of the autistic child's theory of mind: Knowledge, belief, and communication. *Child Development, 60*, 689–700.

Perner, J., & Lang, B. (2000). Theory of mind and executive function: Is there a developmental relationship? In S. Baron-Cohen, H. Tager-Flusberg, & D. J. Cohen (Eds.),

Understanding other minds: Perspectives from autism and developmental cognitive neuroscience (2nd ed., pp. 150–181). Oxford, UK: Oxford University Press.

Perner, J., Lang, B., & Kloo, D. (2002). Theory of mind and self-control: More than a common problem of inhibition. *Child Development, 73*, 752–767.

Perner, J., Leekam, S., & Wimmer, H. (1987). Three-year-olds' difficulty with false belief: The case for a conceptual deficit. *British Journal of Developmental Psychology, 5*, 125–137.

Perner, J., & Ruffman, T. (2005). Infants' insight into the mind: How deep? *Science, 308*, 214–216.

Perner, J., Ruffman, T., & Leekam, S. (1994). Theory of mind is contagious: You catch it from your sibs. *Child Development, 65*, 1228–1238.

Perner, J., Sprung, M., Zauner, P., & Haider, H. (2003). *Want that* is understood well before *say that, think that* and false belief: A test of de Villiers' linguistic determinism on German-speaking children. *Child Development, 74*, 179–188.

Perner, J., & Wimmer, H. (1985). "John thinks that Mary thinks that": Attribution of second-order beliefs by 5- to 10-year-old children. *Journal of Experimental Child Psychology, 39*, 437–471.

Perren, S., & Alsaker, F. (2006). Social behavior and peer relationships of victims, bully victims, and bullies in kindergarten. *Journal of Child Psychology and Psychiatry and Allied Disciplines, 47*, 45–57.

Perry, M., & Fantuzzo, J. (2010). A multivariate investigation of maternal risks and their relationship to low-income, preschool children's competencies. *Applied Developmental Science, 14*, 1–17.

Peterson, C. (2000). Kindred spirits: Influences of siblings' perspectives on theory of mind. *Cognitive Development, 15*, 435–455.

Peterson, C., & Siegal, M. (1995). Deafness, conversation and theory of mind. *Journal of Child Psychology and Psychiatry, 36*, 459–474.

Peterson, C., & Siegal, M. (2002). Mindreading and moral awareness in popular and rejected preschoolers. *British Journal of Developmental Psychology, 20*, 205–224.

Peterson, C., & Slaughter, V. (2003). Opening windows into the mind: Mothers' preferences for mental state explanations and children's theory of mind. *Cognitive Development, 18*, 399–429.

Piaget, J. (1926). *The language and thought of the child.* London, UK: Kegan Paul.

Piaget, J. (1932). *The moral judgement of the child.* New York, NY: Academic Press.

Piaget, J. (1952). *The origins of intelligence in children.* New York, NY: International Universities Press.

Pianta, R. (1992). *The Student–Teacher Relationships scale.* Unpublished manuscript, University of Virginia, Charlottesville.

Pillow, B., & Henrichon, A. (1996). There's more to the picture than meets the eye: Young children's difficulty understanding biased interpretation. *Child Development, 67*, 802–819.

Plomin, R., & Dale, P. (2000). Genetics and early language development: A UK study of twins. In D. Bishop & L. Leonard (Eds.), *Speech and language impairments in children: Causes, characteristics, intervention and outcome* (pp. 35–51). Oxford, UK: Psychology Press/Taylor & Francis.

Plotnik, J., de Waal, F., & Reiss, D. (2006). Self-recognition in an Asian elephant. *Proceedings of the National Academy of Sciences of the United States of America, 103*, 17053–17057.

Pons, F., Harris, P., & de Rosnay, M. (2004). Emotion comprehension between 3 and 11 years: Developmental periods and hierarchical organization. *European Journal of Developmental Psychology*, *1*, 127–152.

Povinelli, D., & Vonk, J. (2004). We don't need a microscope to explore the chimpanzee's mind. *Mind and Language*, *19*, 1–28.

Preacher, K., & Hayes, A. (2004). SPSS and SAS procedures for estimating indirect effects in simple mediation models. *Behavior Research Methods, Instruments and Computers*, *36*, 717–731.

Premack, D., & Woodruff, G. (1978). Does the chimpanzee have a theory of mind? *Behaviour and Brain Sciences*, *4*, 515–526.

Pyers, J., & Senghas, A. (2009). Language promotes false-belief understanding: Evidence from learners of a new sign language. *Psychological Science*, *20*, 805–812.

Rabbitt, P. (Ed.). (1997). *Methodology of frontal and executive function*. Hove, UK: Psychology Press.

Raikes, H., & Thompson, R. (2006). Family emotional climate, attachment security and young children's emotion knowledge in a high risk sample. *British Journal of Developmental Psychology*, *24*, 89–104.

Rakoczy, H. (2008). Pretence as individual and collective intentionality. *Mind and Language*, *23*, 499–517.

Rakoczy, H., Tomasello, M., & Striano, T. (2004). Young children know that trying is not pretending: A test of the "behaving-as-if" construal of children's early concept of pretense. *Developmental Psychology*, *40*, 388–399.

Randell, A., & Peterson, C. (2009). Affective qualities of sibling disputes, mothers' conflict attitudes, and children's theory of mind development. *Social Development*, *18*, 857–874.

Rasmussen, C., Wyper, K., & Talwar, V. (2009). The relation between theory of mind and executive functions in children with fetal alcohol spectrum disorders. *Canadian Journal of Clinical Pharmacology*, *16*, 370–380.

Razza, R., & Blair, C. (2009). Associations among false-belief understanding, executive function, and social competence: A longitudinal analysis. *Journal of Applied Developmental Psychology*, *30*, 332–343.

Reddy, V. (2008). *How infants know minds*. Cambridge, MA: Harvard University Press.

Reddy, V., & Trevarthen, C. (2004). What we can learn about babies from engaging with their emotions. *Zero to Three*, *24*, 9–15.

Redmond, S., & Rice, M. (1998). The socioemotional behaviors of children with SLI: Social adaptation or social deviance? *Journal of Speech, Language, and Hearing Research*, *41*, 688–700.

Repacholi, B. (2009). Linking actions and emotions: Evidence from 15- and 18-month-old infants. *British Journal of Developmental Psychology*, *27*, 649–667.

Repacholi, B., & Gopnik, A. (1997). Early reasoning about desires: Evidence from 14- and 18-month-olds. *Developmental Psychology*, *33*, 12–21.

Repacholi, B., & Meltzoff, A. (2007). Emotional eavesdropping: Infants selectively respond to indirect emotional signals. *Child Development*, *78*, 503–521.

Repacholi, B., & Slaughter, V. (Eds.). (2003). *Individual differences in theory of mind*. Hove, UK: Psychology Press.

Repacholi, B., & Trapolini, T. (2004). Attachment and preschool children's understanding of maternal versus non-maternal psychological states. *British Journal of Developmental Psychology*, *22*, 395–415.

Robins, B., Dautenhahn, K., Boekhorst, R. T., & Billard, A. (2005). Robotic assistants in therapy and education of children with autism: Can a small humanoid robot help encourage social interaction skills? *Universal Access in the Information Society, 4*(2), 105–120.

Ronald, A., Happé, F., Hughes, C., & Plomin, R. (2005). Nice and nasty theory of mind: Genetic and environmental contributions. *Social Development, 14*, 664–684.

Roncadin, C., Guger, S., Archibald, J., Barnes, M., & Dennis, M. (2004). Working memory after mild, moderate, or severe childhood closed head injury. *Developmental Neuropsychology, 25*, 21–36.

Root, C., & Jenkins, J. (2005). Maternal appraisal styles, family risk status and anger biases of children. *Journal of Abnormal Child Psychology, 33*, 193–204.

Rosen, C., Schwebel, D., & Singer, J. (1997). Preschoolers' attributions of mental states in pretense. *Child Development, 68*, 1133–1142.

Rosen, W., Adamson, L., & Bakeman, R. (1992). An experimental investigation of infant social referencing: Mothers' messages and gender differences. *Developmental Psychology, 28*, 1172–1178.

Ruffman, T. (1996). Do children understand the mind by means of simulation or a theory? Evidence from their understanding of inference. *Mind and Language, 11*, 388–414.

Ruffman, T., Perner, J., Naito, M., Parkin, L., & Clements, W. (1998). Older but not younger siblings facilitate false belief understanding. *Developmental Psychology, 34*, 161–174.

Ruffman, T., Slade, L., & Crowe, E. (2002). The relation between children's and mothers' mental state language and theory-of-mind understanding. *Child Development, 73*, 734–751.

Russell, J. (1996). *Agency: Its role in mental development*. Hove, UK: Lawrence Erlbaum Associates, Ltd.

Russell, J., Mauthner, N., Sharpe, S., & Tidswell, T. (1991). The "windows task" as a measure of strategic deception in preschoolers and autistic subjects. *British Journal of Developmental Psychology, 9*, 331–349.

Rutter, M. (1989). Isle of Wight revisited: Twenty-five years of child psychiatric epidemiology. *Journal of the American Academy of Child and Adolescent Psychiatry, 28*, 633–653.

Ryle, G. (1949). *"Descartes' myth". The concept of mind*. Chicago, IL: University of Chicago Press.

Sabbagh, M., & Taylor, M. (2000). Neural correlates of theory-of-mind reasoning: An event-elated potential study. *Psychological Science, 11*, 46–50.

Sabbagh, M., Xu, F., Carlson, S., Moses, L., & Lee, K. (2006). The development of executive functioning and theory-of-mind: A comparison of Chinese and US preschoolers. *Psychological Science, 17*, 74–81.

Salmivalli, C., Lagerspetz, K., Björkqvist, K., Österman, K., & Kaukiainen, A. (1996). Bullying as a group process: Participant roles and their relations to social status within the group. *Aggressive Behavior, 22*, 1–15.

Sambeth, A., Ruohio, K., Alku, P., Fellman, V., & Huotilainen, M. (2008). Sleeping newborns extract prosody from continuous speech. *Clinical Neurophysiology, 119*, 332–341.

Saxe, R., & Powell, L. (2006). It's the thought that counts: Specific brain regions for one component of theory of mind. *Psychological Science, 17*, 692–699.

Schick, B., de Villiers, P., de Villiers, J., & Hoffmeister, R. (2007). Language and theory of mind: A study of deaf children. *Child Development, 78*, 376–396.

Schwartz, D. (2000). Subtypes of victims and aggressors in children's peer groups. *Journal of Abnormal Child Psychology, 28*, 181–192.

Schwebel, D., Rosen, C., & Singer, J. (1999). Preschoolers' pretend play and theory of mind: The role of jointly constructed pretence. *British Journal of Developmental Psychology, 17*, 333–348.

Searle, J. (1983). *Intentionality: An essay in the philosophy of mind*. New York, NY: Cambridge University Press.

Sénéchal, M., Lefevre, J., Thomas, E., & Daley, K. (1998). Differential effects of home literacy experiences on the development of oral and written language. *Reading Research Quarterly, 33*, 96–116.

Shallice, T., & Burgess, P. (1991). Higher cognitive impairments and frontal lobe lesions in man. In H. Levin, H. Eisenberg, & A. Benton (Eds.), *Frontal lobe function and dysfunction* (pp. 125–138). Oxford, UK: Oxford University Press.

Sharpe, H. (2008). *Aggressive, unfriendly and prosocial behaviour in preschoolers' dyadic interactions: Investigating the role of moral reasoning and pretend play*. Dissertation, University of Cambridge, Cambridge, UK.

Shatz, M., Diesendruck, G., Martinez-Beck, I., & Akar, D. (2003). The influence of language and socioeconomic status on children's understanding of false belief. *Developmental Psychology, 39*, 717–729.

Shatz, M., & Gelman, R. (1973). The development of communication skills: Modifications in the speech of young children as a function of listener. *Monographs of the Society for Research in Child Development, 38*, 1–37.

Sinclair, D., & Murray, L. (1998). Effects of postnatal depression on children's adjustment to school: Teacher's reports. *British Journal of Psychiatry, 172*, 58–63.

Sirois, S., & Jackson, I. (2007). Social cognition in infancy: A critical review of research on higher order abilities. *European Journal of Developmental Psychology, Special Issue on Social Cognition During Infancy, 4*, 46–64.

Slade, L., & Ruffman, T. (2005). How language does (and does not) relate to theory of mind: A longitudinal study of syntax, semantics, working memory and false belief. *British Journal of Developmental Psychology, 23*, 117–141.

Slaughter, V., Dennis, M., & Pritchard, M. (2002). Theory of mind and peer acceptance in preschool children. *British Journal of Developmental Psychology, 20*, 545–564.

Slomkowski, C., & Dunn, J. (1996). Young children's understanding of other people's beliefs and feelings and their connected communication with friends. *Developmental Psychology, 32*, 442–447.

Smith, P., Madsen, K., & Moody, J. (1999). What causes the age decline in reports of being bullied at school? Towards a developmental analysis of risks of being bullied. *Educational Research, 41*, 267–285.

Sobel, M. (1982). Asymptotic confidence intervals for indirect effects in structural equation models. In S. Leinhardt (Ed.), *Sociological methodology* (Vol. 13, pp. 290–312). San Francisco, CA: Jossey-Bass.

Sommerville, J. A., Woodward, A. L., & Needham, A. (2005). Action experience alters 3-month-old infants' perception of others' actions. *Cognition, 96*, B1–B11.

Song, H., Onishi, K., Baillargeon, R., & Fisher, C. (2008). Can an agent's false belief be corrected by an appropriate communication? Psychological reasoning in 18-month-old infants. *Cognition, 109*, 295–315.

Southgate, V., Senju, A., & Csibra, G. (2007). Action anticipation through attribution of false belief by two-year-olds. *Psychological Science, 18*, 587–592.

Sparrow, S., Balla, D., & Cicchetti, D. (1984). *Vineland Adaptive Behaviour Scale (Survey Form)*. New York, NY: American Guidance Survey.

Speltz, M., Deklyen, M., Calderon, R., Greenberg, M., & Fisher, P. (1999). Neuropsychological characteristics and test behaviors of boys with early onset conduct problems. *Journal of Abnormal Psychology, 108*, 315–325.

Spencer, S., Zanna, M., & Fong, G. (2005). Establishing a causal chain: Why experiments are often more effective than mediational analyses in examining psychological processes. *Journal of Personality and Social Psychology, 89*, 845–851.

Sprong, M., Schothorst, P., Vos, E., Hox, J., & de Engeland, H. (2007). Theory of mind in schizophrenia: Meta-analysis. *British Journal of Psychiatry, 191*, 5–13.

Steele, H., Steele, M., Croft, C., & Fonagy, P. (1999). Infant–mother attachment at one year predicts children's understanding of mixed emotions at six years. *Social Development, 8*(2), 161–178.

Steele, M., Steele, H., & Johansson, M. (2002). Maternal predictors of children's social cognition: An attachment perspective. *Journal of Child Psychology and Psychiatry and Allied Disciplines, 43*, 861–872.

Stocker, C., & Youngblade, L. (1999). Marital conflict and parental hostility: Links with children's sibling and peer relationships. *Journal of Family Psychology, 13*, 598–609.

Stone, V., Baron-Cohen, S., & Knight, R. (1998). Frontal lobe contributions to theory of mind. *Journal of Cognitive Neuroscience, 10*, 640–656.

Sullivan, K., Zaitchik, D., & Tager-Flusberg, H. (1994). Preschoolers can attribute second-order beliefs. *Developmental Psychology, 30*, 395–402.

Sutton, J., Smith, P., & Swettenham, J. (1999a). Bullying and "theory of mind": A critique of the "social skills deficit" view of anti-social behaviour. *Social Development, 8*, 117–127.

Sutton, J., Smith, P., & Swettenham, J. (1999b). Social cognition and bullying: Social inadequacy or skilled manipulation? *British Journal of Developmental Psychology, 17*, 435–450.

Symons, D., & Clark, S. (2000). A longitudinal study of mother–child relationships and theory of mind in the preschool period. *Social Development, 9*, 3–23.

Tager-Flusberg, H. (2000). Language and understanding minds: Connections in autism. In S. Baron-Cohen, H. Tager-Flusberg, & D. Cohen (Eds.), *Understanding other minds: Perspectives from developmental cognitive neuroscience* (pp. 124–149). Oxford, UK: Oxford University Press.

Tager-Flusberg, H. (2001). A re-examination of the theory of mind hypothesis of autism. In J. Burack, T. Charman, N. Yirmiya, & P. Zelazo (Eds.), *The development of autism: Perspectives from theory and research* (pp. 173–194). Oxford, UK: Lawrence Erlbaum Associates, Inc.

Tager-Flusberg, H., & Joseph, R. (2005). How language facilitates the acquisition of false-belief understanding in children with autism. In J. Astington & J. Baird (Eds.), *Why language matters for theory of mind* (pp. 298–318). Oxford, UK: Oxford University Press.

Tager-Flusberg, H., & Sullivan, K. (1994). A second look at second-order belief attribution in autism. *Journal of Autism and Developmental Disorders, 24*, 577–586.

Tager-Flusberg, H., & Sullivan, K. (2000). A componential view of theory of mind: Evidence from William's syndrome. *Cognition, 76*, 59–89.

Talwar, V., Murphy, S., & Lee, K. (2007). White lie-telling in children for politeness purposes. *International Journal of Behavioral Development, 31*, 1–11.

Tardif, T., Fletcher, P., Liang, W., Zhang, Z., Kaciroti, N., & Marchman, V. (2008). Baby's first 10 words. *Developmental Psychology, 44*, 929–938.

Tardif, T., Shatz, M., & Naigles, L. (1997). Caregiver speech and children's use of nouns versus verbs: A comparison of English, Italian, and Mandarin. *Journal of Child Language*, *24*, 535–565.

Taylor, M., & Carlson, S. (1997). The relation between individual differences in fantasy and theory of mind. *Child Development*, *68*, 436–455.

Tennyson, A. (1850). *In memoriam*. London, UK: Edward Moxon & Co.

Teti, D., Sakin, J., Kucera, E., & Corns, K. (1996). And baby makes four: Predictors of attachment security among pre-school age firstborns during the transition to siblinghood. *Child Development*, *67*, 579–596.

Tizard, B., & Hughes, M. (1984). *Young children learning*. London, UK: Fontana.

Tomasello, M., Carpenter, M., Call, J., Behne, T., & Moll, H. (2005). Understanding and sharing intentions: The origins of cultural cognition. *Behavioral and Brain Sciences*, *28*, 675–691.

Tomasello, M., & Haberl, K. (2003). Understanding attention: 12- and 18-month-olds know what is new for other persons. *Developmental Psychology*, *39*(5), 906–912.

Tomasello, M., Kruger, A., & Ratner, H. (1993). Cultural learning. *Behavioral and Brain Sciences*, *16*, 495–552.

Tomblin, J., Records, N., Buckwalter, P., Zhang, X., Smith, E., & O'Brien, M. (1997). Prevalence of specific language impairment in kindergarten children. *Journal of Speech, Language, and Hearing Research*, *40*, 1245–1260.

Tremblay, R., Japel, C., Perusse, D., McDuff, P., Boivin, M., Zoccolillo, M., Montplaisir, J., et al. (1999). The search for the age of "onset" of physical aggression: Rousseau and Bandura revisited. *Criminal Behavior and Mental Health*, *9*, 8–23.

Trevarthen, C., & Hubley, P. (1978). Secondary intersubjectivity: Confidence, confiding, and acts of meaning in the first year. In A. Locke (Ed.), *Action, gesture and symbol: The emergence of language* (pp. 183–229). San Diego, CA: Academic Press.

Trionfi, G., & Reese, E. (2009). A good story: Children with imaginary companions create richer narratives. *Child Development*, *80*, 1301–1313.

Turnbull, W., Carpendale, J., & Racine, T. (2008). Relations between mother–child talk and 3- to 5-year-old children's understanding of belief: Beyond mental state terms to talk about the mind. *Merrill-Palmer Quarterly*, *54*, 367–385.

Van IJzendoorn, M., Schuengel, C., & Bakermans-Kranenburg, M. (1999). Disorganized attachment in early childhood: Meta-analysis of precursors, concomitants, and sequelae. *Development and Psychopathology*, *11*, 225–249.

Van Overwalle, F. (2009). Social cognition and the brain: A meta-analysis. *Human Brain Mapping*, *30*, 829–858.

Varley, R., & Siegal, M. (2000). Evidence for cognition without grammar from causal reasoning and "theory of mind" in an agrammatic aphasic patient. *Current Biology*, *10*, 723–726.

Varley, R., Siegal, M., & Want, S. (2001). Severe impairment in grammar does not preclude theory of mind. *Neurocase*, *7*, 489–493.

Veenstra, R., Lindenberg, S., Oldehinkel, A., de Winter, A., Verhulst, F., & Ormel, J. (2005). Bullying and victimization in elementary schools: A comparison of bullies, victims, bully/victims, and uninvolved preadolescents. *Developmental Psychology*, *41*, 672–682.

Verkuyten, M. (2001). Global self-esteem, ethnic self-esteem, and family integrity: Turkish and Dutch early adolescents in The Netherlands. *International Journal of Behavioral Development*, *25*, 357–366.

Vinden, P. (2001). Parenting attitudes and children's understanding of mind. A comparison of Korean American and Anglo-American families. *Cognitive Development*, *16*, 793–809.

Volling, B. L., & Belsky, J. (1992). The contribution of mother–child and father–child relationships to the quality of sibling interaction: A longitudinal study. *Child Development, 63*, 1209–1222.

Vygotsky, L. (1962). *Thought and language*. Cambridge, MA: MIT Press.

Walker, S. (2005). Gender differences in the relationship between young children's peer-related social competence and individual differences in theory of mind. *Journal of Genetic Psychology, 166*, 297–312.

Wang, Y., & Su, Y. (2009). False belief understanding: Children catch it from classmates of different ages. *International Journal of Behavioral Development, 33*, 331–336.

Watson, A., Nixon, C., Wilson, A., & Capage, L. (1999). Social interaction skills and theory of mind in young children. *Developmental Psychology, 35*, 386–391.

Weinberg, M., Olson, K., Beeghly, M., & Tronick, E. (2006). Making up is hard to do, especially for mothers with high levels of depressive symptoms and their infant sons. *Journal of Child Psychology and Psychiatry and Allied Disciplines, 47*, 670–683.

Wellman, H. (1979, October). *A child's theory of mind: The development of conceptions of cognition*. Paper presented at The Growth of Insight in the Child, Madison, WI.

Wellman, H., Cross, D., & Watson, J. (2001). Meta-analysis of theory of mind development: The truth about false belief. *Child Development, 72*, 655–684.

Wellman, H., & Lagattuta, K. (2000). Developing understandings of mind. In S. Baron-Cohen, H. Tager-Flusberg, & D. Cohen (Eds.), *Understanding other minds: Perspectives from developmental cognitive neuroscience* (pp. 21–49). Oxford, UK: Oxford University Press.

Wellman, H., Lopez-Duran, S., LaBounty, J., & Hamilton, B. (2008). Infant attention to intentional action predicts preschool theory of mind. *Developmental Psychology, 44*, 618–623.

Wellman, H., & Miller, J. (2006). Developing conceptions of responsive intentional agents. *Journal of Cognition and Culture, Special Issue on Folk Conceptions of Mind, Agency and Morality, 6*, 27–55.

Wellman, H., & Miller, J. (2008). Including deontic reasoning as fundamental to theory of mind. *Human Development, 51*, 105–135.

Wellman, H., & Phillips, A. (2001). Developing intentional understandings. In B. Malle, L. Moses, & D. Baldwin (Eds.), *Intentions and intentionality: Foundations of social cognition* (pp. 125–148). Oxford, UK: MIT Press.

Wellman, H., Phillips, A., Dunphy-Lelii, S., & LaLonde, N. (2004). Infant social attention predicts preschool social cognition. *Developmental Science, 7*, 283–288.

Welsh, M. C., Pennington, B. F., & Groisser, D. B. (1991). A normative-developmental study of executive function: A window on prefrontal function in children. *Developmental Neuropsychology, 7*, 131–149.

Werner, N., & Crick, N. R. (1999). Relational aggression and social-psychological adjustment in a college sample. *Journal of Abnormal Psychology, 108*, 615–623.

Whiten, A. (2000). Social complexity and social intelligence. *Novartis Foundation Symposium, 233*, 185–196.

Wiebe, S., Espy, K., & Charak, D. (2008). Using confirmatory factor analysis to understand executive control in preschool children: I. Latent structure. *Developmental Psychology, 44*, 575–587.

Wilkinson, R., & Pickett, K. (2009). *The spirit level: Why more equal societies almost always do better*. London, UK: Penguin.

Winner, E. (1988). *The point of words: Children's understanding of metaphor and irony*. Cambridge, MA: Harvard University Press.

Wittgenstein, L. (1958). *Philosophical investigations* (G. E. M. Anscombe, Trans.). New York, NY: Macmillan.

Woodward, A. (2003). Infants' developing understanding of the link between looker and object. *Developmental Science, 6*, 297–311.

Wu, S., & Keysar, B. (2007). The effect of culture on perspective taking. *Psychological Science, 18*, 600–606.

Wundt, W. (1921). *Völkerpsychologie. Eine Untersuchung der Entwicklungsgesetze von Sprache, Mythos und Sitte. Erster Band: Die Sprache*. Stuttgart, Germany: Kröner. (Original work published 1900)

Zahn-Waxler, C., & Radke-Yarrow, M. (1990). The origins of empathic concern. *Motivation and Emotion, 14*, 107–130.

Zelazo, P. (1999). Language, levels of consciousness, and the development of intentional action. In P. Zelazo, J. Astington, & D. Olson (Eds.), *Developing theories of intention: Social understanding and self control* (pp. 95–118). Oxford, UK: Lawrence Erlbaum Associates, Inc.

Zelazo, P., & Frye, D. (1998). Cognitive complexity and control: II. The development of executive function in childhood. *Current Directions in Psychological Science, 7*, 121–126.

Zelazo, P., Frye, D., & Rapus, T. (1996). An age-related dissociation between knowing rules and using them. *Cognitive Development, 11*, 37–63.

Zelazo, P., & Müller, U. (2002). Executive function in typical and atypical development. In U. Goswami (Ed.), *Handbook of childhood cognitive development* (pp. 445–469). Oxford, UK: Blackwell.

Ziatas, K., Durkin, K., & Pratt, C. (1998). Belief term development in children with autism, Asperger syndrome, specific language impairment, and normal development: Links to theory of mind development. *Journal of Child Psychology and Psychiatry and Allied Disciplines, 39*, 755–763.

Ziv, M., Solomon, A., & Frye, D. (2008). Young children's recognition of the intentionality of teaching. *Child Development, 79*, 1237–1256.

Author index

Subject index